Star Spangled Scandal

CHRIS DeROSE

National Bestselling Author of
The Presidents' War and *Founding Rivals*

★ ★ ★ ★ ★ ★ ★ ★ ★

Star Spangled
SCANDAL

★ ★ ★ ★ ★ ★ ★ ★ ★

Sex, Murder, and the Trial
that Changed America

REGNERY
HISTORY

Regnery History™ is a trademark of Salem Communications Holding Corporation
Regnery® is a registered trademark of Salem Communications Holding Corporation

Cataloging-in-Publication data on file with the Library of Congress

ISBN 978-1-62157-805-5
ebook ISBN 978-1-62157-895-6

Published in the United States by
Regnery History
An imprint of Regnery Publishing
A Division of Salem Media Group
300 New Jersey Ave NW
Washington, DC 20001
www.Regnery.com

Manufactured in the United States of America

10 9 8 7 6 5 4 3 2 1

Books are available in quantity for promotional or premium use. For information on discounts and terms, please visit our website: www. Regnery.com.

For Hannah DeRose, my wife, who showed me how happy a man can be. I love you beyond measure, today and for all time.

CONTENTS

ACT II
The Trial of Daniel E. Sickles for the
Murder of Philip Barton Key... 163

YEAR of meteors! brooding year!
I would bind in words retrospective,
some of your deeds and signs:
O year all mottled with evil and good!
year of forebodings!
As I flit through you hastily, soon to fall and
be gone, what is this book,
What am I myself but one of your meteors?

—"Year of Meteors, 1859–60"
by Walt Whitman, *Leaves of Grass*

—

Overture—
Opening Night

It was a pleasant Sunday afternoon in Washington. Two gentlemen in top hats encountered one another. "How do you do?" asked Barton Key, extending his hand.

"Villain, you have defiled my bed," said Daniel Sickles. He pointed a pistol at Key and fired.

"Murder!" cried Key, United States Attorney for the District of Columbia. "Don't shoot me. Don't murder me."

Key's cries went unheeded. There was another shot. Key fell to the ground. Sickles advanced on him slowly and fired again. Key lay mortally wounded on his back. His killer stood triumphantly over his body.

Applause!

The curtain dropped on Act II of *Sickles: Or, the Washington Tragedy!* playing at the National Theatre. Nightly re-enactments of Key's shooting were met with "enthusiastic" clapping by the whitest kid gloves in Boston. The Brahmins in all their finery cheered the death of a man who had been prominently among the living two months earlier.[1]

But a lot had happened since then. America had spent that time in the thralls of an illicit affair, savage killing, and sensational trial, grasping after every detail. The shooting touched off a national conversation on male honor, female virtue, marriage, fidelity, and the rule of law. Newspapers covered the story with more speed and space than any that had come before. The *Evening Star* declared that the name "Daniel Sickles" was "oftener pronounced than that of any other one living."[2]

The jury had announced its verdict two weeks earlier, closing the matter for official purposes. But the public was not ready to let go.

It was "the sole topic of conversation wherever men meet, or women either," in boardrooms, boudoirs, and bars. It was discussed in Spanish, German, and French, in London pubs and cafes on the Champs Elysees, and on the beaches of Bermuda and Hawaii. Closer to home, it displaced coverage of violence in Kansas, the breakdown of politics in Washington, the fracturing of the Democrats, and the ascendancy of the Republicans.[3]

Helen and Lucile Western, known as "the Star Sisters," rushed their play into production. David Hanchett, a Shakespearean tragedian, was cast in the role of vengeful husband. Rehearsals were held during the trial, and the script was updated accordingly. Audiences loved it. Others were horrified. People were similarly divided over the whole Sickles matter.[4]

As one critic wrote of the play: *de gustibus non est disputandum*: "in matters of taste, there can be no dispute."[5]

ACT I

The Washington
Tragedy

Chapter One

A Reckless Gaiety

Thursday, February 24, 1859

—

*"Over that gay and brilliant company how near
and fearful a doom impended!"*
—The *New York Times*

D aniel Sickles could see the White House from his window. He
dressed the part of an up-and-coming congressman—as he had
well before he was one—and went downstairs to greet his wife and
daughter. Many members of Congress came to the capital without
their loved ones. But Sickles found life "dull" and "wearisome"
without his wife Teresa and daughter Laura.[1]

Laura was six, restored to health after a bout of fever and chills.
Her baptism was coming soon. And President James Buchanan
would serve as godfather.

When their morning meal was finished, Sickles boarded his
coach and traded the peace of home for the frenzy of the House of
Representatives. Teresa and Laura were headed for Centre Market,
an errand another hostess might have left for servants.

Congress was in the final days of session, scrambling to put
together the national budget on their way out of town. Some were
looking to save money by shutting down the Navy Yards. Like the
one in Brooklyn, critical to national security as well as Sickles's

constituents. When critics of the Navy Yards tried to force a vote, Sickles leapt to his feet, reminding them that they "could remain in session as long as they like." The House agreed to defer action to the following day.[2]

Sickles left the Capitol and traveled up Pennsylvania Avenue. The historic Ewell House, leased by Sickles, was just north of the White House and among the most prestigious addresses in the capital. An invitation there meant an evening with senators, congressmen, diplomats, journalists, cabinet members, and, sometimes, the president. It was the perfect place for a party, such as the one underway when he arrived.[3]

Sickles entered his home to the sounds of laughter, talking, and the clinking of glasses, the merry scene illuminated by gaslight and reflected in chandeliers and mirrors. Buchanan's Washington was a return to form after the bleak Franklin Pierce presidency, where the social scene suffered from a first lady mourning the death of her son. William Stuart, correspondent for the *New York Times*, wrote: "I have never known Washington more delightful." Henry Watterson, the young reporter for the Philadelphia *Press*, proclaimed "Mr. and Mrs. Sickles" the "universal favorites," providing "the most generous welcome in Washington."[4]

Sickles spotted his wife among the colorful dresses and dark suits, greeting guests in her "sweet" and "amiable manner." People who never set foot in Washington could read about Teresa's beauty in national newspapers: her "Italian luster and depth of eye" and "delicacy of feature" making her "remarkable...for something especially soft, lovely, and youthful."[5]

Tonight's guest of honor was Madame James Gordon Bennett, wife of the powerful publisher of the *New York Herald*. To be sure, there had been differences in the past: names were called ("Double Dealing Dan"), accusations made, and a libel lawsuit filed. But it had been sorted out. Bennett had more readers than anyone in Gotham, and Sickles's rapid rise had been faithfully chronicled. This dinner party was intended to cement their nascent alliance. Draped in jewels and dressed in the latest French fashion, Madame Bennett was among "the most brilliant and best in Washington society." Only yesterday she had been feted at the White House, and tomorrow she would dine with the diplomatic corps. But tonight, she was at the Ewell House.[6]

Also there was Chevalier Henry Wikoff, a living, breathing sign that you had arrived at the best party in town. Heir to a Philadelphia fortune, kicked out of Yale for "riding with a young lady," he began his Washington social career in the days of Andrew Jackson. From there, he gained prominence in courts throughout Europe, from King Louis in Paris to the Pope in the Vatican to the Czar in the Kremlin.

In London, he became attaché of the American delegation, where he met the Duke of Wellington and King William IV, and he briefly became a spy for the British against the French. He became friends with the Bonaparte family, "who were then between empires," particularly Louis, and wrote a biography of him. Wikoff returned to America as the manager of Fanny Elssler, the famed dancer, with whom he engaged in a turbulent and long-lasting romance. Wikoff had been engaged to the niece of a senior London banker. When she broke it off and moved, Wikoff found her, and, well… "kidnapped" was the word they used. Wikoff made the most of fifteen months in a Genoese prison, writing a bestselling account: *My Courtship and its Consequences.* James Bennett nicknamed him "Chevalier" because of his foreign affect and adventures throughout Europe. The sobriquet became true twelve years later when he was knighted by the king of Spain.[7]

Partisanship was at a high that winter and North-South relations at a low. But people who would not meet elsewhere could do so in the Sickles's home. In addition to Bennett and Wikoff, there were

Republicans and Yankees, like Congressman Anson Burlingame of Massachusetts and his substantial mutton chops and Alabama Belle Virginia Clay, wife of a leading Democratic senator. Clay was surveying the scene from a red sofa in the back parlor. In a matter of weeks, that couch's history would become a matter of scintillating trial testimony.[8]

Clay likened Washington society to its topography: "many small circles and triangles, into each of which run tributary streets and avenues." She remembered those days as a time of "general prosperity and competitive expenditure. While a life and death struggle raged between political parties, and oratorical battles of ominous import were fought daily in the Senate chamber and House, a very reckless gaiety was everywhere apparent in social circles."[9]

Virginia Clay remembered for the rest of her life how Teresa looked that night. "More lovely than usual," exotic, but "young and fair." Neither she nor her circle believed "the rumors which were then in circulation."

She never saw Teresa again.[10]

There were toasts and cheers and more laughter and conversation over "the most elegant and stylish" dinner served in Washington that winter. It was ten o'clock before they knew it and time for the next event. The crowd poured out of the house and climbed into carriages for Willard's Hotel and their nightly hop. Teresa offered to take several guests in their personal coach. Go on ahead, Sickles said—I'll walk and catch up with you.[11]

If dinner was for gossip and dealmaking, the nightly hops were a place to let loose and a "time for banalities." One reveler saw it like a battle: the reconnaissance, as the crowded ballroom floor divided by sex, making "observations as to the best point of attack"; "feelers are thrown out" by "promenading close to each other, followed by general skirmishing" in the form of small talk. "It's quite warm this evening," "A very pleasant affair this," "Were you at so and so's?" An hour into the battle, those sitting on the sidelines—the reserves—are sent in. It seems fitting for people who would be killing one another in two years.[12]

Teresa arrived with her party and scanned the ballroom. Philip Barton Key II, US Attorney for the District of Columbia, was hard to miss. The "handsomest man in all Washington society," an "Apollo in appearance," "well formed," and "athletic," with a "well-trimmed mustache," Key was also a sartorial standout, known for his foppish attire, such as white leather tights and high boots.[13]

"Barton" to those who knew him had "a sad yet handsome face." Social arbiter Virginia Clay declared him "foremost among the popular men of the capital," "a favorite with every hostess of the day," "clever at repartee," and "a generous and pleasing man." He was a sought-after dance partner, known for his "presence, tall stature, winning manners," and "easy, fashionable air." "Fitted by nature to gain the affections of a woman," those he fancied were immediately the "subject of conversation to the lovers of scandal."

And for some time, his fancy had an unusual focus.[14]

The Sickles had become fast friends with Key on their arrival in Washington. A widower, he escorted Teresa on the social circuit while Dan was detained in the House. Key and Teresa sat next to each other on a couch. The two engaged in a lively conversation, oblivious to the ball that surrounded them and the looks and whispers cast in their direction.[15]

As Sickles prepared to leave for Willard's, a messenger came to the door and handed him a basic yellow envelope. He tucked it into his jacket unopened and thought no more of it. Sickles walked outside, turning left on Pennsylvania Avenue, heading toward the hop.[16]

The brass band blasted music as gaslights masked the hour. The partiers—fueled by champagne—quadrilled, waltzed, and polkaed.

Key took leave of Teresa when Sickles arrived. They came home late from the hop.[17]

Teresa went upstairs to sleep and Sickles to his study to catch up on correspondence. He remembered the letter in his pocket. It crinkled when he unfolded it:

> Dear Sir: With deep regret I inclose to your address the few lines but an indispensable duty compels me so to do seeing that you are greatly imposed upon.
>
> There is a fellow I may say for he is not a gentleman by any means by the [name] of Philip Barton Key & I believe the district attorney who rents a house of a negro man by the name of Jno. A Gray situated on 15th street between K and L streets for no other purpose than to meet your wife Mrs. Sickles.
>
> He hangs a string out of the window as a signal to her that he is in and leaves the door unfastened and she walks in and sir I do assure you he has as much the use of your wife as you have. With these few hints I leave the rest for you to imagine.
>
> Most respectfully Your friend R. P. G.

It is unclear what "R. P. G" thought they had left to the imagination.

A man could waste a lifetime accrediting every bit of gossip coursing through Washington. And it wasn't the first time someone had tried to start trouble between Sickles and Key. Last time, there was at least a name attached to the charge; a man—if you could call him that—who backed down when confronted.

Normally, Sickles would have introduced the letter to his fireplace. But it was gnawingly specific. He could verify whether it was true.

And he would have to. The answer, once found, would greatly relieve or utterly destroy him.

A sleepless night lay ahead.

Chapter Two

"A Skeleton Sketch
of My Life"

There was a time, in his turbulent teenage years, when Daniel Sickles's problems were limited to a domineering father and an overattentive mother. They sent him to Glens Falls Academy, two hundred miles north of Manhattan. There his troubles grew to include a headmaster tasked with smoothing out his rougher edges. He didn't stay long.[1]

Rather than retreat home, Sickles walked across town and applied for work at the newspaper. It was a struggling weekly whose misfortune opened the door for a young academy reject with no relevant experience. Its routine mergers and changes in ownership were reflected in its unwieldly name: the *Warren Messenger and Glens Falls Advertiser.*

Sickles worked as a "printer's devil," a time-honored apprenticeship once held by Benjamin Franklin. Sickles was tasked with carefully laying type with black-stained hands while his nose filled with the pungent smell of ink.

From the small village on the Hudson, he absorbed the news of the world, letter by letter. The German states created a free trade union on a path to unification; President Andrew Jackson was censured by congress for draining the National Bank; Jackson's opponents formed the Whig Party; slavery was abolished in the British Empire; anti-abolition riots raged in New York City; and Cyrus McCormick (who would later intersect with Sickles in a way neither could imagine) applied for a patent on his mechanical reaper. Sickles returned to Manhattan after eighteen months with a better education than that offered by the academy.[2]

In New York, Sickles worked for a printer on Fulton Street. At night, he ran around the notorious Five Corners, free from his parents, with disposable bank notes in his pockets. But no matter what he'd gotten into the night before, he was renowned for hard work and accuracy.[3]

Across the river in Brooklyn, Sickles delivered his first speech: a full-throated "Houzee!" for the presidential bid of Martin Van Buren. Van Buren was a fellow New Yorker, made of the same stock as the original Dutch settlers, like his own ancestors, the Van Sickelns.

"Who is that young man?" asked one of his listeners, who was old enough to remember speeches for George Washington. "If he lives he will be great."[4]

Sickles's father, George, was a real estate investor. Riding the latest upswing and hedging against the next crash, he bought a farm across the Hudson in Livingston, New Jersey. It took all his negotiating skills, but his son agreed to join him there. Sickles endured his bucolic exile for a year before hitting the road. With the tall sails of the Hudson River in view, it was a miracle he lasted that long.[5]

With his belongings tied in a handkerchief and "a few shillings in his pocket," Sickles left the farm. And he just kept walking—until he found himself in Princeton, "hungry and dusty." The local newspaper had no openings. They hired him anyway.[6]

When he had saved a dollar, he set forth for Philadelphia. He had underestimated the cost, however; he'd spent a quarter of his money by the time he reached Bristol. Sickles explained his problem to an innkeeper. He was cared for that evening and left in the morning "… with a loaf of bread under his arm and sixpence in his pocket." When he knocked on a farmhouse door outside Philadelphia and asked for a glass of water, the woman who answered insisted on giving him milk.

Arriving in the city with no place to stay, he called at a fashionable boarding house. "Yes, you shall stay with me," said the landlady, as if it could never be doubted that she would admit a young man with no luggage or money. Sickles stayed in the attic at first until one of the lodgers, so impressed by the young man, invited him to share the finest suite. Sickles found work at *Burton's Gentleman's Magazine.* It was a literary monthly that would soon feature Edgar Allan Poe as editor, and it was the first outlet for several of Poe's stories, including "The Fall of the House of Usher." Before long, Sickles heard from his father: if Sickles would return to New York, his parents would assist him with his education.[7]

In New York City, Sickles was lodged with the Da Ponte family to prepare for college. The household at 91 Spring Street consisted of Lorenzo DaPonte, the patriarch; his three sons; his daughter Maria; and their families. Maria was presented as adopted but was suspected to be every bit a natural Da Ponte, the result of an encounter when Lorenzo was in his 60s. She was married to Antonio Bagioli, a famed composer and music teacher from Italy, and they had a little girl named Teresa.[8]

A new, very different apprenticeship began for Sickles. Lorenzo Da Ponte had been born to a Jewish family in Venice, but his father converted to Catholicism for a woman. Other considerations were secondary to those of the heart, a lesson absorbed by little Lorenzo and one he may have passed on to his family. Da Ponte became a priest, taught languages, and made his first attempts at poetry, including a tribute to wine.

He passed on priestly pursuits for nights of gambling, drinking, and women. The staid merchant princes of Venice eventually had enough. Citing his mistress, two children, and possible residence in a brothel, Da Ponte was convicted of "public concubinage" and "abduction of a respectable woman" and banished from the City of Canals for fifteen years.

The fallen priest found his way to Vienna as the poet laureate of Emperor Joseph II. There he collaborated with Wolfgang Mozart, putting words to the music of *The Marriage of Figaro*, *Don Giovanni* (inspired by his friend Casanova), and *Cosi Fan Tutte* (*Women Are Like That*). Leaving the theater amidst a sex scandal, he found his way—circuitously, of course—through the courts of Europe and finally to Manhattan, where he became a professor of Italian at Columbia. He introduced opera to the island and managed to keep the New York Opera Company open for two years before it was liquated to pay debts.

At the foot of the old maestro, Sickles learned of the world's highest pursuits—and the lowest.[9]

Sickles, scion of new (and occasionally no) money, a journeyman printer and academy dropout, would have to keep pace in a household where philosophy, music, wine, and politics were debated in Italian, French, English, and Spanish. At the end of the summer of 1838, in his ninetieth year, Da Ponte wrote his last song, "Parti de la Vita" ("Farewell to Life"), and died the following day. He was buried in an unmarked grave—a nod to Mozart, the man whose genius ensured that his work would live forever.[10]

The head of the household was now Lorenzo Da Ponte the Younger, a man of such intellectual achievement that only a father such as his could overshadow him. It was the son, a professor of *belle letters* (literary works) at the University of New York,[11] who oversaw Sickles's admission to college.

Six days before finals, to coerce the administration on some matter or another, the entire faculty resigned, except Da Ponte. Finals consisted of a personal exam in the student's field of study. Da Ponte agreed to examine *every* student in *every* subject. He would rely on his closest pupil: "Dan, I can examine all the classes with your help." Successful, Da Ponte was rewarded with the chair of philosophy, the first such post in the Americas; and Sickles was rewarded with all the privileges of the university.[12]

Lorenzo the Younger was blessed with his father's genius but not his longevity. On a winter's night in 1840, students gathered in the university chapel and adopted a resolution, expressing "deep regret of the afflictive death of our much esteemed and respected professor," a "model for exertion and source of encouragement and counsel."

Sickles never returned to the University of New York.[13]

It was time to move on again. Sickles had decided on a career as a lawyer. He studied law under Benjamin Franklin Butler, attorney general for Presidents Jackson and Van Buren. Sickles passed the Bar in 1843 and opened a law office: *Daniel Edgar Sickles, Esq., Counselor at Law, 79 Nassau Street.*[14]

Sickles proved his mettle early by winning a major patent claim. Daniel Webster, Secretary of State and one of the nation's finest lawyers, was one of three commissioners who heard the case. He singled out Sickles for praise. Sickles soon developed a reputation for his "fine legal mind," "graceful and effective oratory," and large fees.[15]

With his education behind him and his legal career underway, Sickles could focus on what he really cared about—politics. In New York City, the road to civic success ran through "the Wigwam" at the corner of Franklin and Nassau Streets, headquarters of the Tammany

Society. Named for a mythical chief of the Delaware Indians, this fraternal organization had evolved into the most powerful political machine in the country. Careers were made or destroyed in the noisy street-level bar and quiet upstairs corridors. Tammany politics were not for the faint of heart: one had to be ready to defend himself with reason—and any other tool available.[16]

Sickles published *The Sober Second Thought*, a popular newspaper promoting "Success! Triumph! Victory!" for James K. Polk's presidential campaign.[17]

Sickles was also a frequent guest at 161 Mercer Street, a house that attracted the elite of politics, business, and the diplomatic corps. Its visitors enjoyed the best wine in the city; looked at themselves in large, gilded mirrors; walked ornate carpets; and left their troubles on rosewood bedsteads. Fanny White, the proprietor, fell for Sickles. Her patrons used their money to widen their circle of intimates. Fanny used their money to try to settle down. She made sure her new beau had the best tailored suits and jewelry to wear. Though he prospered in the law, Sickles had nothing on the most successful madam in Manhattan. Only Sickles could patronize a high-priced bordello and come out ahead.

Kindred spirits, they followed their own paths in life and twisted setbacks to their favor. Fanny, born Jane Augusta Funk, was from a good family, was a gifted pianist and poet, and had many prospects for love. All of that changed in the face of false promises from an older man and an encounter she couldn't take back. Disgraced and disowned, she followed the one path open to her. Four years later, she was running her own establishment. On one date, she and Sickles drank their way through the saloons of the Eighth Ward. Women weren't allowed, a problem temporarily solved by Fanny dressing as a man. She had assumed so much of a man's role in the 1840s—financially independent, in charge of her personal life—that slipping on a man's clothes seemed minor. But Fanny's feminine qualities were not easily concealed, and their detection earned them an overnight trip to the local jail.[18]

In 1846, twenty-seven-year-old Sickles was elected to the New York Assembly. Sickles was unsurpassed as a "debater and parliamentary leader," in the eyes of Governor William Marcy. Fanny came to visit him in Albany, much to the chagrin of his hotel messmates. He gave her a tour of the Capitol, which ended abruptly, just before the sergeant at arms got involved. Sickles didn't care. His colleagues went to places like hers and did things in Albany their wives wouldn't appreciate.

And how did they even recognize Fanny?[19]

From his childhood home in Manhattan to Glens Falls and Philadelphia to the courthouse and Tammany and now at the seat of power in Albany, Sickles did things his own way. He wrote a friend: "I cannot play the courtier to the multitude, much less to individuals...I know all the consequences...and have many a long year since resolved to enjoy it even at the price which must be inevitably paid...I do not deem it a wise course, nor approve it, nor recommend it to any friend; but I've adopted it: it is mine, and I will follow it come what may."[20]

Soon Sickles found a new love with someone he had known a long time. Fanny White learned of the courtship and gave Sickles a taste of a bullwhip, a singular event in the history of New York's Carleton Hotel.[21]

Years later, as a member of congress, at the height of his political power and domestic felicity, Sickles wrote a letter to a friend about an upcoming profile of him in the *New York Sunday Courier*, in an age where such treatments of any politician were exceedingly rare. The story would serve as "a skeleton sketch of my life," he wrote.

But some of the more interesting details would, by necessity, not be included.[22]

Chapter Three

Teresa

—

"The Helen of our melancholy Iliad."
—diary of Laura Crawford Jones

ST. JAMES'S PALACE, LONDON, March 30, 1854
Remember what you were told.

Teresa Bagioli Sickles followed every step on her way to see the Queen. The train of her dress was folded over her left arm as she approached the throne room. The long, red chamber was dotted with colorfully costumed functionaries: Ladies of the Bedchamber, Yeoman of the Guard, and Mistress of the Robes. As she crossed the threshold, she dropped her train, as instructed, and Lords-in-Waiting used wands to smooth it out behind her.

At the other end of the room was Queen Victoria, in a dress of white poplin, satin, opal, a diamond diadem, and feathers. From her throne, she reigned over the Pyramids, the Cape of Good Hope, and the Taj Mahal—from Canada to Australia.

Teresa was getting close to the Queen. All she had to do was follow the people ahead of her. The French ambassador presented an aristocrat from Hanover. Countess de Lavradio introduced the wife of a Brazilian naval officer. Now it was her turn. Lady Clarendon, wife of the foreign minister, would present Teresa.

A card with her name on it was handed to another Lord-in-Waiting, who read it aloud: "Mrs. Daniel E. Sickles, wife of the Secretary of the American Legation."

Teresa curtseyed as low as possible, almost kneeling. Victoria extended her hand. Teresa kissed it, rose, curtseyed to Prince Albert, and made her way out, keeping her face toward the Queen as she left the room. She could hear the name of her mother, who was presented next.[1]

Most diplomatic wives would be lost among the viscounts and marquesses and the different languages and cultures at court. Teresa was different: "[b]rilliant, beautiful, and highly educated," the perfect balance of firmness and feminine grace.[2]

Daniel Sickles had factored in her earliest memories and impulses. She had been little when he boarded with them, but he was a frequent visitor as she grew older. First, he came to see her parents, Antonio and Maria, the last link to those happy days when her uncle and grandfather were alive. Eventually, she realized, he was there to see her.

He asked her to marry him. She wanted to. Her father objected. She was too young, he said. She was seventeen and didn't know her own mind.

But who was he to advise caution?

Antonio Bagioli arrived in the New World as the conductor of a touring symphony. He stopped at 91 Spring Street to pay homage to the great Da Ponte, but his attention quickly turned from father to daughter. He remained while his opera company went on to Havana. Teresa arrived four years later, the result of a decision to marry no less practical than the one she now intended to make with Dan.[3]

Teresa married Sickles in secret, on September 27, 1852, in a civil ceremony performed by the Mayor of New York. Her parents knew when they were beat: they were in attendance six months later when she married him again, this time before the Catholic Archbishop.

Thus, the Sickles's union began with the sanction of the highest civic and ecclesiastic authorities in the city.[4]

Chapter Four

Men of Force
and Originality

Sickles had married the one woman he could not live without. And he now planned his political comeback after a defeat for state senate. Elections were just ahead—Franklin Pierce versus Winfield Scott and the charred remains of the Whig Party. Sickles focused on helping the Tammany slate win the city.

Empire State Democrats won up and down the ballot. Sickles was appointed Corporation Attorney, a plum position litigating on behalf of New York City.[1]

Shortly thereafter, Sickles was at a dinner party where he met John Forney, a powerful newspaper publisher and Clerk of the US House of Representatives. Forney had an unexpected proposition.

"How would you like to be Secretary of Legation under Mr. Buchanan, the new Minister to London?" he asked.

James Buchanan was headed across the Atlantic with a long list of challenges and needed a talented young man to serve as senior aide. Buchanan had asked Forney if he had anyone in mind for the job. Forney knew that Buchanan was hard to please and would blame him for any disappointment. He hesitated in recommending anyone. On meeting Sickles, he changed his mind.

"What's the pay?" Sickles asked. After all, he had a child on the way.

"$2,500 a year."

"Why, bless you, my dear fellow, that would hardly pay for my wine and cigars. My annual income is fifteen times more than that. I could not think of such a sacrifice."

But Sickles did think about it.[2]

James Buchanan had been a national leader for as long as Sickles could remember. He had served with every president since James Monroe, in the House and Senate, as Jackson's minister to Russia, and he had been a contender for the presidency as far back as 1844.

In 1844, James K. Polk, the former Speaker of the House, was nominated on the eighth ballot and won on the ninth. Polk made Buchanan secretary of state, the most important position in his cabinet. Together, they oversaw the annexation of Texas, the settlement of Oregon's boundaries, and a successful war against Mexico that extended America to the Pacific. In 1848, the Democrats passed on Buchanan again, to their detriment. Lewis Cass lost Buchanan's home state of Pennsylvania, and with it, the election, to the Whigs and General Zachary Taylor.

The Whigs were torn apart by the Compromise of 1850. Things looked good for the Democratic nominee in '52, and Old Buck, as Buchanan was called, had reason to think it might be him. He ran a close second to Lewis Cass for nineteen ballots, overtaking him on the twentieth, leaving Stephen Douglas and the others in the dust. But on the thirty-second ballot, they traded places again. Then, on the thirty-fifth ballot, dark horse Franklin Pierce was placed in nomination for President.

Franklin Pierce? He'd been the youngest Speaker of the New Hampshire House at age twenty-six, the youngest U.S. congressman at age twenty-eight, and the youngest U.S. senator at age thirty-two. He'd also been out of office for ten years. His wife hated politics and forced his resignation after five years in the Senate. Popular, handsome, long out of sight but not out of mind, Pierce was exactly the kind of candidate who could carry the convention.

And he did, on the forty-ninth ballot.[3]

At age forty-eight, President Pierce added another "youngest" to his list. He also hoped to be the first president since Jackson to win re-election. Buchanan was a threat, and Pierce determined to ship him off to London. Buchanan raised objections, and Pierce answered them. Buchanan made unprecedented demands, and Pierce agreed. Buchanan couldn't turn down the president, particularly after he had been so accommodating. He was heading back to Europe and would need a capable aide.

Sickles found Forney the day after their initial meeting: he would interview with Buchanan after all. He boarded a train for Lancaster, Pennsylvania, on July 29.

Buchanan knew Sickles's reputation as "a brilliant lawyer, politician, and man of the world" with "a host of friends and not a few enemies, like all men of force and originality." The two made an instant impression on one another. Buchanan felt Sickles's "manners, appearance, and intelligence [we]re all that could be desired."[4] The job was his. Washington's *Daily Union* praised Sickles as "a firm, fearless, and uncompromising national democrat," a "gentleman of experience, ability, and great decision of character." The *Philadelphia Inquirer* thought Buchanan had chosen a "most accomplished assistant," an "elegant scholar, a fine linguist, a sound lawyer, and a finished gentleman."[5]

Not everyone shared their enthusiasm. "I want to be with you as much as possible," Teresa wrote Dan. "I wish to be near and with you. I hate the idea of your going away without me, and know that I would not have you if it were in my power. You know what is best—and I shall act as you wish me to however much I may dislike it. God only knows how I can get along without you."[6]

Sickles concluded his business in New York and said goodbye to Teresa and their new baby, Laura Buchanan Sickles. They would join him when she was old enough for travel. He left on August 20 and arrived at Merseyside ten days later.[7]

The Sickles spent their first anniversary separated by the Atlantic. Buchanan noticed his aide was "very anxious" for Teresa and Laura to join them. Sickles searched each day for mail addressed in her familiar, elegant script with a New York postmark and a letter inside addressed to "my own dear darling Dan."[8]

Sickles lived in London's Clarendon Hotel with Buchanan while they searched for permanent lodgings. Their time together confirmed Buchanan's opinion of Sickles: a "very agreeable and an able man," with "much energy of character [who] will make a favorable impression here."[9]

Teresa and Laura arrived that spring, as hoped, and just in time. Harriet Lane, the bachelor Buchanan's niece, was the hostess of the delegation. As Teresa arrived, Harriet returned to America. Teresa, as wife of the second ranking diplomat, assumed Harriet's place. She had gone from her father's house to her husband's house but now held a position equal to her talents, advancing America's interests at Queen Victoria's court. "Her" joyful personality charmed as much as her "brilliance," in the words of one courtier. The grand dames of English society, Ladies Palmerston and Clarendon, befriended her. There were balls at Buckingham Palace and banquets at Mansion House with the Lord Mayor of London. Then there were trips to Paris and the Hague, where Teresa "excited interest in every one who met her." Teresa, feeling her power for the first time as she dazzled leaders of Europe, could never have known that these would be the "best days of her life."[10]

It was a wonderful time to be in London and an even better time to be away from America. On February 13, the London *Morning Chronicle* reported "A very strong opposition" to Stephen Douglas's plans to organize the Kansas Territory. "The whole question of slavery and abolition will be opened up" because the bill "repeals the Missouri compromise." By virtue of that compromise, which had held the country together since 1820, slavery was prohibited in all of Kansas and Nebraska. Now Douglas proposed to leave it up to the settlers.[11]

The Kansas-Nebraska Act was passed 37-14 in the Senate and 113-100 in the House. There may have been bitterer days in Congress, but no one could remember them. The opposition to Kansas-Nebraska—Whigs, Northern Democrats, and Free Soilers, formed a new political party—the Republicans.

★ ★ ★

They ruined the Star Spangled Banner!

Sickles was getting increasingly angry at the host of this alleged Fourth of July party. George Peabody, an American living in London, had invited 150 people to the Garter Hotel for the occasion. There were life-sized portraits of the Queen and Prince flanking a small image of George Washington. From there, offenses accumulated: no visible honors to Franklin Pierce, a toast to the Queen *before* the President, and an Englishman given the right to toast Washington! Sickles opened the program pamphlet—featuring both the American eagle *and* British lion and unicorn—and saw that the lyrics to the national anthem had been edited to remove offensive references to the British. When Peabody played his redacted version of the anthem, Sickles stood up and walked out of the room. The incident made headlines in America. Most agreed with the *Louisville Courier*, applauding Sickeles's refusal "to play the fawning minion to Royalty."[12]

In August, British newspapers were filled with speculation: Sickles was on his way to Washington, but what for? He briefed President Pierce and the Secretary of State and prepared a detailed memorandum "On the State of Europe." He accomplished all this so quickly he returned on the same steamer that brought him. Sickles carried instructions to the American ministers at London, Paris, and Madrid to develop a plan to acquire Cuba from the Spanish. Sickles, whose rise had coincided with the Manifest Destiny, enthusiastically supported Cuban acquisition. American ministers gathered in Ostend, Belgium, on October 9 and prepared a policy statement declaring Cuba's addition to the United States as important as that of any state. Pierre Soule, American minister to Spain, was a Louisianan who wanted Cuba for the purpose of expanding slavery and increasing its support in Congress. He was also not shy about sharing his viewpoint. These private proceedings became public, and the policy of Cuban acquisition became inextricably tied to slavery. The fallout in the north was dramatic, giving fuel to the new Republican Party and further damaging the Democrats.[13]

The first election in Kansas, to send a territorial representative to Washington, was a violent charade. The pro-slavery faction won, using threats, voter fraud, and ballot box stuffing that would shame the most cynical pol at Tammany Hall. Of 2,871 votes cast, only 1,114 were legal.

The Democrats paid the price that November, losing seventy-four seats in the House of Representatives (nearly half their total number).

Republicans and other opponents of the president's Kansas policy won 108 seats. Buchanan and Sickles were experienced politicians. They could see the spiraling disaster and what it meant for them. If Democrats were to have any chance of holding the presidency, they would need a candidate untainted by the mess in Kansas. Pierce had sent Buchanan off to end his presidential prospects. Now he was the party's only hope.

Buchanan was well-insulated in London. But for Sickles, there were other considerations: money, Teresa missing her family, and the fact that he could only be someone else's person for so long. Plus, Buchanan needed friends to lay the groundwork for his presidential campaign.

On December 14, 1854, Buchanan wrote to Forney: "I am warmly and strongly attached to [Sickles]. He is a man of fine talents, of excellent manners, and of a brave and loyal temper." Sickles "possesses qualifications both of mind and manners for a much higher place than that of Secretary of Legation." On that, they could both agree.

Sickles left for home the following day, and wasted no time in reminding New York of his return. He was elected to the state senate, returning to provincial Albany with the shine of Queen Victoria's court. He worked feverishly on several issues: revising the code of criminal procedure; tightening inspections of state poor houses and jails; and the creation of Central Park, a place the *Tribune* predicted would "become the pride and ornament of the city."[14]

James Buchanan arrived in New York on April 23, 1856, and was greeted like a conquering hero. Sickles had organized a welcome befitting a future president, inviting Democratic leaders from across the country. It appeared Buchanan's moment had finally arrived.[15]

Chapter Five

A Key of the Keys
of Maryland

May 20, 1856

S enators, diplomats, and the distinguished society of Washington were in a frenzy, thunderously applauding and waving hand-kerchiefs. Two of the greatest opera stars in the world, Mademoi-selle Parodi and Madame Strakoselt, were on stage, belting out the beloved words of the national song:

> O, say does that Star Spangled Banner yet wave
> O'er the land of the free, and the home of the brave?

There to acknowledge this energetic outpouring was Philip Barton Key II. Key, son of Francis Scott Key, was "most deeply moved by the homage to the memory of his father's genius." The constitutional rule against royalty could not prohibit America's love for famous families. And in the unofficial aristocracy of Washington, Key was a King.[1]

He was a *Key*, of the Keys of Maryland. Fifty years before Independence, British Brothers Henry and Philip planted their branch of the family on the banks of the Potomac. From Philip sprung a line of colonial high sheriffs and privy councilors, revolutionaries, legislators, congressmen, and judges. The Keys recycled names so much that their family tree looked like a giant series of tributes. The first Philip Barton Key fought with the British during the Revolution. But his Loyalist sins were forgiven, and the young republic availed itself of his many talents. He was mayor of Annapolis, appointed a federal judge by John Adams, and served three terms in Congress. He had also trained his promising nephew, Francis Scott Key, as a lawyer. Despite his grandiose name, he went by "Frank."

In the dark days of the War of 1812, with the Capitol and White House in ruins, Frank learned that his friend, Dr. William Beanes, was captured and held aboard a British ship. Frank risked his safety, traveling under a flag of truce, to negotiate for his release. The Admiral told Frank that Fort McHenry would fall within a day and Baltimore within two. This preview also meant that Frank would be their hostage until the battle was finished.

The British fired rockets for the next twenty-seven hours. Morning light, however, revealed the waving broad stripes and bright stars of the flag above the fort. Frank wrote a poem about what he had seen and published it in the local newspaper. Set to the tune of "To Anacreon in Heaven," the song of a London drinking club, "The Defense of Fort McHenry" became "The Star Spangled Banner." Frank had outdone his ancestor John Key, poet laureate to King Edward IV, in composing the anthem of a great country.

Four years later, in 1818, Frank and Polly Key welcomed Philip Barton, the eighth addition to their family. This was Philip Barton II, not to be confused with his great-uncle, who was also the II, or Jr., his cousin. He would be known by his middle name.

Barton had been in Washington nearly his entire life, starting with McVean's Academy in Georgetown. After boarding school at

Highland Gymnasium in New York, he returned to the capital, where his father had been appointed US Attorney by President Jackson.

Frank remained in office under Van Buren, survived the thirty-one-day presidency of William Henry Harrison, but was sacked by his successor, John Tyler. He may have been the author of the national anthem, but he was still a Democrat. "We regret that this change...is necessary," said the *New York Tribune*. "The author of the Star-Spangled Banner ought to be a Whig."

Back in private practice, Frank traveled to Fort Madison, Iowa, for a federal case on behalf of the New York Land Company. Barton went with him.

Father and son took a train from Baltimore to Philadelphia and travelled from there to Pittsburgh by a canal barge, pulled by a mule (the barge on the water, the mule on land). Pious Frank woke his son early for church and wrote home excited for a second worship service that evening.

The two ate well and slept as comfortably as they could, making their way west. It took four days to reach Cincinnati by riverboat. From there, they traveled to St. Louis, where they boarded a steamer for Iowa.

Barton was fascinated by the booming Mississippi River town and made plans to stay. The frontier was far enough that he could finally step out from his father's shadow. No one would know or care who he was, and he could prove what he was made of, to others as well as himself.

But his father's gravitational pull proved too strong. Frank died suddenly, two years later, at the age of sixty-three. Barton inherited his father's law library and the "hope [Barton] will make such use of it as will enable him to assist his younger brother and sisters and the children of his brother John."[2]

Barton had some early success as a lawyer. Two tailors made a pair of pantaloons for a man and sent them with a delivery boy, with instructions not to turn them over without payment. The intended recipient was offended and refused the delivery. The tailors sued him and won. The buyer hired Key, and on appeal, the court ruled that, because they had used credit in the past, the tailors had an obligation to discuss terms beforehand, reversing the judgment.[3]

The Keys were not only a prominent family, they also married well. Barton's aunt was the wife of Roger Taney, Chief Justice of the US Supreme Court. His sister wed Congressman George Pendleton of Ohio. In 1845, Barton married the beautiful Ellen Swann, daughter of the President of the Bank of Baltimore. Ellen was known for her sweetness, and, in the observation of Jesse Benton Fremont, who knew her well, she "was loved and made happy to a degree few women ever reach." They were soon joined by the first of five children.[4]

Key became an intricate part of capital life. He was appointed by President Polk and confirmed by the Senate as the new US Attorney. At twenty-eight, he was even younger than his father when he held the post. The *Alexandria Gazette* noted: "Mr. Key is the son of the late F. S. Key." As if anyone needed reminding.[5]

He was one of seven riders selected to escort the new president to town. He also served on committees to celebrate Washington's Birthday and memorialize Jackson's death.

Key was an "excellent story teller," "uncouth in speech and rough in address," who would show up at dinner "with a riding whip under his arm." This behavior would've rankled had it come from someone of lower standing. From Key, it was charmingly eccentric. *Oh, that's just Barton!* Riding boots at dinner? *There goes Barton again!*

The culture of Washington was Democratic, Southern, and unapologetically pro-slavery. To maintain his position, Barton would have to vigorously protect the institution.[6]

On April 13, 1848, Washington was caught up with torchlight celebrations in honor of France becoming a republic. As they returned home from an evening celebrating liberty, over forty families realized their slaves were missing. A black cab driver, in exchange for a reward, told the slaveowners what they wanted to know: he had transported a number of them to a ship known as the *Pearl*, which was on its way north to bring them to freedom.[7]

One of the dispossessed owners had a steamboat, for which a crew of thirty-five volunteers was quickly assembled, "armed to the teeth with guns, pistols," and "bowie knives," and well-provisioned with "brandy and other liquors." The *Pearl* was captured and returned to Washington. Nights of riots followed, vandalizing the offices of antislavery newspapers and attacking the homes of abolitionists.[8]

The ship's captain, Daniel Drayton, was consigned to a cell with nothing but a "night bucket" and cut off from the rest of the world. Drayton was a semi-literate small-time seafarer from Philadelphia, and Barton Key was determined to know who had financed and planned the escape. Key found a friend of Drayton's from Boston; he was allowed repeated visits with him, during which Drayton was encouraged to give up his co-conspirators. An offer of $1,000 was delivered by one of his jailors. Drayton was not interested.[9]

One lawyer after another declined to represent Drayton before David Hall accepted. During their first meeting, Key walked into the room, advising Hall to "leave the jail and go home immediately." People "outside were furious, and he ran the risk of his life."

Hall replied that events had taken a bad turn when a lawyer could not speak with his client.

"Poor devils," Key said of Drayton and his crew. "I pity them— they are to be made scape-goats for others." Drayton remembered that Key pursued him with "rancor, and virulence, and fierce pertinacity," and that it "did not look much like pity."[10]

Unable to break Drayton, Key won a grand jury indictment against him on seventy-four counts of transporting a slave. Drayton faced execution without "benefit of the clergy." Many crimes carried the death penalty. This may have been the only one attempting to issue an eternal sentence. Drayton faced a minimum sentence of twenty years and a $15,000 fine for every slave, enough to keep him behind bars for the rest of his life. He noted that not even Methuselah of Old Testament longevity could serve out an 800-year sentence.[11]

Key also obtained forty-one indictments for larceny, one for every identified owner. Drayton's counsel accused Key of self-interest, referencing the $10 fee associated with every indictment.

The first trial against Drayton, for transporting two slaves of Andrew Houver, opened on July 27. James Carlisle joined the defense team, hoping to show the country that Washington could put on a fair trial. Carlisle, though a close friend of the prosecutor, thought Key's opening statement was zealous and "vehement."

Slaves, Key argued, were not common property. With their ability to think, they were less secure than other forms of property; therefore, the jury must subject violators to the most serious consequences. "Suppose a man were to take it into his head that the northern factories were very bad things for the health of the factory girls, and were to go with a schooner for the purpose of liberating those poor devils by stealing the spindles, would not he be served as this prisoner is served here?

"Let it be known from Maine to Texas to the earth's widest limits," Key said, "that we have officers and juries to execute that law, no matter by whom it may be violated!" Key called Drayton "a liar, a rogue, a wretch."

Carlisle took exception to this, saying, "I do not dispute the learned gentleman's right" to use those words. "It is a matter of taste."

Key bristled. "Was I, instead of calling him a liar, to say, 'he told a fib?'" Key then mocked Drayton's fear of dying in the penitentiary. "Don't you think he ought to?" Key asked the jury.

To convict Drayton, the jury had to find that he intended to sell the slaves for profit rather than set them free. The sole evidence on this point was the claim of a single witness that Drayton told him he would make a fortune selling the slaves in the West Indies (despite the fact that the *Pearl* was a bay craft, unfit for sea travel). This witness would soon abandon his story, saying that he couldn't remember whether Drayton had said it.

The next day, with the jury considering the first case, Key began another prosecution against Drayton for transporting William Upperman's slaves. Late in the afternoon, the jury in the first case reached their verdict—guilty. Four jurors in favor of acquittal had been told it would not be "consistent with their personal safety and business interest to persist in disappointing the slave-holding public." But they couldn't intimidate everyone. The first two trials against Drayton's co-conspirator ended in acquittals, the first after a half-hour's deliberation, the second after ten minutes.

Drayton's convictions were reversed on appeal. Key hired another lawyer, Richard Cox, at an additional cost to taxpayers, and retried him. The juries instantly acquitted Drayton on both charges. Key was ready to bargain. He would drop the transportation charges if Drayton pled guilty to larceny. Drayton had little choice. Judge Thomas Crawford fined him $10,060 and sentenced him to jail until it was paid. He spent years there, suffering abuse at the hands of the pro-slavery marshal, until Millard Fillmore pardoned him.

No amount of shilling for the slave power could save Key when the Whigs won the White House. He was forced to hang out a shingle on C Street and advertise his services in "the Courts of this district," adjourning counties, and to anyone with claims before congress or the executive branch.[12]

Pierce restored him as US Attorney four years later. The newspapers reported that he was the "son of Mr. Francis S. Key, author of 'Star Spangled Banner.'" As if anyone needed reminding.[13]

Two years later, Ellen Key fell sick. She and Key were having a conversation when Ellen put her hand to her breast and complained of a sudden pain. "What's that?" she asked. Key watched helplessly as she uttered her final words. He saw her for the last time at the Green Street Presbyterian burial ground, surrounded by their four children and their extended family. He had loved her like no woman on earth and doubted he could be that happy with another. [14]

Chapter Six

A Violent Year

On May 5, 1856, hundreds of armed pro-slavery men surrounded Lawrence, Kansas. The capital of the antislavery movement surrendered peacefully. Their homes and businesses were looted and burned and the presses of their newspapers were thrown in the river.

Charles Sumner of Massachusetts took the senate floor two weeks later. It was ninety degrees in the crowded chamber. Sumner condemned "the crime against Kansas" at length and in vivid tones. Two days later, Congressman Preston Brooks of South Carolina, nephew of a senator who had been criticized by Sumner, crossed the Capitol and ambushed Sumner at his desk. Brooks hit him repeatedly over the head with his solid wooden cane until it shattered. Sumner suffered permanent injury to his nervous system, and it would take years before he returned to the Senate.

Barton Key, who had sought 110 indictments against Captain Drayton, charged Brooks with simple assault and battery. Brooks was allowed to make a long speech defending himself at trial. Key made no objection and did not otherwise put on much of a case. Judge Crawford sentenced Brooks to a $300 fine, and he walked out of the courtroom. Brooks resigned his seat in Congress and was overwhelmingly returned in a special election. Canes flooded in through the mail to replace the one he had broken over Sumner's skull.[1]

★ ★ ★

Buchanan's forces, meanwhile, were huddled in Washington. John Forney, the original tie between Buchanan and Sickles, would serve as campaign manager with Sickles as his top lieutenant. Together they traveled to the convention in Cincinnati. Buchanan maintained a strong lead over fifteen ballots, with Pierce sinking and Douglas far behind. The convention adjourned for the night. When it reconvened in the morning, Pierce's name was withdrawn. Instead of being the first president since Jackson to win re-election, he became the only elected president refused re-nomination by his own party.[2]

Two weeks later, Key tried his second high-profile case of the summer. Philemon Herbert was a gambler, a violent drunk, and, incidentally, a congressman from California. After a late night out, he showed up at the Willard Hotel demanding breakfast, more than a half hour after the last breakfast was served.

"Go get us some breakfast or go away from here, you damned Irish son of a bitch," said Herbert, throwing a plate at a waiter, Thomas Keating. Keating threw a chair at Herbert. The waiter and the congressman scuffled. Another waiter swung a chair at Herbert, hitting Keating by mistake. Keating took another chair to the head when one of Herbert's friends intervened. Keating lost his grip on Herbert, who pulled out a Derringer, placed it to his chest, and fired. Keating asked for a priest with his dying words. Herbert turned himself in and was bailed out. That night, he had dinner with Barton Key, who would be prosecuting his case.[3]

A formidable legal team assembled to protect Herbert. Despite this, Key refused the assistance of co-counsel until just before trial. The Dutch ambassador to the United States was a witness and willing to testify. There were diplomatic hurdles that had to be cleared, and Key ensured that the trial would start before this could happen. Herbert was a Democratic congressman and voted with the president. Also, the 1856 presidential election was a three-way contest: ex-president Millard Fillmore running on the Know Nothing ticket, in addition to John C. Fremont as the first Republican nominee, and Buchanan for the Democrats. If no one received a majority of Electoral Votes, the House would decide, and Herbert's vote would be desperately needed. What was the life of an Irish waiter next to all this?

The *New York Times* wrote that the trial had been politicized "by those whose only duty was to administer stern justice, regardless of all personal or party consequences." Judge Crawford effectively instructed the jury that Herbert had acted in self-defense. Despite this, they deadlocked. A second trial was quickly put together. Three fourths of the jury were made up of anti-Catholic, anti-Irish Know Nothings, a number so far out of their proportion in the District that they were clearly selected for that purpose. A friend of Herbert was placed on the jury by Judge Crawford despite his admission that he was biased in his favor. Every witness agreed that Herbert was the aggressor. Crawford instructed the jury that if Herbert was in danger when he fired the shot, he acted in self-defense. The jury was ordered to disregard the fact that Herbert had struck the first blow and that any danger was entirely of his own making. The *Washington Reporter* said that Key's prosecution was "unworthy of a public officer."[4]

What was the point, the *Tribune* wondered, after Brooks's slap on the wrist and Herbert's acquittal, "of calling congressmen to legal account for ruffianly and sanguinary acts of violence."[5]

The newspapers had run rumors all summer that Sickles intended to run for Congress. They were skeptical, considering the rewards awaiting him should Buchanan win. But they misjudged Sickles, who would rather be his own man. Sickles was nominated for Congress by a Democratic convention on October 10. The *Herald* predicted he would be "gloriously beaten." Sickles and his supporters flooded the district, down Houston, Hammersley and Broadway, with handbills touting him as the "true, tried and personal friend" of James Buchanan.[6]

Tammany Hall was "well filled" on election night, the "yelps and yells and hoorays" interrupted only to hear more good news. Sickles was going to Congress, winning with 5,897 votes, more than 3,760 over his closest opponent.[7]

On November 6, James Buchanan addressed a group that had come to his estate to congratulate him: "It is my sober and solemn conviction that" if "the Northern sectional party [Republicans] should succeed, it would lead inevitably to the destruction of this beautiful fabric reared by our forefathers, cemented by their blood, and bequeathed to us as a priceless inheritance."

This had been essentially the Democratic platform in 1856. They may have criminally mismanaged the country, but the alternative was civil war. The economy was doing well, and just enough Americans were willing to keep the status quo to put Buchanan in the White House.

But the writing was on the wall: Republicans had swept New England and won New York, Iowa, Wisconsin, Michigan, and Ohio. If they could find a candidate who could carry Pennsylvania and either Indiana or Illinois, they would prevail without a single vote in the south.

Nevertheless, Sickles was on his way to Washington. Before he was even sworn in, the Democrats in the state legislature nominated him for the US Senate. They were badly outnumbered by Republicans, and he lost, 77 to 38.[8] But it was a tremendous vote of confidence and a sign of bigger things ahead.[9]

Congressman Daniel Sickles.

The new title fit like the top hat and frock coat he wore in the Inaugural Parade. The Marine Band serenaded the cheering thousands, a harmony of pageantry and military might saluting the peaceful transition of power and the dawn of a new presidency. Even the sun came out and paid its respects.[10]

The general optimism that pervaded the day was not shared by Barton Key. He rode in the parade at the head of the Montgomery Guard, a 100-man militia unit he commanded. Dressed sharply in his green and gold uniform with feathered cap, atop his grey horse, Lucifer, he looked like a modern-day knight.[11]

Watching his uncle, Chief Justice Taney, swear in the new president, Key wondered how he could keep his job. Buchanan and Pierce were both Democrats, but they had fought for control of the party. Buchanan won and would be well within his rights to send Pierce appointees packing.

Buchanan's inaugural ball was the grandest in the history of Washington. Six thousand attendees paid ten dollars apiece to enter a specially built hall in Judiciary Square near the courthouse and jail. Dan and Teresa Sickles loomed large: the energetic, well-dressed Manhattan congressman and the twenty-year-old graceful Italian beauty, both intimates of the new president.

The Sickles visited with Tammany friends like Samuel Butterworth, a Democratic stalwart who had served as Van Buren's US Attorney for Mississippi and who hoped to fare even better under Buchanan. Butterworth's fine suit was accessorized by a bandage around his leg. He and another Tammany man, in their excitement to collect the spoils of office, had overdone their celebration on the train from New York, resulting in a dropped firearm and an unfortunate injury. But damned if he was going to miss the party![12]

Washington was a foreign world to the Sickles. There were unfamiliar faces to recognize, names to learn, and motives to uncover. It was a sea of narrow top hats and wide dresses, filled with elected officials, lobbyists, clerks, reporters, job seekers, society ladies, and peripheral hangers-on. But on that day, their new environs seemed to present more possibilities than threats.

There were new friends to make, like Jeremiah Black, the attorney general; Senators John Slidell and Stephen Douglas; and a host of other luminaries who paid their respects to the Sickles. And their new city seemed to know how to put on a party. There was $3,000 worth of wine, 400 gallons of oysters, and 1,200 quarts of ice cream. The president and his niece Harriet joined the party near 11:00 p.m. as the orchestra played "Hail to the Chief." Buchanan led the room in a cotillion.[13]

While in town for the inauguration, the Sickles were the guests of Jonah Hoover, US Marshal for the District of Columbia. Presidents came and went in Washington. But people like Hoover stayed. He was popular, "remarkably pleasant in his manners, generous almost to a fault, and a Democrat dyed in the wool." He was a member of the Democratic National Committee, "Well known in political circles throughout the country," and "an influential man at the White House" whenever a Democrat was in residence. When Hoover was awarded the post of marshal, it was written: "No office will pay him for his invaluable services to the party." He was only thirty-six.[14]

People like Hoover thrived on knowing just the right person to contact in any situation. He introduced Barton Key to Daniel Sickles. Key, he explained, was his "most intimate friend." He hoped to remain as US Attorney. Would Sickles be willing to intercede with the president on his behalf? Sickles agreed, gladly.[15]

Shortly after, Hoover had a card playing party at his home—gentlemen only. Sickles told Key that he had made his case to Buchanan and "believed the President would reappoint."

"Thank you for your intercession," said Key. "I hope you will persist in urging my claims."[16]

Neither could have imagined that in two years' time, at the courthouse where Key worked every day, their meeting and friendship would be the subject of a speech by John Graham, a bear-like lawyer from the city of New York, defending Sickles for his life:

"Now what were the relations of Mr. Key to Mr. Sickles? We shall show you what those relations were. So far as Mr. Sickles was concerned they were those of sincere friendship. So far as Mr. Key was concerned they were those of professed or avowed friendship. It has been said by the Psalmist, 'for it was not an enemy that reproached me, then could I have borne it. Neither was it he that hated me that did magnify himself against me. Then I would have hid myself from him. But it was thou—a man mine equal, my guide and my acquaintance. We took sweet counsel together, and walked into the house of God in company.' The wrong of a stranger may be borne with patience, but the perfidy of a friend becomes intolerable."

Chapter Seven

The President's Park

The Sickles had breathed in an intoxicating preview of life in Washington. But the thirty-fifth Congress would not meet until December, nine months away. When they returned, they would need a place to live.

Lafayette Square was the most prestigious address you could have without winning the White House. It was the home of vice presidents, cabinet members, senators, and emissaries of great foreign powers. To list its former residents was to call the roll of prominent Americans: James Madison, Martin Van Buren, Henry Clay, Daniel Webster, and John C. Calhoun. Dolly Madison, America's last living link to the Founders, had stayed there until her death, eight years earlier.

Washington was the ninth capital of a young nation. During most of that time, Lafayette Square had been a sleepy graveyard with apple trees. Its first above-ground residents were the laborers who built the White House, living in mud huts among brick kilns and lime pits.[1]

It was intended to be part of the White House grounds. Thomas Jefferson rejected this idea, directing Pennsylvania Avenue to cut across, opening "President's Park" to the public. The huts and debris gave way to a series of beautiful homes and a black iron gate around the park at its center. In 1824, it was named in honor of the Marquis de Lafayette, who, along with a rowdy retinue, was partying his way through the United States in the lead up to the semi-centennial.

The centerpiece of Lafayette Square was a park with a statue of Andrew Jackson on horseback. In Clark Mills's fifteen-ton master-piece, the horse is rearing on its hind legs, and the general is holding his hat in a greeting. To get the pose right, Mills taught a horse to stand on two legs as a model. Audiences, looking at the first equestrian statue in the United States, were sure that it would fall over and were shocked when Mills threw himself against it to prove its stability. It had been unveiled four years before the Sickles arrived, on the forty-eighth anniversary of the Battle of New Orleans. Four cannons captured by Jackson in battle guarded the statue in each direction. Nearby was the Wishing Tree, a chestnut imported from London's Hyde Park and believed to have mystical properties. Its leaves were boiled to make healing teas, and its chestnuts baked to predict the future. Visitors would sit beneath the tree and wish for good things, all wishes to be made silently and never shared.

Sickles found the perfect home: Ewell House, at Number 14 Jackson Place. A beautiful white house with two stories, a basement, an attic, and a "square central hall," it would be the ideal place to live and entertain. Three secretaries of the Navy had lived there, along with two senators and an attorney general. And now, Congressman Daniel Sickles with his wife and daughter were to take up residence. He hired Barton Key to negotiate the lease of the home.

The builder of the house, Dr. Thomas Ewell, was a Navy surgeon, trained at the University of Pennsylvania (and father to Confederate

General Richard Ewell). He opened his practice in America's new capital and placed his house on the west side of the square. His proposal to build a great hospital for Georgetown and Washington went nowhere. Alcohol dulled his genius and ultimately destroyed his career. Soon, all his great plans were reduced to a newspaper advertisement: due to "overwhelming losses and disappointments" and creditors prosecuting him "to the utmost extremity of the law," he was unable to meet his obligations. Ewell House was sold to pay some of these obligations, and he was locked in a debtors' prison.

Ewell's oldest children could remember their neighbor, Stephen Decatur, being brought back to his home to die. Decatur, hero of the War of 1812, was wounded in a duel, and his screams and cries could be heard until 10:30 that night, when he died at the age of forty-one.

He was another man who had chased his ambitions all the way to Lafayette Square and who would make it no farther.[2]

Chapter Eight

The Investigation

Two years later—Friday, February 25, 1859

The House of Representatives opened in prayer at 11:00 a.m. Members debated a proposal to reduce government salaries until the budget was balanced.

Sickles was nowhere to be found.[1]

He arrived at the Capitol after noon. The House floor and hallways were busy, noisy, and no one had any clue to his private panic.

Sickles was searching for George Wooldridge. The thickly mustached Wooldridge was tall, his powerfully built upper body a contrast to his shriveled legs. He carried himself through the world on crutches, a result of infant paralysis that limited his ability to walk. Wooldridge had been born in a saloon and grew up to manage one—Ellsler's, a watering hole and brothel popular with Tammany men. Wooldridge invested his earnings in starting the *Sunday Flash*, covering "Awful developments, dreadful accidents," and scandalous revelations of people's private lives "with all the horror, satire, sagacity, humor, experience and fun necessary for the proper treatment of these important subjects." On that day, he was about to enter a story more sensational than anything he had ever printed.[2]

Most newspapers relied on subscriptions and advertising. Wooldridge found the real money was in blackmail. He moved in low circles and knew the secrets of men who couldn't afford to read about them in the *Flash*. The publishers found themselves defendants in the first obscenity trial in New York City. Wooldridge was a survivor, turning state's evidence against his partners in exchange for a dismissal. On the stand, he defended the newspaper as having done "more good in correcting vice and shaming profligacy than all the sermons preached by all the paid and pretended moralists of the church put together."

After the trial, Wooldridge opened the *Libertine*, a similar paper featuring woodcut "pleasure pictures." The law caught up with him again, resulting in a sixty-day stay on Blackwell's Island. It was an occupational hazard, but after his fifth indictment, this time for defaming a dancer, Wooldridge decided on a new line of work. He set out for Europe as the business manager of the Virginia Serenaders, the first minstrel show. He reappeared a decade later in Albany as the doorkeeper of the Assembly, where he befriended State Senator Sickles. When Sickles was elected to congress, he placed his friend as a deputy clerk in the House map room.

Sickles found Wooldridge behind the speaker's chair.

"George, I want to speak to you on a painful matter; late last night, I received this letter." Wooldridge thought his friend "appeared different from what he had been the day before...very much affected and distressed."[3]

Sickles read from the parchment, slowly breaking down until he burst into tears. Unable to finish the final lines, he handed the letter to Wooldridge. "I would not have given it another thought," Sickles said. "But its detail made it simple to verify and impossible to disregard."

Sickles told Wooldridge of his trip that morning to the house mentioned in the letter and his conversation with the neighbors. Barton Key had indeed rented it out, and a woman "was in the habit of going there. My hope is that this is not my wife but some other woman. As my friend, you will go there, and see whether it is or not. Get a carriage, we'll go, and I'll show you the house."

Washington was a patchwork of neighborhoods, from brilliant marble edifice to the gritty, muddy dwelling places of the tradesmen. On their two-mile ride, Sickles and Wooldridge passed from one to the other. Sickles pointed to the house at 383 15th Street. They drove past without stopping and returned to the Capitol, where Sickles was urgently needed.

The Naval Appropriations Bill was back on the floor. Sickles proposed an amendment to maintain the yards at Pensacola, Norfolk, New York, Mare Island, and Sackett's Harbor, telling his colleagues, "There never had been a time when a strong Navy was more necessary than now."

He was questioned by Congressman John Millson of Virginia. "But sir, it is a truth that in this country, with a very small Navy, we have more Navy Yards than the great naval powers of the world," more "than either England or France."

"We have not half the number that England has," Sickles said. "She has eight within the British Isle." Not everything called a "Navy Yard" was the same. "I am not speaking of colonial dockyards, where occasional ships of war may undergo repairs, but I am speaking of the great establishments for the constitution of war vessels." Sickles rattled off the challenges and opportunities that required a strong fleet: European navies off the waters of Mexico, Haiti and St. Domingo in a state of revolution, commercial trading routes in Central America and new ones in China and Japan, and increasing hostility with Spain.

Meanwhile, Wooldridge's investigation was off to a promising start. Everyone he met had something to say about the house and the people who used it. Key was the man in question. There was no doubt about that. Workers of the capital may have been invisible to the US Attorney, but they could see him. An acquaintance of the owner said that Key claimed to be renting the house for a member of Congress. The man and the woman met there two or three times a week, starting in January. Their most recent rendezvous had been on Thursday. Wooldridge's informants agreed that it was the same woman every time, though she covered herself in a veil or a shawl.

Wooldridge wrote down descriptions of her outfits in a notebook. To be certain, he would have to catch them in the act. Wooldridge walked on his crutches across the street from Number 383 and knocked on the door. He told the woman his business and asked if he could rent a room in her home. The owner was a single mother, and the money would help. She agreed. Wooldridge returned to the Capitol and shared what he had learned. Sickles thought the outfits worn by the mystery woman resembled clothes belonging to Teresa. Wooldridge promised an update after the next day's surveillance.

The following day, a Saturday, two Washington newspapers, the *Star* and the *States*, carried a curious advertisement among ads for competing undertakers; weather reports from "stormy, cool" New York, rainy Lower Peach Tree, Alabama, and "clear, pleasant" Cincinnati; a promotion for a sermon on "Sinful Pleasures" delivered to the Young Men's Christian Association; and a funeral notice for Mary Quincy, "for many years a teacher in Washington." A finger graphic pointed to the text:

> R.P.G., who recently addressed a letter to a gentleman in
> this city, will confer a great favor upon the gentleman to

whom the letter was addressed by granting him an early, immediate and confidential interview.[4]

It was the first modest manifestation of the Sickles story in print—one that would soon consume more column inches than any previous event in history.

Sickles answered the first roll call of the morning. The Navy Yard debate continued. "Mr. Chairman," Sickles began, "this is not the first time that the Brooklyn Navy-Yard has been selected as a point of attack from the other side of the House."[5]

Wooldridge sat in his rented room, watching out the window while Sickles defended American naval power. Quiet. No signs of life. At least he was indoors. After a dull day staring at an empty building, he returned to his boarding house. There was a note waiting from Sickles: "Be exceedingly tender in the prosecution of your inquiries. I have reason to believe my wife is innocent."

Wooldridge ate dinner and walked to the Capitol. Sickles and Wooldridge met once again behind the Speaker's Chair. Wooldridge gave him an update, such as it was. Sickles shared his news with excitement. Teresa couldn't have been the woman with Key on Thursday. Her whereabouts were accounted for the entire day. And the neighbors said that it was always the same woman. So it must be someone else.

Wooldridge steeled himself. Earlier that day he had learned his initial report was wrong. And didn't realize the significance. Key's most recent visit to the house was Wednesday, *not* Thursday. Wooldridge watched Sickles absorb the blow. It unmanned him completely, he thought. Wooldridge managed to move Sickles to a private room, where the weight of it came crashing down. Sickles sobbed uncontrollably.[6]

Chapter Nine

New Latitudes

Winter of 1857–58—One year earlier

B arton Key bundled up and boarded an icy steamship. Days later, he could put his coat away and leave his porthole open. At night, he could stand on the deck and look at the big moon and vivid stars and feel the warm trade winds and watch the sun rise from the same spot. It was still winter, but it didn't feel like it.

It had been years since he'd traveled, when he and his father had ventured into the heart of the country. Now there was the Morro Castle, the oldest building he'd ever seen, the massive fortress that guarded the harbor of Havana. The masts of the ships in port looked like a dense forest. He could see working men in little boats with oranges and bananas, wearing straw hats and blue and white checked shirts.

A man boarded the steamer, wearing a white linen suit and straw hat with a red cockade and chewing a cigar—how you would expect a Cuban functionary to look. He was a health officer and had to clear passengers for arrival. Key hadn't felt healthy for quite some time. In fact, he had hoped this trip would restore him.

Key walked the narrow streets of the old city. He could smell cigars and flowers, and he saw mango and palm trees for the first time. There were beggar girls playing tambourines and lottery vendors selling tickets. The billiard halls and cafés were filled with people. In the cobbled Plaza des Armas, he could hear a military band play for an hour at night. There were at least fifty instruments, maybe more.

Near the water were the Banos de Mar, little square pools cut into the rock, filled with seventy-two-degree water from the Gulf Stream. There were holes big enough to let the water flow in and out but small enough to keep the sharks out.

Key had taken a proper vacation in a healing climate, but he felt no better. As the steamer headed north, he passed the lighthouse at Cape Hatteras, the final resting place for so many sailors. The year had been full of struggles, but at least he'd kept his job. Maybe 1858 would be better.[1]

Daniel and Teresa Sickles entered Washington society in earnest in December of 1857, more than a year after his election and nine months since the Inauguration.

On February 2, Buchanan sent congress the application of Kansas to join the union, with a pro-slavery Constitution adopted by force and fraud.[2]

There were days of acrimonious debate. It was after 2:00 a.m. on the House floor. Members smoked, slept at their desks, came and went from the bar. A fight broke out between members.

It was a "truly fearful contest," where "blows were given and taken indiscriminately." Sickles thought the congressmen pounded "each other with little skill, but with much enthusiasm, making blood fly in every direction." Finally, one congressman grabbed the hair of another and found himself holding nothing but a wig. "A mighty shout of laughter filled the hall." The melee ended.[3]

The breakdown in Congress had not yet infected the social scene. Virginia Clay felt "the surface of society in Washington" was "serene and smiling, though the fires of a volcano raged in the under-political world." There were balls and parties; hops and dinners; and plays, operas, and symphonies. Clay said that she felt so tired at night that she couldn't wiggle an antenna.[4]

Teresa held receptions on Tuesdays and dinners on Thursday evenings. As Ladies Palmerston and Clarendon had done in London, the grand dames Mathilde Slidell and Virginia Clay adopted Teresa in Washington.

Teresa's hectic calendar was relayed to a high school friend: "Tomorrow night Mrs. [Stephen] Douglas's party will be a perfect crush. So many invitations are out and we were invited to dine at [Senator] Gwin's but Miss Gwin is quite ill and the dinner is therefore postponed. On Thursday we have another large dinner party. I was invited to one yesterday but was too ill to go."

Teresa's entertainments were the equal of anyone's. And they were far from free. The lease on the Ewell House was $3,000 a year, equal to Sickles's congressional salary. Teresa had $5,000 worth of jewelry and a "splendid carriage with outriders." To maintain their lifestyle, Sickles had to keep his law practice in New York, which took him away from the capital more than he liked.[5]

Chapter Ten

Vile Calumnies

March 1858

Stephen Beekman was "violently in love" with Teresa. Now she was off riding horses with Barton Key, outside the city on the road to Bladensburg. By Beekman's count, this was the third time since Dan Sickles went to New York on business. He watched them go inside a hotel and waited for them to come out—an hour and a half later. He was furious. Key had bragged to him once: "I only need thirty-six hours with any woman to make her do what I please." Now it seemed he was right.

At first, Teresa and Key rode in a group, along with Congressman John Haskin of New York and reporter John McElhone of the *Congressional Globe*, out to Potomac Falls. Then it was the two of them. What had happened that first day? Maybe the others had cancelled. Or maybe Key had suggested they ride alone. But what Beekman knew for sure was that Sickles was out of town and this was the *third time* Teresa was out with Key.[1]

Beekman became too upset to keep it to himself. He went to Willard's where he saw Marshal Bacon, a young clerk at the Interior

Department. He and Bacon were loosely connected through New York and Albany circles and had met at the Sickles home. Bacon took him aside, out of earshot of everyone else. What did he think about Mr. Key's attentions toward Mrs. Sickles? Bacon affected a "confidential tone," and made "several very indelicate remarks about Mrs. Sickles." He then asked for Beekman's opinion of her. Beekman gave it to him.

Before long, Beekman was summoned to the Sickles home. Sickles asked: "What did you say about my wife in connection with Mr. Key's name?"

"Trifling jokes." Beekman said. And "that I had noticed a flirtation going on." But "I had uttered no charges, no facts, no inferences even injurious to Mrs. Sickles, but merely generalities, without the slightest design or malice. What I had said I had said and am personally responsible for."

Beekman walked out of the house, never to return.

Jonah Hoover, who had made the connection between Sickles and Key, brought the matter to Key's attention. Key was determined to discredit the whole thing as idle gossip. He sat down at his desk and spread out a piece of buff paper with his family crest at the top: a dragon with a key in its mouth.

He wrote first to Wooldridge, who had brought Beekman's chatter to Sickles: "Will you please state in writing what communication you made to [Sickles] concerning me and also give me your authority for making such communications?"

Key thought Wooldridge would back down. But if Key had spent his life among the highest society, Wooldridge had spent his among the lowest. His replied: "Marshal J. Bacon informed me on Tuesday afternoon, March 23, that Mr. Beekman said that Mrs. Sickles [and Mr. Key] had been out riding on horseback three different times...during Mr. Sickles's last absence to the city of New York," that they had "stopped at a house on the road towards Bladensburg," "that Mrs. Sickles had a room there and remained one hour and a half," and that he had no doubt there was an intimacy" between the two. "There was much more of the same kind of conversation." For good measure, Wooldridge added, Bacon told him that Key had bragged that he could make any woman do whatever he wanted within thirty-six hours.

Key took this letter and forwarded it to Bacon, who also stuck to his story. "In the main," Bacon replied, "his statement is correct." I learned these things from Mr. Beekman. "I stated at the time to Mr. Wooldridge and now repeat, that I did not believe there was any truth" to it and "deemed it a fabrication."

Beekman thought the matter behind him until there was a knock on his door. It was Jonah Hoover with a note from Key. Are you "responsible for the vile calumnies?" Key demanded "an immediate answer."

Beekman responded: "I disavow that I was ever their author, and pronounce everything therein as a lie, and also the statement of Mr. Bacon that I was their author." Perhaps Beekman didn't want to get involved, didn't want to admit how he knew, or didn't want to fight a duel with Key. But he had folded.

Key forwarded his response to Sickles with a note: "My Dear Sir," he wrote. "You will perceive the effort to fix the ridiculous and disgusting slander on me" was unsuccessful. Jonah Hoover delivered the chain of letters, from Wooldridge to Bacon to Beekman, to the Ewell House.

"I have always liked Mr. Key," Sickles said, and "thought him a man of honor. This thing shocked me when I first heard of it." But due to Beekman's disavowal and Key's assurances, Sickles was "willing to meet him as formerly."[2]

Beekman saw Bacon at Willard's and charged him, cane in hand, "intending to apply it to him promptly," along with some "rather harsh epithets." Bacon pleaded with him: could they please discuss it outside? Beekman realized that a public beating would attract unwanted attention. Outside, Bacon said that "he must have been beside himself" and "would never injure [your] character for anything." He promised to retract everything. In writing, tomorrow.

But he didn't. Bacon managed to avoid Beekman until the latter returned to New York.

Chapter Eleven

The Last Dance

April 18, 1858

For Lo! Amid the night of faction's din,
A bright idea lights the mind of Gwin,
And see, responsive to her welcome call,
All parties vie to grace her Fancy Ball.
—"A Metrical Glance at the Fancy Ball"

It wasn't the best time for a party. The Douglas Democrats hated Buchanan Democrats for trying to impose slavery where it wasn't wanted. The Buchanan Democrats hated Douglas Democrats for not following the party line. The bitterly divided Democrats agreed that they hated the Republicans. The Republicans hated both factions of the Democratic Party. Eight days earlier, after months of bitter debate, the House repudiated the president and rejected the admission of Kansas under the Lecompton Constitution.

But the invitations had already gone out.

Mary Gwin was determined to host a masquerade ball, the grandest in the history of Washington. William, her husband, was a medical doctor who had represented Mississippi in congress. He moved to California in 1849, made a fortune in gold mining, and returned to Washington as one of California's first two senators. Gwin was more popular in Washington this time around, spending $75,000 a year on entertaining (twenty-five times a congressman's

63

salary). The ball was the most eagerly anticipated event that anyone could remember, and a massive economic stimulus for tailors and seamstresses.[1]

Mary greeted her guests as Queen Maria Theresa, wife of Louis XIV, whose extravagance had bankrupted France.

Little Red Riding Hood—Teresa Sickles—arrived on her own. The poet John de Havilland published a thirty-page poem about the ball. He looked at Teresa and thought:

> Lo! Little "Riding Hood," with artless grace,
> Reveals the sweetness of her childish face

There was a cavalier, matador, and ranchero, mingling with a Quaker and a Tartan. Some went for the abstract, such as sunrise, liberty, winter, night, and the nine of clubs. Some women went for royalty, from a French marchioness to an Indian princess, while others came as an English bar maid, a Spanish peasant girl, or a gypsy. There was some amusing overlap in costumes: four of the diplomatic corps dressed as the French mime, Pierrot.

Barton Key was dressed as an English Huntsman:

> Here "English Hunters" run their game to earth,
> And strike the "Key" note of their jovial mirth

Alice Key Pendleton, his sister, dressed as the Star Spangled Banner itself: a white satin gown, a golden eagle, a tricolor sash, and a crown of thirteen stars.[2]

> ... by proud hereditary right, our "Starry Banner" floats
> in living light ...

President Buchanan wore a black suit and white cravat.

> Lo! In the centre, he who calmly bears, Upon that snowy
> head, the nation's cares ...

He and the senators in attendance, such as William Seward, Jefferson Davis, and Gwin, were among the few out of costume.

The Huntsman and Little Red Riding Hood danced the fastmoving gallop across the room.[3]

> Where Impudence and Pertness takes the floor ...

Mary Gwin had triumphed.

> The frolic subjects of the sportive Queen, whose kindness
> rules the gay, fantastic scene ...

Descriptions of her ball made their way into newspapers across the country. It figured prominently in memoirs of the time. Many would remember it not for its opulence, but as the last time in history that many of those in attendance met on cordial terms.

> But this is not the time to moralize; the buzz and glitter
> claim our ears and eyes ...

The Huntsman and Little Red Riding Hood left together at 2:00 a.m. Beekman's loose talk and Key's desperate epistolary campaign had occurred only three weeks earlier. The situation called for extreme caution. They seemed to have none at all. Key and Teresa waded through a sea of the best carriages in Washington to hers.

Teresa instructed her coachman, John Thompson, to take them to the National Hotel. "Drive down H or I Street," she added. It was an indirect route. When they arrived, Thompson sat for what felt like a long time. He had picked up his mistress, who had a man in the coach with her who was not his master. He did not know what was happening inside. Finally, Key exited, bidding her goodnight. Thompson drove Teresa home.[4]

> ... pained with beauty, the full heart, oppressed,
> Demands the relief of nature—rest.

★ ★ ★

Henry Watterson was a nineteen-year-old reporter, the correspondent of the Philadelphia *Press*, run by John Forney, who had introduced Sickles to Buchanan.

He felt awful, and illness was only part of it. In bed at his room in Willard's, he was reading about Senator Gwin's ball in the newspapers and staring at his Spanish cavalier costume that, thanks to his severe indisposition, would never be worn.

Watterson was surprised when Teresa Sickles came to see him just to check in and see what he needed. It was true what they said about her: she would treat a servant with the same kindness and respect as a king.[5]

There was speculation that Sickles might not seek a second term. He was under consideration to serve as ambassador to Spain in order to negotiate the purchase of Cuba. It was an issue he cared about and was closely identified with. But there were many reasons to stay. Sickles had distinguished himself as a national star in the six short months that Congress had been in session. He was a force to be reckoned with on issues of consequence, independent of his relationship with the president. He had traveled to Spain and knew they were unlikely to sell. That made it a bad tradeoff for leaving center stage.

The reason to go, to take his wife and daughter and leave Washington, to return to the world of diplomacy where they had thrived and been happy, had not yet come into focus and would not until it was too late.

Congress adjourned on June 14, and the Sickles returned to New York. It was time to campaign for re-election, and the split in the party assured that he would face a Democrat as well as a Know Nothing opponent. Bob Wood, his Democratic challenger, was noted for being "Successful in business," "very rich," "sport[ing] a fine moustache," and owning a pair of horses." The newspapers predicted Sickles's defeat.[6]

But on election night, he stood on the balcony of Gardiner's Hotel, his campaign headquarters, while 3,000 supporters, accompanied by three bands, congratulated him on his victory. Among the banners made for the occasion was this: "The Hon. D. E. Sickles—triumphant over a base combination of moral and political depravity and corruption." Daniel Sickles acknowledged this impressive display of support. "I thank you for the cordial manner in which you have honored me by your enthusiastic congratulations. We had, indeed, a hot contest. It is gratifying to know that we made no concessions." Concessions were never really his thing. Every sort of opposition "was openly defied and crushed."[7]

Chapter Twelve

No. 383
15th Street

John Thompson drove Teresa to the meeting place. Key was already there, as usual, with his horse, Lucifer, tied to a post. Key helped her down from the carriage. They walked together through the old iron graveyard gate and down the gentle slopes toward the Anacostia River, out of Thompson's sight.

Victorians believed in a thin curtain separating the living from the dead. They replaced the austere, square church burial yards with parks, paths, and trees, a place of beauty where people could experience closeness to loved ones or simply pass a pleasant afternoon.

William Swinton, a stonecutter who helped build the Capitol, became the first permanent resident in 1807, marked by a sandstone tablet with colonial calligraphy. Originally known as the Washington Parish Burial Ground, it was designed for everyday residents like Swinton. But the city was filled with Congressmen months out of the year, Congressmen who frequently died in office, and shipping caskets presented logistical and hygienic issues. Their increasing presence gave the cemetery its name and endowed it with a certain éclat, so that the prominent families of the district built vaults and mausoleums there. Invitations to the best party in Washington, it appeared, mattered even after death. Now there was row after row of cenotaphs, square memorials with pointy tops, one for every congressman who was buried there over the past twenty-five years.

Surrounded by weeping willows, away from the prying eyes of Thompson and the other servants, Key believed they could finally be alone. Then they saw Congressman Haskin and his wife out for a walk. They would need someplace safer.

George Brown, the White House gardener, could be sure of one thing. If something out of the ordinary happened in his neighborhood, he would hear about it. Nancy, his wife, made it her business to know. Philip Barton Key had come by earlier that day, asking if the John Gray house was occupied. He had said it was for a congressman. Or maybe a senator. Nancy told him that nobody lived there and told him to contact the owner. She gave him his address at his new place on Capitol Hill.

It wouldn't be long before he would see her again, somewhere safer, Key thought.

John Gray was surprised to find the US Attorney at his door. Was his house on 15th Street still for rent?

It was. Fifty dollars a month.

Key said that it was needed for a Mr. Wright, a member of Congress from Massachusetts.

Gray returned to the house three weeks later to deliver wood. He had not been back since.

The whole thing was strange.

The Club House was a private home on the east side of Lafayette Square, across the park from the Sickles. It was "much frequented by fashionable young bloods of the town, statesmen, and literati," and amply supplied with booze and manly bluster.[1]

Albert Megaffey was a member. He was a contractor, didn't work in politics, and had greater liberty to speak frankly with Key. On a night of drinking and storytelling at the Club House, he told him what people were whispering: Key, you've been overly attentive to Teresa Sickles.

Key was indignant. I have a great friendship with her, he replied. I entertain nothing but "paternal feelings toward her," he said, as with "a child." Nothing but "kind and fatherly feelings." He had said the same thing to Jonah Hoover during the Beekman blowup. Megaffey tried another tack as time passed and the situation became more conspicuous: Key, you will "get into danger or difficulty about the matter."

But Key seemed impervious to danger.

As a younger man, Key had gone to great lengths to participate in a duel. Under the headline, "Hold Him Tight!" it was reported: "All Washington city, and a considerable part of creation, were thrown into an excitement," by rumors of an impending duel between Barton and Captain May of the Navy. May, a disappointed suitor to Key's then fiancée, had publicly insulted him at a Baltimore hotel.

Their friends raced to the magistrate's office, hoping to have them arrested to prevent a duel. Key traveled to Washington in disguise and took a room at Brown's Hotel. When the marshals found him there, he announced that he would do violence to anyone who opened the door. Key attempted to leave through a window, then climbed back in once he realized someone was stationed outside. He opened the door and threw a deputy marshal to the floor, along with James Carlisle, his friend and fellow lawyer. Barton ran downstairs and leapt onto his horse, escaping. Yet despite Key's best efforts—and news stories from Philadelphia to Boston—the duel never happened.[2]

Key's brother had died in a duel eight years earlier. There was an initial round of fire, but he and John Sherburne were unharmed: "Mr. Key, I have no desire to kill you."

"No matter," Daniel Key said, "I came to kill you." In the second round, Key was shot through the lower part of his chest. He died where he fell, twenty minutes later. The Keys pursued Sherburne, "most vindictively, threatening to assassinate" him. One of their "most influential friends" went to President Jackson to have him dismissed from the Navy. "No, by God!" said Jackson. "I wish he had shot the whole family."[3]

Nearly ten years later, the house of Senator Thomas Hart Benton caught fire. The firemen looked on helplessly, frozen water in their hoses, along with a "vast throng" gathered outside. "Volumes of suffocating smoke drove back all who tried to enter," wrote Jesse Benton Fremont, his daughter. As people cried out warnings, Barton Key ran into the house to save a portrait of Benton's deceased wife. When he reappeared, there was a "great shout of relief." Key emerged, singed and scorched, "his eyes alight with joy." Instead of a portrait of Benton's wife, however, he had accidentally saved a painting of the senator as a younger man.[4]

Whether it was being shot or burned, Key had long ignored signs of danger. The affair was increasingly "well known" at the Club House and a frequent "topic of conversation." Key greeted all warnings with an "air of haughty bravado" and refused to listen to "remonstrance from any quarter."

Key did, however, drop his denials. "Sickles's wife is my whore!" he bragged.

His friends warned, "Something dangerous will grow."

"Give me a French intrigue," Key said. "A fig for common license! French intrigue and romance, with a good spice of danger in it!"

What if Sickles found out?

"I am prepared for any emergency," Key said, tapping the left breast of his coat. Besides, "Sickles is a damned Yankee and would do nothing if he did find it out."[5]

Wednesday, February 24, 1859—
The Day before the Letter

The ritual began early in the New Year. A tall, well-dressed gentleman appeared, conspicuous in a neighborhood of free blacks, poor whites, and their modest houses, mud huts, and stables. He approached the front door of 383 15th Street and opened it with a key. Stuck between K and L Streets, it was among the more presentable brick buildings in the area, two stories tall, its shutters tightly closed as if keeping a secret. No one had lived there for some time. An unseen hand would drop a string below a second story shutter. Smoke would rise from the chimney. As if conjured out of air, the woman in black would arrive and pass through the back gate.[6]

John Seeley, his wife, and his daughter watched it all from their second-story window. They saw the woman entering the house. John could see her mouth below her short veil. "She looked like a person badly frightened," he thought. "Severely threatened." The neighborhood welcomed this break in the day, peeking out windows and looking up discreetly from yardwork. What happened inside No. 383 was in line with their imaginations.

This had been going on all winter, but today was different. The neighbors noticed a ghostly figure, tightly wrapped in a shawl, watching silently from across the street. Neither the man nor the woman had seen the specter as they entered the house. But he had noticed them. A woman on the street saw the Man in the Shawl walking quickly toward her: "Is the house occupied or not?" he asked, his face hidden behind the shawl.

"Yes, sir," she answered.

"Very well, that's all I want."[7]

Teresa could remember when Key had told her about the house and the exhilaration of meeting him there for the first time. There was no chance of being seen by a Stephen Beekman or a gossipy servant. Within these walls, there was no danger of interruption. There were two rooms and a kitchen on the first floor, neither of them in use. It was carpeted, and lightly furnished with some chairs and a bookcase.

Teresa walked to the top of the stairs to a room with a bureau and a bed. It was one piece of furniture too many. After an hour, they left the house, he from the front, she from the back. The Man with the Shawl had watched them leave. He walked toward Key, said something that only he could hear, and quickly walked away.[8]

Chapter Thirteen

An Improper Interview

Saturday, February 26, 1859 — Two Days after the Letter

S ickles came home in the early evening to a different house than the one he had left. Inside was the wife who had betrayed him—not an accused wife or a possibly unfaithful wife, but a guilty wife. The lovers had met on *Wednesday*, not *Thursday*. The words were still ringing in his ears. Only minutes before, he had been at the Capitol with Wooldridge, crying in a private room off the House floor because his entire world had come apart.

Bridget Duffy was a young, dark-haired Irish maid who worked for the family. She thought it strange that Sickles walked straight upstairs without eating. He eventually rang for food. "His manner and appearance seemed troubled."

Teresa was sitting in her room, completely unaware. Everything changed in an instant. Her husband walked in and accused her of betraying him with Barton Key. She denied it. He replied with specifics. Wednesday. Two o'clock. 383 15th Street. A woman in a black velvet shawl with bugle trim.

"I am betrayed and lost!" Teresa said. She felt dizzy. The image of her angry husband faded to black.

Teresa came to and realized it was no dream. She was terrified he would hurt her. Sickles assured her that he would not and that he believed her to be the victim of a scoundrel. But he wanted to know everything. A confession. In writing.[1]

Teresa might have obliged him anything. There was guilt and shame, but also relief. For the first time in a year, she had nothing to hide. Teresa sat at her desk and stared at the blank page in front of her. Soon it would be covered in ink and all the truth would be out. For how long have you been going to that house? Dan wanted to know. What did you do there? Where was Laura during this time? Has it happened in this house?

> I have been in a house in Fifteenth street with Mr. Key; how many times I don't know; I believe the house belongs to a colored man; the house was unoccupied.
>
> Commenced going there the latter part of January; have been in alone, and with Mr. Key; usually stayed an hour or more; there was a bed in the second story.
>
> I did what is usual for a wicked woman to do; the intimacy commenced this winter, when I came from New York, in that house; an intimacy of an improper kind; have met half a dozen times or more at different hours of the day; on Monday of this week, and Wednesday also; we arranged meetings when we met in the street, and at parties; never would speak to him when Mr. Sickles was at home, because I knew he did not like for me to speak to him; did not see Mr. Key for some days after I got there; he told me he had hired the house as a place where he and I could meet; I agreed to it; I had nothing to eat or drink

there; the room is warmed by a wood fire; Mr. Key generally goes first; have walked there together, say four times;
I do not think more.

I was there on Wednesday last, between two and three;
went there alone;

Laura was at Mrs. Hoover's; Mr. Key took her and left
her there at my request; from there I went to Fifteenth street
to meet Mr. Key; from there to the milk woman's; immediately after Mr. Key left Laura at Mrs. Hoover's I met him
in Fifteenth street.

Went in by the back gate; went in the same bedroom,
and there an improper interview was had; this occurred on
Wednesday, 23 February, 1859.

Mr. Key has kissed me in this house a number of times.
I do not deny that he has had connection in this house, last
spring a year ago, in the parlor, on the sofa. Mr. Sickles
was sometimes out of town and sometimes in the Capitol.
I think the intimacy commenced in April or May 1858. I
did not think it safe to meet him in this house, because
there are servants who might suspect something.

As a general thing have worn a black and white woollen
plaid dress and beaver hat trimmed with black velvet. Have
worn a black silk dress there also; also a plaid silk dress,
black velvet cloak trimmed with lace, and black velvet
shawl trimmed with fringe. On Wednesday either had a
cloak trimmed with lace and black velvet, or a shawl
trimmed with fringe. On Wednesday I either had on my
brown dress or black and white dress, beaver hat and velvet
shawl. I arranged with Mr. Key to go in the back way, after
leaving Laura at Mrs. Hoover's. The arrangement to go in
the back was either made in the street or at Mr. [Senator

Stephen] Douglas's as we would be less likely to be seen. The house is in fifteenth street, between K and L, on the left hand side of the way. Arranged the interview for Wednesday in the street, I think, on Monday. I went in the front door. It was open; occupied the same room; undressed myself and he also; went to bed together.

Mr. Key has ridden in Mr. Sickles's carriage, and has called at his house without Mr. Sickles's knowledge, and after my being told not to invite him to do so, and against Mr. Sickles's repeated request.

She signed the letter with her maiden name, "Teresa Bagioli." A legalistic postscript followed:

This is a true statement written by myself, without any inducement held out by Mr. Sickles of forgiveness or reward, and without any menace from him. This I have written with my bedroom door open, and my maid and child in the adjourning room, at 8 1/2 o'clock in the evening. Miss Ridgeley is in the house within call.

Teresa Bagioli

Lafayette Square, Washington D.C., February 26, 1859

A second postscript was added.

Mr. and Mrs. Pendleton dined here two weeks ago last Thursday, with a large party. Mr. Key was also here, her brother, and at my suggestion, he was invited because he lived in the same house, and also because he had invited

Mr. Sickles to dine with him, and Mr. Sickles wished to invite all those from whom he had received invitations; and Mr. Sickles said, "do as you choose."

It was signed again, "Teresa Bagioli. Written and signed in the presence of C. M. Ridgeley and Bridget Duffy."

C. M. Ridgeley, known as "Octavia," was Teresa's closest friend and a frequent house guest, a beautiful blue-eyed blonde around her age. Her father had died in the Mexican War, and she lived alone with her mother. She and Bridget were called into the room to sign the letter, attesting to its authorship. They quickly learned the reasons for the raised voices and sobbing.[2]

Sickles asked Teresa for her wedding ring. She slipped it off her finger, where he had placed it six years ago, and handed it to him. He left her room.

Teresa refused to lie in the bed with Octavia. To punish herself, she sprawled on the floor with her head propped up on the rung of a wooden chair. From her room, Bridget drifted to sleep amid the sounds of Teresa and Dan sobbing from their separate rooms.[3]

Chapter Fourteen

Sunday in Lafayette Square

Sunday, February 27, 1859

T he day opened quiet, clear, and pleasant.[1]

Key walked into the basement of the Willard Hotel. He was greeted by the staff of the barber shop, free black men in "clean white jackets and aprons," and seated in a chair. He relaxed as they spread a fragrant cream across his face. He daydreamed of Teresa, close by, in the home of her husband on Lafayette Square.

The straight razor scraped his cheeks and chin. The barber cleaned up his face. If he saw her today—and he was determined to see her— he would be fresh and smooth shaven. Key encountered Mayor James Berrett and S. S. Parker outside the barber shop. He bowed to Parker and spoke for a moment with the mayor. Key then made a joke that came completely out of nowhere—something about Sickles killing him. It seemed strange but insignificant in the moment. If Key finally understood that he was playing with fire, he didn't seem bothered by it.[2]

Samuel Butterworth, visiting from New York, was seated in the parlor of Senator Gwin. With them was Robert Walker, the former senator and treasury secretary, who as governor had brought free elections to Kansas before resigning over the Lecompton Constitution. Butterworth was the Tammany stalwart who had been accidentally shot on the train ride to Buchanan's inauguration. As hoped, he benefited from the new administration as the Superintendent of the New York Assay Office, responsible for testing the purity of American coins.

A messenger arrived at Gwin's house for Butterworth. He read the letter:

Dear B.—Come to me right away.

He showed the letter to Gwin and Walker. "What can Mr. Sickles desire?" Butterworth excused himself and headed to the Ewell House.

★ ★ ★

Bridget Duffy had plenty to pray for that morning at Mass. The previous night, she had witnessed Teresa's confession and fallen asleep to the sounds of the Sickles wailing in separate rooms. She returned home unsure of what awaited her. Bridget walked upstairs to clean Sickles's room. It was empty.

Sickles entered suddenly, crying and sobbing, his hands tearing his hair from his head. "God, witness my troubles!" he begged.

Butterworth let himself into the house and searched for Sickles. He walked upstairs and opened the door to his room.

Sickles lay on the bed with his head buried in a pillow. "I am a dishonored and ruined man and cannot look you in the face," he explained. Sickles poured out the revelations of recent days: the anonymous letter, the desperate investigation, the rendezvous house, the encounters *in his own home*, the confrontation, and the confession.

Butterworth could do little to make him feel better. But he did have thoughts on how to proceed. Send Teresa back to New York. It was near the end of session and would not raise suspicion. Travel to Europe during the recess of Congress. Arrange a separation. File for divorce. Almost no one will know the truth of the matter.

"My friend, I would gladly pursue this course, but so abandoned, so reckless have Key and my wife been, that all the negroes in that neighborhood, and I dare not say how many other persons, know all about the circumstances."

If true, that certainly narrowed their options, thought Butterworth. He went downstairs to find Wooldridge newly arrived. "This is a terrible affair," said Wooldridge. He didn't know the half of it. Butterworth handed him Teresa's confession.

Butterworth excused himself to get a drink. If Sickles asks, tell him I'll return. His destination was the Club House.

It was a three-minute walk across the park, around 700 feet, from the Ewell House to the Club House. As Butterworth crossed the Jackson statue, the White House was directly to his right, just across Pennsylvania Avenue, and the Club House straight ahead, across from the Sickles home. The crooked trees that dotted the square had yet to regain the leaves they had lost in autumn. Butterworth crossed Madison Lane, the street that made up the eastern boundary of the square and entered the Club House.

Key headed to Lafayette Square and drew a handkerchief from his pocket. He waved it in the air, hoping she would see it. A couple he knew passed through the park after church at St. John's. He stopped to speak with them for a moment, waving his handkerchief toward the Ewell House, his eyes on Teresa's second-story window. Key pulled at opposite ends of the handkerchief, tightening and holding it in the air. There was no response.

Key saw a young woman he knew and walked alongside her for a bit. "I am despondent about my health," he said, "and very desperate. Indeed, I have half a mind to go out on the prairies and try buffalo hunting. The excursion would either cure me or kill me, and, really, I don't care much which."[3]

Key was oblivious to what was happening inside: penitent Teresa prone on the floor of her room, Sickles agonizing his way around the house. All Key could think about was seeing her. He did succeed in attracting one member of the Sickles family. Dandy, their dog, walked over to Key and greeted him familiarly.

Butterworth swallowed an ale at the Club House bar. Poor Sickles. Everything gone in an instant. He walked back to the Ewell House and encountered Wooldridge in the library. Key had passed the house, Wooldridge said. Twice. Waving his handkerchief. Butterworth scarcely had time to think as Sickles bounded in on them.

"The villain has just passed my house." Sickles said. "I have seen the scoundrel making signals. My God! This is horrible."

"Mr. Sickles, you must be calm," Butterworth said, "and look this matter square in the face. If there be a possibility of keeping the certain knowledge of this crime from the public, you must do nothing to destroy that possibility. You may be mistaken in your belief that it is known to the whole city."

"No, no, my friend, I am not." Sickles said. "It is already the town talk."

"If that be so," Butterworth said, "there is but one course left for you, and as a man of honor you need no advice."

Butterworth left the Ewell House, retracing his steps toward the Club House down Pennsylvania Avenue, across the south side of Lafayette Square. He encountered Key at the southeast corner of Lafayette Square, on Madison Lane and Pennsylvania Avenue.

"Good morning, Mr. Butterworth," Key said. "What a fine day we have."

"Have you come from the Club?" Butterworth asked.

"I have."

Butterworth inquired after a sick friend. "Is Stuart in his room?"

"Yes, and he is quite unwell."

"I am going to see him," Butterworth said, excusing himself. "Good morning." Turning toward the Club, Butterworth saw Sickles walking quickly toward them, coming down Madison Lane from the north.

"How are you?" Key asked Sickles, extending his hand.[4]

"Key, you scoundrel, you have dishonored my house. You must die."

"What for?" Key asked.

Sickles pointed a pistol at him and fired. The sound shattered the Sunday afternoon quiet, bouncing off the mansions of Lafayette Square and the White House.

Key reached into his coat pocket, pulling out a pair of binoculars, and "rapidly advanced" on Sickles. Key grabbed a fistful of his coat collar and tried to strike him with the binoculars. Key hung on, knowing that everything he had in the world depended on his doing so. He had been surprised, but he was uninjured, and, now fully aware of what was happening, had a real chance of surviving.

Sickles backed up into the street and wrested himself free. He drew a pistol from his overcoat and "presented it at Key," who backed up toward the Club House. Key threw the binoculars at Sickles as he fired again. It was an uneven trade. The binoculars hit Sickles, without conspicuous effect. Key was wounded. "Don't shoot me!" he said, staggering toward the sidewalk and taking refuge behind a tree.

"Murder!" he yelled. "Don't murder me! Murder!" Sickles advanced on him at close range and fired again. Key wilted, falling on the sidewalk, clutching his groin, landing hard on his elbow. "Don't kill me!"

"You villain, you have dishonored my house, and you must die!" Sickles repeated. And again. Sickles advanced with no special hurry and pointed his gun.

"I am murdered!"

Sickles fired again, flattening Key on the sidewalk as his chest filled with blood.

Sickles came closer until he was standing directly over Key. He aimed the gun directly at his head. *Click.* Misfire.

Sickles felt a hand on his shoulder. Francis Doyle had come running from the Club House, begging him not to fire again. "He has defiled my bed," Sickles said.

Thomas Martin had also come from the Club House and knelt beside Key's body. He looked up inquiringly toward Sickles.

"He has violated my bed."[5]

Martin asked for help in carrying Key to the Club House. They were aided by William Bonitz, a twenty-year-old White House clerk. Martin asked Key if he had anything to say, perhaps to his children, or an explanation of what happened. Key made no response.

A crowd began to gather. "Is the damned scoundrel dead?" Sickles asked no one in particular. Butterworth gently linked arms with Sickles and guided him away.

Where does a congressman go in this city to turn himself in for a murder? Sickles and Butterworth decided on the home of Jeremiah Black, Attorney General of the United States.

Bonitz, bearing the signs of having carried a bloodied man, ran into the White House and found the president in his study, getting ready for church. Buchanan nearly collapsed when he heard the news. "I must see Sickles at once," he said.

Bonitz had seen a great deal since arriving from Germany three years before. He had made his way from North Carolina to a job with Senator

Jefferson Davis in Washington. A year later, he was working in the White House. Now he had witnessed a congressman kill the US Attorney.

Buchanan warned him that "as the principal witness he would be put in jail without bond," and that he must "leave Washington immediately." It was a lie. But if his friend Sickles was going to survive this, Bonitz's testimony wouldn't help. He handed Bonitz some money and hunted around for a souvenir. Buchanan settled on his personal shaving razor, of the finest Sheffield steel, that he had brought home from England. He thanked Bonitz for his service as they said goodbye. Bonitz hid for the rest of the day, planning to catch an excursion boat to Norfolk that evening. He was robbed at gunpoint as he walked through Lafayette Park. The man took the money the president had given him, which for some reason he had kept separate from a money belt he was wearing, where he still had $500.*

Richard Coolidge, assistant surgeon of the Army, thought nothing of Sunday afternoon gunfire in Washington—until he heard people running. He left his room at 820 H, seven blocks away, and followed the gathering crowd to the Club House. Running inside, he saw Key on the floor, his head propped up on the rung of a chair.

Coolidge felt for a pulse. Nothing. Key breathed twice and never again.

Washington policemen James Suit and William Daw were the first to respond to the shooting. Members of the crowd directed and then followed them to the home of Jeremiah Black on Franklin Square. The door was answered by the attorney general himself. The officers asked for Sickles. Black went upstairs and personally brought him down. Sickles went willingly. He asked if he could return home to set some affairs in order before going to jail. The officers agreed to

---

* Bonitz's grandson, John Bonitz, is alive and graciously made time for the author. He knew exactly why I was calling when I said, "I want to talk about Daniel Sickles." Bonitz still has the razor given to his grandfather by James Buchanan. He provided me with a copy of his grandfather's diary and a statement from his father repeating what Bonitz had told him of the shooting and his return to North Carolina.

accompany him, and they along with Butterworth headed for the Ewell House.

★ ★ ★

Thomas Woodward was surprised to see a carriage outside his home in Georgetown. On a Sunday?

It was Francis Doyle. Are you the coroner?

I am.

I need you to come with me.

★ ★ ★

At Brown's Hotel on Pennsylvania Avenue, Virginia Clay was getting ready for church. Her husband, Senator Clement Clay, "burst into the room, his face pale and awe-stricken."

"A horrible, horrible thing has happened, Virginia!" Sickles "has killed Key, killed him most brutally, while he was unarmed!"[6]

Lawrence Branch, a North Carolina congressman who was a regular at Teresa's parties, sat and wrote a letter to his wife. "What is the world coming to?"[7]

In Senator Gwin's parlor, where Butterworth had been passing a pleasant morning just hours earlier, a servant entered. "Mr. Sickles has just shot Barton Key dead."

"What was the cause?" Walker asked.

"Did you never hear the stories as to Mr. Key and Mrs. Sickles?" someone said.

"No." Walker answered. It seemed he was the only one.

This scene was replayed in similar fashion in thousands of rooms across the District. Coroner Woodward arrived to find that the Club House had lost some of its exclusivity. Over a hundred people were lurking about the building. Washington City had morphed into something like a vast stage with multiple scenes playing out at once and the audience having to decide which was the most worth watching.

A more modest crowd was in the room with Key's body. It was Woodward's responsibility to determine the cause of death. He announced a coroner's inquest, a spontaneous trial where he would pull men from the crowd to serve as jurors, who would examine evidence and question witnesses. The proceeding began with Key still in his place on the floor.[8]

Sickles pulled in front of his home to find a swarm of curiosity seekers. He made his way inside, Officers Daw and Suit with him, as well as Butterworth. He asked to go upstairs and see Teresa. They asked his pledge not to harm her. He agreed. The word of a man who had, an hour before, publicly executed the US Attorney was considered enough to guarantee the safety of Mrs. Sickles.

Teresa had not left her room since last night's confession. Suddenly, her husband was back, standing in front of her.

"I have killed him."

Robert Walker raced to the Club House, then Black's, then Sickles's. He entered amidst "Great buzz and confusion" and saw a familiar face.

"My friend, you should not grieve so deeply," Butterworth said. "It is deplorable, but Mr. Key deserved his fate."[9]

Sickles was also there to greet him. "A thousand thanks for coming to see me under these circumstances." Without warning, Sickles threw himself on the sofa and covered his face with his hands. Twisting in violent spasms, he "broke into an agony of unnatural and unearthly sounds, the most remarkable" that Walker had "ever heard—something like a scream interrupted by violent sobbing." He believed that Sickles would lose his mind and nearly sent for a doctor.

Sickles cried for his wife and his daughter. What would happen to them?

Walker thought it was the most terrible thing he had ever seen in his life.[10]

Police Chief Goddard and Mayor Berrett arrived. "I was just making some little arrangements here," Sickles said, "preparatory to coming to you to surrender myself into your custody."[11]

The final party at the Sickles home was drawing to a close. There were famous names: Governor Walker, the Police Chief, the Mayor, Butterworth. There were random faces. The hostess was nowhere to be found. Nobody seemed happy.

The most famous host in Washington had one last task to perform. He opened a bottle of brandy and offered it to his guests. All but Butterworth declined to drink with him. With that, the final party at the Ewell House came to an end.[12]

The police had not anticipated the crowd outside, which they now estimated at 150 people. Daw worried that "some of the mob would shoot Mr. Sickles." Suit put his hand on his pistol and said that "he could shoot as well as any of them." Sickles was led through a sea of people, any one of whom could have meant him harm. They boarded the carriage without incident.

Sickles, the mayor, the police chief, and two officers left for their next stop. Walker, frightened over Sickles's mental state, also went along. People lined the streets as if it were a one carriage parade, hoping to glimpse Sickles on his way to jail. The prisoner stuck his head out the window and waved to one of his friends.[13]

The Club House was "surrounded by an immense crowd, eager to view the body of the ill-fated Key." Inside, the coroner's inquest was a straightforward, if macabre, affair. The reporter for the *Evening Star* thought Key appeared in a "gentle slumber," but for the blood.

Standing over Key's body, one witness after another testified to the essentials.

Then Butterworth was sworn. He testified to Key's final conversation and what followed. Were you aware of Mr. Sickles's intentions? Butterworth refused to answer. The inquest was to determine the cause of death, he said, and nothing more. "It is sufficient to state simply that Mr. Sickles shot Mr. Key, who fell dead."[14]

The coroner's jury reached a verdict. "Philip Barton Key came to his death from the effect of pistol balls fired by the hands of Daniel E. Sickles."[15]

Washington City did not have a morgue. Key was brought back to his home on C Street to await burial.

Four blocks to the north, at 4th and G, Sickles could see his destination: "The Blue Jug." Three stories of badly painted stucco surrounded by a 20-foot wall. *Harper's* called it "one of the worst constructed and most miserably arranged in the country."[16]

Congress debated condemning the building for almost a decade. "The miserable structure" was the creation of Robert Mills, who designed the Treasury Building and Washington Monument. It was not his most aesthetic work. It wasn't meant to be.[17]

An "evil smell" and the sound of "howling inmates" announced that you were close to the Jug.

Sickles was escorted past the wall as the gate shut behind him. He was led inside the building. Another door closed. "The wretched air of the prison is perfectly poisonous." The Jug was badly overcrowded with petty grifters, runaway slaves, and violent criminals, as many as twelve to a cell, locked away to rot. He could hear their cries bounce off the dark walls as if they were already in Hell.[18]

Sickles passed through a labyrinth before arriving at his dirty, dingy cell. Only rats and roaches would choose to live in such as place.

And many of them did. There was no sewage, bath, water, or ventilation. Guards slept with their guns beside them.[19]

Walker stayed at the jail with Sickles. There were violent sobs and convulsions. His body would get rigid and his hands would go to his head. He sobbed bitterly. In a moment of lucidity, Sickles asked the jailor: "Haven't you a better room to put me in?"

"No," said the jailer. "This is the best place you members of Congress have afforded us."[20]

★ ★ ★

Octavia Ridgeley had picked the wrong weekend to visit. Teresa wouldn't eat and couldn't sleep. She was in a state of constant agony. Octavia thought she might lose her mind or maybe even kill herself. Teresa prayed for oblivion—to simply cease to exist. She would settle for leaving Washington and never seeing the city again.

Sickles received a surprise visitor at the jail, a "little man" dressed in black. Sickles didn't know him. It was late. But he wasn't exactly able to choose his company. And besides, he needed a favor.

Reverend Haley was a Unitarian minister. Sickles sent him to check in on Teresa. Teresa in turn asked Reverend Haley to carry a letter to her husband. He agreed to wait while she hurriedly wrote down her thoughts. She implored her husband's pardon and promised better times ahead. "Would he return her wedding ring?" she wondered.

Haley returned to the jail with the letter.

Sickles read her note. Teary eyed, voice trembling, he explained: I have no resentment toward Teresa. But too much has happened. Regardless of whether he ever left that jail, he was "determined to see her no more." Sickles firmly blamed Key for what had happened. Had they not met, she would never have been disloyal. "Poor child," he said.

Sickles wrote a four-page letter to Teresa. She was at liberty to return to their home in New York and to take Laura with her as soon as she was able.[21]

Sickles's friends complained to Bejamin Perley Poore, correspondent of the *Boston Journal*, about Reverend Haley and his "persistent efforts" to "bring himself into notice." Haley told reporters what he said to Sickles, what Sickles said to Teresa, and what both said to him. "It is astonishing what pains some people take to get their names into the newspapers," wrote Poore.[22]

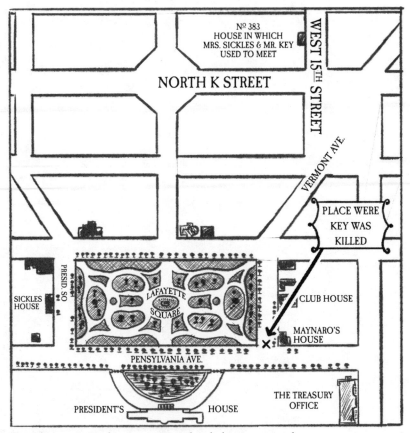

Pan of streets in Washington connected with the recent tragedy.

Intermezzo

Chapter Fifteen

Special by Magnetic Telegraph

*"There has been an almost unparalleled excitement
in the public mind ever since the news of the shooting
down of Philip Barton Key in the street by Daniel E.
Sickles spread abroad upon the wings of the telegraph."*
—Leslie's Illustrated

It may have been the biggest story in America's short history. William Henry Harrison, president of the United States, died after thirty-one days in office. On April 4, 1841, a letter with this sad detail was sent to Cincinnati where it was published. A newspaper across the river in Louisville picked up the story. A copy of that paper was mailed to St. Louis, where the story was printed. Copies of St. Louis newspapers were carried by steamship to Jefferson City. Only then—eleven days after the fact—did the news of the president's death reach Missouri's capital.[1]

Information made its way slowly across the country. That it traveled at all was in large part due to newspaper exchanges, allowing publishers to share copies of their work without paying postage. Benjamin Franklin, deputy postmaster for the colonies, codified this tradition. In the year Harrison died, there were an astonishing seven million exchanges.[2]

In December 1842, Samuel Morse connected two committee rooms of Congress by a wire. He used electric charges to send signals from one room to another, which could then be translated from dots and dashes to English. Morse wanted funding to deploy this technology on a wider scale. Four years earlier, Congress had rejected his request. Now, by a vote of 89-83, with 70 abstentions, they approved $30,000 for Morse's project. Many members considered it a joke. One introduced an amendment to fund telekinesis instead.

Morse believed he could win over a skeptical Congress by breaking a political story. His line from Washington to Baltimore was nearly complete when, on May 1, 1844, the Whig National Convention nominated Henry Clay for president. Morse transmitted the news along the wire, beating the train by sixty-four minutes.

When the line was completed three weeks later, he wrote from the Supreme Court chamber, "What hath God wrought." The possibilities of this new device were quick to present themselves: people on either side of the line could play chess with one another; a message from the Washington police caught a criminal in Baltimore; a Baltimore merchant verified the creditworthiness of a man who had written him a check; a family was able to dispel a rumor that a loved one had died in Baltimore. It was greeted with a shrug. Most could not imagine news so important that they couldn't wait for it.

The Magnetic Telegraph Company was founded in 1845, with 50% of its stock held by Morse and the other inventors and 50% sold to finance construction of lines to Buffalo, Philadelphia, Boston, New York, and the Mississippi River.

Thousands of miles of new lines were opened and maps of telegraph stations were out of date almost as soon as they were printed. By 1850, there were twelve thousand miles of wire. That number had more than doubled two years later.

Telegraph operators became skilled and could hear the messages in their heads simply by listening to the machine. Abbreviations were agreed upon: "G A" (dash dash dot, dot dash) meant "Go ahead." Operators along the same line would tell jokes, stories, and play checkers while they waited for messages.

As with subsequent inventions, people used the telegraph to improve their dating prospects. Couples met over the telegraph, inspiring a bestselling novel: *Wired Love, a Romance of Dots and Dashes.*

A Boston woman was determined to marry a man against her father's wishes. The father placed the young man on a steamer to London. At his stopover in New York, he found a surprising message waiting for him: present yourself at a telegraph office with a magistrate. They married over the wire, she in Boston, he in New York.[3]

Before long, newspapers were carrying "The News by Telegraph," short snippets with basic details.

As the telegraph was opening new and faster channels of communication, a similar revolution was taking place among the press. The entire concept of "news" was being redefined. Commercial papers were focused on ships, their destination and cargo, and the prices of cotton, flour, or gold. These reports were expensive, costing around six cents. They made their money primarily through subscriptions and were obtained at a local office. There were also political papers, financed by parties and other interests and focused narrowly on promoting and polemicizing candidates. For newspapers that appealed to a more general audience, their subject matter was strictly local. One enterprising journalist pitched his editor on covering a speech in a neighboring town. He was turned down: "Somebody will send us something about it in two or three days."[4]

This stodgy regime was challenged by the rise of the Penny Papers. The New York *Sun*, founded in 1833, candidly staked their fortune on covering "the calamities of others." There would be "murders, suicides, and crime, [and] stories about animals."

The business papers had an average circulation of 1,700. The *Sun* quickly reached 10,000. Because of its wide readership, it could make its money from advertising and, therefore, sell newspapers for almost nothing. Newsboys appeared throughout the city to move copies. The first generation of American reporters were hired and sent out to find stories. Freedom from political parties or mercantile interests allowed for investigative journalism, targeted at exposing corruption.

James Gordon Bennett, former editor of a pro-Jackson political paper, entered the fray two years after the *Sun*. The first edition of Bennett's *Herald* featured "a murder and death by suffocation, the explosion of a steamboat, a balloon ascension, horse racing, romantic poetry, and police court reports." Bennett correctly saw that people wanted more from newspapers: yes, fires and suicides; but also politics, news from abroad, and the price of cotton.

The "lightning press" arrived in 1846. Paper could be run through cylinders at 20,000 sheets per hour, allowing for larger circulations and later printing. Ten years later, the circulation of the major New York papers was 57,840 for the *Herald*, 50,000 for the *Sun*, 42,000 for the *Times*, and 29,000 for the *Tribune*.

Meanwhile, the telegraph had scaled. Mergers and acquisitions of the scattered telegraph companies, increased proficiency of operators, and the advent of better batteries and cables dramatically lowered the cost of transmission.

Real-time national networks of communication, rapid and inexpensive printing, and the pages of the popular press were dry kindling for a media firestorm.

Daniel Sickles fired the spark on February 27, 1859, and that evening there was a rush on the Washington telegraph office. William Stuart, correspondent for the *New York Times*, had spent the day like all his colleagues: darting around town, interviewing witnesses, visiting the scenes of the drama, melding it into a coherent narrative, and doing so in time for tomorrow's edition. His hard work finished, he did not envy the people on the other end of the wire. They would have to rework the newspaper and set the type for a story that took two entire broadsheet columns and part of a third. The telegraph could process 2,000–2,500 words per hour at a cost of anywhere from 150 to 218 dollars.[5]

As Stuart was leaving, he ran into Congressman John Haskin, who was there to notify Sickles's father in New York.[6]

News of the shooting had traveled through Washington by word of mouth, the oldest news network. It would proceed from there to millions by the newest.

★ ★ ★

Simeon was in the habit of doing what he had to. He had immigrated from Germany to England and from there to Boston, where his mother and step-father told him, though he was a little boy, that he was on his own. He found a job making walking canes, and once he had saved two dollars, he set out, making his way to New York. He sold papers, blackened boots, and assisted merchants in the marketplace. When he had earned enough for that day's food and shelter, he went to school. Simeon lived at the News Boys' lodging house, where he slept on the hard floor near the warm stove rather than the cold but more comfortable bed.

A few weeks earlier, he and a group of boys had gone to the Children's Aid Society searching for additional work for a train ticket west. Selling newspapers, they said, was a bad business.[7]

On the morning of February 28, Simeon and the ragtag army of newsboys fanned out through New York, in the markets and crowded streets and squares of the city. "Dreadful tragedy!" they called out. "Shocking homicide at Washington. Philip Barton Key shot dead in the street by Daniel E. Sickles. Sad story of domestic ruin and bloody revenge." The *Times* printed "a very large extra edition," that "was absorbed at an early hour," and soon, no copy could be found for sale anywhere in the city.[8]

The *Evening Post*, founded by Alexander Hamilton, would find a ready audience for today's edition. "A dreadful homicide was committed at Washington by a person who, to the discredit of this city, is one of its representatives in congress."[9]

This scene of sensational headlines and newspapers selling as fast as people could buy them played out throughout the country:

"A Murder at Washington."
  —*Boston Journal*

"A member of congress kills the seducer of his wife."
  —*Daily Pennsylvanian*

"ASSASSINATION"
  —*Daily Standard* (Bridgeport, Connecticut)

"Terrible Tragedy."
  —*Baltimore Sun*

"Tragedy in Washington"
  —*Louisville Daily Courier*

"Terrible Tragedy at Washington."
  —*Cincinnati Commercial Tribune*

"Shooting Affair."
—*Daily Journal* (Wilmington, North Carolina)

Most newspapers would settle on daily coverage under the headline "The Sickles Tragedy" or "The Washington Tragedy." The Washington *Evening Star* sold more copies than at any point previous in its history. The second day of coverage came under the headline "The Homicide," as if it were the only one in the world. For purposes of their readership, it may as well have been.[10]

The initial accounts, thrown together in the late afternoon on Sunday and telegraphed before that evening's deadline, were surprisingly detailed: there were eyewitness accounts of the shooting; and reports of the affair between Key and Teresa, Key's handkerchief signals in Lafayette Square, the secret rendezvous house, and the anonymous letter.[11]

There were also plenty of errors: Teresa had been arrested, Teresa was pregnant, Butterworth had been arrested, President Buchanan had visited Sickles in prison.[12]

The *Boston Journal*, in their first sentence on the shooting, made sure to mention that Key was the "son of the author of the Star Spangled Banner."[13]

Sickles believed he was the last to know of the affair, and he was not far off. The *New York Herald* reported: "gossip had made free with Mrs. Sickles's name in connection with Mr. Key for more than a year." While Sickles was out of town last week, "the attendance of Mr. Key at his house was even more unremitting than usual."[14]

Laura Crawford Jones, the young daughter of Georgetown's mayor, wrote in her diary that the lack of effort to hide their romance reflected poorly on Key. "For my part, I should have been more wary, I think, if I had been engaged in such an affair. His whole conduct shows how little he really cared for her, the recklessness with which he carried on his amours showed he had no real regard for her."[15]

★ ★ ★

William Stuart was an Irishman who had known both kinds of luck. In the past year, he'd produced a theatrical hit—followed by a major flop. Now he was in Washington, planning his next great play and hoping to get by as a correspondent for New York newspapers. Correspondents in 1859 were exactly that: people who wrote letters. And with Congress leaving town in a week, demand for dispatches from Washington was drying up. But the dramatist would now have the chance to share the most incredible real-life drama with the world. Nobody knew political scandal better than he did. For starters, William Stuart was not his real name.

Edmund O'Flaherty was born near Galway thirty-eight years earlier. He'd been an elected member of the UK Parliament and had served as income tax commissioner for Ireland. He was famous for his warmth, kindness, and largesse, the source of which no one could seem to figure out. In the spring of 1854, as Daniel and Teresa Sickles were winning over London, O'Flaherty disappeared. One step ahead of creditors, he boarded a steamer at Havre under the name "William Stuart" (Captain William Stuart). He was penniless, but an east side tenement was preferable to an English gaol.[16] He wrote articles for the *New York Tribune* on English politics (the editors found him surprisingly knowledgeable) and theater criticism for five dollars apiece. Stuart longed for Broadway glory of his own. He saved and raised enough money to rent Wallack's Theatre. There he produced some modest hits and major flops. Now here he was, correspondent for the *New York Times* in the nation's capital. With congress on the edge of adjournment, demand for DC stories was drying up, and he faced going broke again. Until the biggest story in the history of the world fell into his lap. How was that for luck? And who better to write about political scandal?[17]

"The vulgar monotony of partisan passions and political squabbles has been terribly broken in upon today by an outburst of personal revenge," Stuart wrote, "which has filled the city with horror and consternation—I cannot, unfortunately add with absolute surprise."

Stuart was not just a gifted writer, he was an intimate of the parties involved. "It was but on Tuesday last that on visiting Mrs. Sickles, Tuesday being her day of reception, I found Mr. Key there, his horse waiting for him at the door. The rooms were filled with a pleasant company, the soft Spring sunlight poured in at the open windows, and Mrs. Sickles herself in all her almost girlish beauty, wearing a bouquet of crocuses, the firstlings of the year, seemed the very incarnation of Spring and youth, and the beautiful promise of life."

Stuart's stories were published anonymously, credited to "Our Special Washington Correspondent." As a theater producer, he knew that the best storytellers were often behind the curtain.

Chapter Sixteen

The Day After

February 28, 1859

"His future promised to be most prosperous; but
l'homme propose, et le Dieu dispose."
—The *New York Herald*

Daniel Sickles woke up in jail, and his skin was dark—covered in bed bugs, "so as to be literally black with them." It wasn't a nightmare. Not the bugs—not any of it. Teresa had carried on an affair—more or less in public—for over a year. And he had killed his former friend on account of it. Now he sat somewhere in the bowels of a disgusting dungeon, staring out behind iron bars, and at some non-distant date, he would be tried for his life.[1]

Sickles's friends tried to keep him company. There was Emanuel Hart, a former Congressman and Supervisor of the Port of New York; Chevalier Wikoff, who was never far from the scene of action; Wooldridge; and Governor Walker. Butterworth was there also, looking "very solemn." The prevailing rumor, which made the papers, was that he had been an accessory to the killing and would soon be joining Sickles in jail. And Reverend Haley was there too, of course.

The federal district court opened on Monday. James Carlisle stood up to speak. The Bar of Washington, he said, had "called upon [him] to discharge a painful duty," to "announce to the Court the death of Philip Barton Key, Esq., the United States Attorney for the District of Columbia. In doing so, all that was good, all that was attractive in his character came so forcibly before" him, that he felt he "could not do justice to the subject."

Chief Justice Dunlap responded with praise for Key's "fine talents," and "many noble, manly, and generous qualities." Out of respect to his memory, the court adjourned until Thursday.

After adjournment, the Bar of Washington met as a group and adopted a resolution: Key was a man "endeared to and respected by us while living, and whose sudden death has filled our hearts with the deepest sorrow and regret."[2]

★ ★ ★

Teresa was "confined to her bed by severe illness." She refused "to see any one"—not that people were beating down her door.[3]

The *Tribune* called it "a sad commentary on the shallowness of the friendships in fashionable circles here, that all of the gay throng which crowded the parlors of Mrs. Sickles on Thursday night last at her levee, but very few have condescended to call upon her in her misfortune."[4]

At the split second of tragedy in Washington, a race began to see who could most quickly build distance from the sufferer, as if it were contagious. Sources told one newspaper: "Any lady who opened her house and gave good dinners can obtain [Teresa's] station." A "Number of gentlemen scoff at the idea that they had ever crossed her threshold. The select circles she did not enter."[5]

Stuart set the record straight in the *Times*. Teresa "certainly did move in the best society, and was generally courted and adored. The idea that she filled a doubtful position in Washington is preposterous. Why is it that poor human nature so loves to shove downhill with accelerated motion every sinning fellow-creature who once is found failing?"

Chapter Seventeen

For the Defense, Part 1

S ickles would need the best defense to have any hope of survival. His legal team gave the outward appearance of being carefully selected. The opposite was true. From the moment of his arrest, Sickles's friends and family began hiring lawyers to defend him. The first were made public in time to make the next day's papers: Edwin Stanton, Daniel Ratcliffe, and Allen Magruder.

Though his lasting fame was in the (near) future, Stanton was considered among "the foremost men in America," and "honest as steel," possessing "an energy to which relaxation is almost pain."

Stanton was thirteen years old when his father, a small-town doctor who excelled at charity but lacked in collecting fees, died. Stanton was pulled from school and apprenticed to a bookbinder. After a grueling three-year apprenticeship, he went to Kenyon College in Ohio. When finances were low, he was forced to drop out and spend another year working for the bookbinder. He finally convinced the guardian of his father's estate to take him on as a legal apprentice.

Like many successful men, he charged ahead as though a return to poverty was chasing him. He assumed more work in the face of family tragedy. When his daughter died, Stanton had her remains sealed in a metal box that he kept in his room. When he lost his wife to tuberculosis, he wandered the house "in a daze carrying a lamp." "Where is Mary?" he asked.

Stanton was known as a lawyer for railroads and major corporate interests. But his rarefied appearance concealed his years as a county prosecutor in Ohio. In private practice, he represented Joseph Thomas against a charge of poisoning his wife, taking a dose of mercuric chloride before the jury to prove it wasn't fatal. He also defended John Gaddis, who had killed his wife with a brick. In that case, he did not attempt a similar demonstration.

Stanton gained the notice of Washington as the lawyer for Caleb McNulty, Clerk of the House of Representatives, charged with stealing $50,000. Stanton's surrogate father, a senator for Ohio, had vouched for McNulty's good character and paid his $20,000 bond. The senator faced a ruined reputation and finances unless Stanton could clear McNulty. Stanton shredded the state's main witness in the "severest" cross-examination one reporter had ever heard. In his closing, he called trial by jury America's most precious asset. McNulty was acquitted and Stanton returned to Ohio.

A lawyer of his talent and ambition could not resist the pull across the river to Pittsburgh. He was soon tasked with a case impacting the future of the city. A planned bridge across the Ohio River to Wheeling threatened to redirect commercial traffic south, cutting off Pittsburgh. He sued on behalf of Pennsylvania, charging that the bridge interfered with interstate commerce because its height would not allow the tallest smokestacks on ships to pass. Stanton took the case all the way to the Supreme Court, where he won. Congress later passed a law allowing the bridge.

Stanton remarried, and he and his young wife decided to move to Washington. He wanted to increase his practice before the Supreme Court, and she looked forward to the excitement of the capital city.

President Buchanan appointed Jeremiah Black as attorney general. Black knew Stanton from his appearances before the Pennsylvania Supreme Court, where he had served as a justice. Black offered Stanton the biggest challenge of his career. Who owned what in California was hardly a federal concern... until gold flakes were found in the river near Sutter's Mill. Someone was needed to sort through the patchwork of Spanish land grants, Mexican titles, and American deeds and determine the true owners of priceless property rights.

Stanton wasted no time after his month-long steamer ride. He traveled to the old capitals of Benicia and San Jose, inspecting dusty records in Spanish and English and collecting nearly 400 folio volumes from throughout the state. He exposed one of the largest claimants as a fraud and quickly restored the rule of law. It had been a task for Stanton's unique talents: an endless capacity for work, a painstaking attention to detail, total incorruptibility, and sheer perseverance. After fifty weeks, he returned to Washington to an increasingly impatient wife and the biggest case of his career.[1]

Sickles's supporters initially tried to hire Jeremiah Black as his lawyer (it was not unheard of for an attorney general to handle private cases). Black declined, but he referred the case to Stanton.

Other friends of Sickles hired Daniel Ratcliffe of Alexandria, Virginia, a seasoned lawyer in the District. When Pierce became president, 9,000 residents petitioned for Ratcliffe to be named US Attorney. Only 2,000 did the same for Key. But Key had the support of the people who mattered and won the job. Ratcliffe served as the solicitor of the court of claims before resuming his private practice.[2]

Allen Magruder had spent most of his twenty-year legal career in Charlottesville, Virginia, before moving north. He joined the case by virtue of his partnership with Ratcliffe.

Samuel Chilton, a former Virginia congressman and longtime lawyer in Washington, was retained by other friends of Sickles.[3]

The group met with Sickles at the jail, wading through the large crowd hanging about outside, "earnestly discussing the sad event." Sickles and his ad hoc legal team were forced to make their first decision. With the inhuman cries of prisoners as ambient noise and the vile smell of the jail in their noses, they advised Sickles to waive a preliminary hearing, his only option for getting out on bail. But it would also reveal arguments and evidence they were reserving for trial. Moreover, the defense believed that time was the enemy. Cool consideration, they felt, would lead to the conclusion that a man could not simply kill whomever he pleased. Also, with Sickles incarcerated, he would have priority in the criminal docket over defendants on bail.

There was a practical consideration as well. Friends of Key were described as "quite indignant" and talked openly of killing Sickles on sight. Key's brother planned "a shooting exercise with the honorable Daniel Sickles for a target," reported one newspaper. "Wonder if he can't hit him without *three* shots."

Sickles's friends believed he was safer in "The Blue Jug."[4]

Chapter Eighteen

Funeral Rites

March 2, 1859

—

"If Sickles is guilty, what is Butter worth?"
—*Bennington Banner*

The role of Samuel Butterworth remained a matter of debate. It had been widely assumed—and reported—that he had known Sickles's intentions and had distracted Key so that he could be shot. Butterworth had heard the rumors and could read the newspapers. He knew it meant a death sentence if a jury believed them. His detailed defense appeared in newspapers on March 2.

Butterworth wrote of his unexpected summons to the Sickles house on the day of the killing. He explained that Sickles walked into the hall and said, "Come, go over with me" to "the Club House," to ask "whether Key has a room there, and for what purpose he uses it."

"I assented," Butterworth wrote, "and walked out into the street, supposing that Mr. Sickles was following me. I left the house for this sole purpose. When I left Mr. S. in the hall I am satisfied that he had no weapons on his person. He was without his overcoat. He said nothing to me about weapons, or the probability of encountering Key." Butterworth described the killing in vivid terms, from the best vantage point of anyone. "I took no part in the contest," he wrote. "I believed them both to be armed. It is not true that I either sought or detained Mr. Key. He first addressed me, and our interview did not last one minute. I have known the late Mr. Key in New York and in Washington during the last ten years, and our relations have ever been of the most friendly character. I did not anticipate a collision on the Sabbath, though I did not doubt that it would take place at an early day. This is the whole of my connection with the unfortunate occurrence." The statement was accompanied by declarations from Walker and Gwin attesting that this was consistent with what they knew and what he told them on Sunday and from Wooldridge, who was present for the final conversation between Sickles and Butterworth.

The *Post* was not satisfied. If every word of Butterworth's story were true, "Did he move hand or foot to prevent this atrocious butchery?"

The *Star* was skeptical: Sickles was "armed with a five-shooter, every barrel loaded, and at least one, if not two, loaded Derringer pistols. They were of course loaded before Butterworth preceded him from the house."

The ostensible purpose for which they left the house made little sense. Sickles had proven the affair beyond all doubt. Teresa had signed a confession. What did it matter if Key had a room in the Club House? Even if Butterworth went along to gratify Sickles, where did he think Sickles was during the three-minute walk across the square?

Butterworth, who seemed to be everywhere on Sunday, was now in hiding, possibly to avoid arrest, to avoid being forced testify against Sickles, or both. The *Tribune* reported, "The most diligent search for him has been made in vain."[1]

He wasn't the only person trying to clear their name. John Gray, owner of the world's most famous assignation house, wrote a letter to the newspapers denying any knowledge of Key's purpose in renting his home.[2]

★ ★ ★

James Carlisle stood outside Washington City Hall. He and Barton Key had tried many cases in that building, some together, some on opposite sides. They had been friends outside of the courtroom. Now he was there to meet colleagues and court officials and to proceed as a group to Key's wake and burial. Carlisle and his colleagues arrived to find C street "thronged" with people vying to enter the memorial service. Key had been popular in life, but not *this* popular.[3]

Carlisle made his way into the living room. The focus was a mahogany coffin, draped in black cloth and mounted in silver. Inside was his familiar friend Key, dressed in a black coat and pants and with white camellias strewn about him. His expressions were so lifelike that is was "difficult for the spectator to realize that [his] once noble form lay in the stillness of death."

For two hours "a motley crowd" of boy and man, rich and poor, black and white, free and slave "poured through the parlor to take a glimpse of the corpse." Reverends Pinckney and Butler performed the funeral rites of the Episcopal Church over his body. The coffin lid was closed. Carlisle and seven other pallbearers carried it to a hearse outside. Visible on top of the coffin was a silver plate: "Phil. Barton Key, died Feb. 27, 1859, aged 39 years."[4]

Key's final carriage ride through Washington was to the depot for a trip to Baltimore aboard the three o'clock train. Crowds followed the hearse all the way there. From the train, Carlisle and the pall bearers entered the Green Street Presbyterian burying ground.

Key would be buried with his wife and one of their children among the leaders of early Baltimore, near Edgar Allen Poe, who had died ten years earlier.

Key's siblings broke the news to their mother gently. Mary Key was not surprised, as they had expected: she had recently dreamed of her son's death. "Apoplexy?" she asked. The siblings went with it. "Did he die in the street?" They answered in the affirmative. Just as she had seen, Mary said.[5]

★ ★ ★

The press reflected the split in public opinion. The *Post* said the *Times* "was fertile in finding excuses for a homicide...deliberately planned and deliberately executed."[6]

The *Times* said that the *Post*, "once regarded as a respectable and responsible organ of opinion, has neither the cheap honesty nor the common courage" to explain how Sickles should have handled the situation.[7]

The *Tribune* split the difference: "We cannot...treat the case as one of cold-blooded murder; but it may nevertheless be one of very culpable, unjustifiable killing. Let us calmly await the result of the legal investigation."[8]

The *Waltham Sentinel* asked whether everyone involved was reading from the "Wicked Bible," a version from 1714 with a printing error that commanded: "Thou shall commit adultery." The Archbishop, who hadn't read the rest of the book, punished the printer for their mistake by fining them into insolvency and sending them to a star chamber.[9]

Chapter Nineteen

Teresa, Part 2

*"Many visitors this evening, everyone still talking of
the dreadful murder of young Key."*
—diary of Elizabeth Lomax

Sickles asked Emanuel Hart to stay at the home with Teresa and Laura until they could return to New York. Ratcliffe told him that witnesses would come to identify Mrs. Sickles and requested that he admit them. The first was Nancy Brown, the neighborhood busybody, who clearly identified Mrs. Sickles as the woman she had seen with Key.

Paradoxically, prevailing opinion seemed to deny Teresa's agency but awarded her the greatest punishment. The *Richmond Dispatch* lamented that Sickles was celebrated in jail, Key was honored with a grand funeral, and that "at the worst, [Teresa] cannot be more debased than the two criminals who have received such tokens of special honor" while she is "excommunicated as a moral leper."[1]

Henry Watterson, the young correspondent for the Philadelphia *Press*, who had been a close friend of Teresa's, said: "She was an innocent child. She never knew what she was doing." Key was "a handsome, unscrupulous fellow who understood how to take advantage of a husband's neglect."

The *Evening Star* blamed Sickles: "Married at the child's age of sixteen to an experienced man of the world, who knew well all the dangers to which the virtue of a young and intensely fashionable wife might be subjected in an ill-ordered household, we cannot acquit the husband of all blame for her ruin. Such ruin rarely, if ever, invades the threshold of the husband who strictly discharges the duty of a head of a family. Nay, we question whether it ever came into the family of a man really careful at all times to protect the honor of his own household."[2]

Some newspapers took the novel position that Teresa was an adult who had done as she wanted.

The *Philadelphia Despatch* wrote: "There may have been instances where young and artless girls, in their pure and trusting confidence, have been heartlessly seduced and betrayed. But in nine cases out of ten what are called *seductions* are caused by the ill-governed passions and advances of the women. It is convenient, after the shame has been made public, for the guilty one to allege that she was seduced."[3]

The *Baltimore Sun* agreed: "She can hardly be said to fall—she steps aside of her own free will and sins deliberately."[4]

Chapter Twenty

Revenge of the Keys

---

*"The friends of Mr. Key will leave no stone unturned
to vindicate his memory, by showing that he did not
deserve his fate."*

—Washington *Evening Star*

Benjamin Perley Poore, correspondent of the *Boston Journal*, reported: "Key has warm friends who will endeavor to cast obloquy on the past character of both Mr. and Mrs. Sickles, in which they will be joined by the faction of New York politicians opposed to him." The "first families of Maryland are striving hard to so arrange matters that Mr. Sickles will be convicted of murder."[1]

The Keys hired investigators to dive into Sickles's past and discredit witnesses for the defense. Their counteroffensive soon appeared in the newspapers: "All the chimney sweepers of the earth might run against [Sickles] without dirtying him, and would come off the worse themselves from the collision."

There were allegations of infidelity: "If Mr. Sickles had been shot thrice for every lady he has been too well acquainted with, what an expenditure of powder and ball! Would he not have resembled a perforated pin cushion?"

They claimed he had "Not the courage of a duelist but of an assassin."[2]

The *Baltimore Exchange* defended Key as "a man wholly incapable of plotting or accomplishing the ruin of any woman. Mrs. Sickles's paramour, it is possible, he may have been—but her seducer, never."[3]

They claimed that Sickles had been censured by the New York Assembly for Fanny White's visit. This has been repeated uncritically in nearly every biography of Daniel Sickles, but it isn't true. The *Journal of the Assembly of New York* records every vote of the seventieth legislature and no motions for censure, against Sickles or anyone else, appear.

There were rumors that Sickles had brought Fanny to London and presented her to Queen Victoria as the wife of James Gordon Bennett. Again, Sickles's enemies as well as his biographers found this too good to verify. Only eight women were presented to Queen Victoria during Buchanan's tenure. All were presented by either the Countess of Clarendon or Harriet Lane. As a man, Sickles could not make a presentation.[4]

In the midst of unprecedented press coverage and public interest, the overcrowded wake, and dueling newspaper articles, there were friends of Key who were trying simply to grieve. Jesse Benton Fremont wrote a friend: "I think I knew Barton in his true and best nature—he was a truly loving and good husband and father and his cruel death came to me with a shock that few could have. Whatever Barton did at the last, his wife was loved and made happy to a degree very few women ever reach. I know them so well and I see plainly she was most happy and beloved.

It seems to me that Mr. Sickles talked too much before acting and acted with a due regard for safety when he did act and the extracting a written confession before two women witnesses from a woman in her state of mind and in the family way was an accumulation of heartless cruelties that show a character to justify his wife's looking elsewhere for something to love."[5]

The *New York Herald*, which had once been Sickles's bitterest critic, found sympathy with him: "It is beyond denial, that whatever may be alleged against [his] early career, his conduct since his advent in Washington has been beyond blame or suspicion. He has never been seen in loose or disorderly company, has never frequented doubtful places, or been known to be engaged in amorous intrigues of any kind. On the contrary, he has sought the best society, has given close and laborious attention to his political duties, and was steadily obtaining a solid and commanding position in social and public life."[6]

This sentiment was echoed in the *Times*: "Few men, I presume, including even the editors of the *Evening Post*, would like to have their past lives rummaged, and all the[ir] indiscretions…dragged forth in such an hour as this, which has overtaken Mr. Sickles…no one in Washington can say that he has ever seen him even in a gambling house, which here is the favorite fashionable resort of men," or a "bar room."

"His whole soul appeared to be centered on ambition, the advancement of his political adherents in New York, and the cultivation of a happy domestic life. To his parliamentary duties he was scrupulously attentive, and he was considered by many, among others by the speaker, as the ablest member of the present house."

And not to take these attacks lying down, Sickles's camp made public a letter from Antonio Bagioli, his father-in-law, who had arrived in Washington: "You have heaped on my child affection, kindness, devotion, generosity. You have been a good son, a true friend, and a devoted, kind loving husband and father."[7]

Chapter Twenty-One

Beekman Returns

Thursday, March 3, 1859

The Washington correspondent of the *Tribune* unearthed a major story. "One is certain of nothing in this scandal loving city," he wrote, "but the few facts which I subjoin are, I believe, authentic," from "persons likely to know," and "corroborated."

"A Mr. B. of New York, whose name it is unnecessary to give in full, being a rather susceptible young man, last session fell violently in love with Mrs. Sickles. He soon became jealous of District-Attorney Key, and watched him." He then told an abbreviated version of the Beekman story that ended with Sickles throwing him out of his house.[1]

Stuart responded in the *Times*, "The Mr. B. referred to is a Mr. Beekman, of New York." Stuart denied that Sickles was abusive to Beekman. Key "obtained, under what influences I know not, an entire retraction." Beekman excused himself "upon the ground that he was drunk, and knew not what he said. Unless Mr. Sickles had been predetermined to believe that the wife to whom he was so devoted was utterly unworthy of his love, how could he have harbored suspicion of her under such circumstances?"[2]

Stephen Beekman responded in the *New York Times* to "several very erroneous statements calculated to do my character great injury." He put the blame squarely on Bacon, who he did not name and referred to as "a clerk in the Interior Department." He claimed that Bacon took him aside and asked him his thoughts on Key's attention toward Teresa. He admitted to "several trifling jokes about the female sex in general, and about her." He claimed to have no suspicions as to Teresa and Key, a position he maintained when summoned to Sickles's house or when he received a letter from Key demanding to know what he'd said.

The *Tribune* reporter also found Key's statement of last summer, hoping for a French intrigue with a good bit of spice and danger. Laura Crawford Jones wrote in her diary: "Poor fellow! He had his wish—the danger was greater than he thought."[3]

★ ★ ★

Advertisers used the tragedy to get the public's attention. One company alleged to be the bug repellent that had cleaned up Sickles's cell: "WHOLESALE DEATH AT THE JAIL, dead cockroaches, bed bugs, and other vermin [lay] in thousands all over the floor," at the hands of "Schwerin's Annihilating Powder: the only sure remedy for extermination."[4]

A Philadelphia clothier claimed that they had sold Sickles "an elegant suit," to "make as respectable an appearance as possible upon his trial."

Then there were ads that simply referenced the case in a headline: THE SICKLES TRIAL—"It is a fact, and no humbug, that if you

want to buy a good article of ready made clothing, very cheap, go to
M. Bohm's Washington Clothing Store."[5]

Chapter Twenty-Two

Sickles in the Pulpit

Sunday, March 6, 1859

———

"In the streets, the law courts, public houses, private dwellings, and, in fact everywhere, it was the prominent topic of conversation."
—*Cleveland Plain Dealer*

Henry Ward Beecher was the pastor of Plymouth Church, Brooklyn. An abolitionist, he had sent rifles to Kansas ("Beecher's Bibles") and ran a prominent stop on the Underground Railroad. It was the first Sunday since the shooting. Pastors like Beecher in pulpits like Plymouth would finally have their say on what their congregations had been talking about all week.

Sickles, Beecher thought, "has made himself obnoxious to the laws of his country" and "to the judgments of God."

> Out of this boiling and uneasy crater, just now comes a fiery flash, a rain of mud, and black clouds, full of sound and bolts hang about it. Pride has reached forth a hand of lust, and vanity has clasped it. Then comes assassination to destroy the guilty plight. The papers are loaded down with the matter. There is not a hamlet or ranch on the continent in which this sore of depravity is not about to drop its ichor.[1]

The *Pennsylvanian* thought Beecher was no better than the press:

Many of the flash preachers are going to preach sermons on Sunday upon the Washington tragedy which is thus a windfall for the cloth, as well as the sensation newspapers. Parson Beecher...scolds the press for giving publicity to criminal transactions, but he has no qualms in preaching on a love and murder affair if it will but fill Plymouth Church—as doubtless it will—to its utmost capacity.

The *Tribune* agreed:

Had we barely published on Monday, the fact that the Hon. Dan Sickles had the day before shot dead in the streets of Washington his intimate personal and political friend, the US District Attorney, and that a well-grounded jealousy was the sole incitement to this crime, we apprehend that our Reverend patron would not have been able to finish his breakfast with that deliberation and calmness which is dictated by the laws alike of hygiene and good breeding, owing to his haste to run around the corner and buy a *Herald*, containing the painfully interesting particulars of this shocking affair. [We] feel it incumbent on us to shield our esteemed patron from this odious necessity.[2]

Reverend Haley told his congregation: the "Sickles affair was the natural result of our social condition. It is an undeniable fact that most women who come here and launch into hotel and fashionable life do not escape scandal.'" He had heard that members of Congress leave their wives at home for that very reason.[3]

On the day of the shooting, a handful of people had been near Lafayette Square. Today, before, after, and instead of church, over 1,000 people milled about, taking in the crime scene. Artists for the illustrated newspapers were sketching the Ewell House, the Club House, and the square. The bark of the tree that Key hid behind was quickly disappearing at the hands of souvenir seekers. One eagle-eyed visitor saw the mark made by a pistol and carved out a block of wood with the ball inside. It was official: no scene was sacred.[4]

Chapter Twenty-Three

Aria

Tuesday, March 8, 1859

"No event that has happened for many years will occasion more wide spread excitement."
—*Daily Standard*

A lice Key Pendleton waited on a train platform with her brother's four children, ages four to twelve; her own two; and the two of her widowed sister on their way to Ohio. The *Star* said that their "chief sympathy" was with these children, who will be "through life as intense sufferers from this affair as any others." They are also "the only parties concerned in it who had no agency whatever in bringing it about."[1]

William Stuart wandered the city of Washington as members made their way out of town. "Our city has now put on its provincial garb," he wrote, "and now appears to be nothing more than a large country town." The departure of Congress and arrival of Lent "have disrobed the metropolis of her proud, flaunting, and important air."[2]

Stuart saw Chevalier Wikoff on Pennsylvania Avenue and at Willard's "discussing the topic of the hour with that mixture of philosophy and pathos which renders his conversation at once so luminously clear and so mystically profound.

"Two more dull and dreary days than the 7th and 8th of March have seldom fallen even on this chosen home of dullness and dreariness," he wrote. "The rain had not the spirit to come down boldly and have done with it, but sneaked down in a stealthy drizzle to the earth." Umbrella sellers and cab drivers "leered triumphant." Carriages "floundered like so many arks along the swamp, miscalled street, of Pennsylvania Avenue."

An Irishwoman with "five prospective little American citizens" sold oranges and oysters at the gate to the Capitol, her last day before closing for the season.

Congress may have closed, but the Capitol bar was open, crowded with "lawyers, politicians, journalists, schemers, dreamers, lobbyists, land-jobbers, slave-dealers, filibusters, reformers, congressmen…all more or less drunk." Upstairs in the drawing room, there was "a bevy of lazy looking ladies lolling in voluptuous rocking chairs, some self-complacent, some helpless and harassed with the die-away disorder of ennui, some cynical and scoffing, but all prettily dressed and borrowing from the enchantment of distance the indescribable look of the 'lady.'"

"The all-engrossing topic of the hour," Stuart wrote, "naturally enough, is the Sickles tragedy, and the smallest detail connected with any of the parties is still caught up with eager curiosity and rapt attention."[3]

They discussed the identity of "R. B. G." There was rumor of a letter sent to Key on the same day, warning him of danger and urging him to quit the affair. Newspapers reported they were the work of a woman "who was jealous of [Key's] attentions to Mrs. Sickles."[4]

There was also the matter of Key's gun. "Few men in Washington do go so unarmed, and Mr. Key had received but the Thursday before a letter warning him of the danger of discovery and of the risks involved in it." Sickles himself seemed surprised that Key reached into his coat and came out with nothing but an opera glass. The consensus seemed to be that Key had changed clothes, fatefully forgetting his weapon. Key "had gone constantly armed for ten days previously." It was thought he left his pistol in another coat.[5]

The *Boston Traveler* concluded that "Men shouldn't change their clothes on a Sunday...If [Key] had been armed, Sickles probably would have been killed." But "as it is, the end may come at the end of a rope."[6]

Stuart continued his trips to see the man of the hour. "Mr. Sickles does not look well," he wrote. Mental suffering and confinement within a prison's walls have tolled severely upon him, paling his cheek and shaking his vigorous constitution."[7]

Sickles tried to limit his visitors to his closest friends and his lawyers. He passed long hours pacing the corridor of the prison "in silent grief." He pressed his head between his hands, as if trying to disappear from the world. Most of the time he wanted to say nothing of his reason for being there. Sometimes he would repeat: "I could not live on the same globe with a man who had thus dishonored me." Sickles tore his hair and lamented the fate of his wife and daughter.

Sickles was visited separately by his parents and Teresa's parents. His mother fainted, while Teresa's mother became frantic, sending him into tears.[8]

Sickles had spent ten nights in his "close and stifling" cell, but the worst part was being cut off from his daughter. He did not want Laura to see this place. But now Teresa was well enough to travel and would be headed for New York on the next morning's train. Sickles asked for Laura to come to him.[9]

"At first the joy of seeing her father engrossed her attention, but soon the strange appearance of things excited her childish wonder." Laura took in the whitewashed walls and the brick floor. The narrow sleeping cot was less than their servants had. The window had a row of iron bars.

Why haven't you come home? Laura asked.

Sickles replied that he had "a great deal of work to do, and cannot leave at present."

Are you coming with mamma and Laura to New York in the morning? Laura asked, slipping into third person.

Not now, but he hoped to see her soon.

Laura asked a hundred "puzzled and excited" questions, which Sickles answered. But "some dark foreboding seemed to fall upon her delicate soul, as if the very proximity of a prison and criminals shocked the purity which could not even comprehend the meaning of crime, for suddenly her fair little face became troubled, and her beautiful large dark eyes filled with tears that multiplied and flowed freely down her cheeks, and, when the fountain was exhausted, were replaced by sobs."

Laura could not explain her sudden sadness and probably did not understand it herself. Sickles handed her a small bouquet of flowers that he had managed to get his hands on. He then watched Laura disappear from sight, not knowing when or whether he would see her again.[10]

Thursday, March 10, 1859

In the early hours of the morning, Teresa, along with her mother, Laura, and two friends, left her home for the first time since the shooting. She had been among the most public of women in the city. Now she was sneaking away with the last minutes of darkness. She walked from her house to the carriage, rode to the train depot, and left Washington for the last time. She had wanted to see her husband, but Sickles was resolute. Such a meeting, he said, "could only inflict torture upon all parties." Teresa and Laura would stay at their home in Manhattan, on the Hudson.[11]

Postmaster General Aaron Brown was in "critical condition." This was bad news for Sickles, as the death of a cabinet member would suspend government operations and further delay his trial. After several days of being sick with pneumonia, he began hemorrhaging and wasn't expected to survive the night. The president and cabinet were with him when he died in the early morning hours of March 10. Thousands gathered in the East Room to watch the body lie in state. The houses of the capital were draped in black. Except for one "desolate" house "on the west side of Lafayette Square," wrote Stuart, "where ambition, love and elegance so lately had its home and its resource."[12]

Chapter Twenty-Four

Seeing the News

Saturday, March 12, 1859

———

"Well, brother what do you think of this
affair at Washington?"
"Perfectly right. I would have done the same myself."
"The Same as which?"
"Either."
"So would I."
—Fictional dialogue in the *New York Picayune*

This was the story the illustrated newspapers were waiting for. *Frank Leslie's* was only four years old; *Harper's* only two. Several smaller and lesser imitators had entered the market, but the big two remained dominant. As the newest arrivals on the media scene, they were subject to criticism by the last wave of media innovators. The *New York Times* called them a "Prostitution of fine art." *Harper's* responded: "This is a newspaper, not a nursery tract or a child's hymn-book...For us, our purpose is to present our readers with an illustrated account of the events of the day, be they what they may." The technology did not yet exist to print photographs, but for the first time in history, readers could see detailed drawings of people and places alongside stories.

They covered the substantive as well as the sensational. In *Harper's* March 12 issue were headlines such as: "Love in a convent";

"Lion at Large on Board Ship" (a situation that had presumably resolved itself by the time of printing); and "A Bride Burned to Death," alongside national and global politics. There were sketches of the closing scenes of congress, Bostonians engaged in the rare sport of ice skating, and Prince Frederick of Prussia presenting his baby to the royal household (Wilhelm II, Kaiser of Germany during World War I).

They were not as nimble as the dailies: drawing, printing, and distribution meant their coverage of "one of the most awful tragedies that ever occurred in this country" took thirteen days to reach subscribers. But they needn't have worried about waning interest. As *Harper's* wrote: "The public mouth is still full of stories about the lamentable affair which took place at Washington on Sunday 27th February; and the public ear, it seems, can not be satisfied with details of the catastrophe."

The illustrated papers made good use of that time and their space to go further in depth than the newspapers. *Harper's* presented a detailed biography of Daniel Sickles, the basis for all that followed to the present day. Under the headline "Drama of crime, retribution and death" appeared drawings of Sickles, Key, and Teresa, arrayed in a triangle with Teresa above and between. Readers could see different vantage points of Lafayette Square: the Sickles's house, the Club House, the scene of the homicide. There was a detailed map of general area, including the White House, the cabinet departments, and their proximity to Sickles's home and the crime scene.

Frank Leslie, a British-born artist who worked for that country's first illustrated magazine, had brought this new medium with him to the New World. He wrote: "Our presses have been going night and day without cessation." By the time we're done, "our edition will have far exceeded two hundred thousand copies," and if they had printed 500,000, they would have sold them all. The illustrations, he argued, were better than "lifeless photographs." They "are living sketches, with all the action of reality."

From an initial printing of 75,000 copies, *Harper's* sold 120,000. *Harper's* made the mistake of featuring reports on the end of Congress on its cover, while *Leslie's* had a sketch of a crazed looking Sickles firing at a prostrate Key (*Harper's* had a similar sketch, but it was further into the magazine). *Harper's* would not repeat their mistake: the next week, Sickles was on the cover, alone in his cell, his hands clasped in prayer and his eyes heavenward, beseeching the almighty for deliverance.[1]

Leslie's touted "the only correct illustrations published; made from sketches by our special artist." This is unlikely, as *Harper's* hired Mathew Brady to take photographs from which drawings were made. On the day of the murder, *Leslie's* artist had sketched Key's vest at the Club House, complete with bullet holes. The steward of the Club House saw no problem with this.[2]

One of the lesser illustrated publications, unable to get their own drawings or looking to save a few bucks, reused images of other people from previous issues. Opera singer Jenny Lind, "The Swedish Nightingale," was used for Teresa. Alfred Bunn, the manager of London's Drury Lane Theater, was passed off as Key. And in an ominous sign, "two criminals recently hanged" were substituted for Sickles and Butterworth.[3]

The *Congregationalist*, a religious newspaper, wrote: "The pictorial journals appear to feel that their harvest time is now at Washington, and that they must put their Sickles in and reap. It is rather a mortifying commentary, however, on the state of the public taste, that there is such an appetite for portraits of the criminals whose doings are now ventilated at the seat of government, and for photographs of the scenes which they have disfigured."[4]

Chapter Twenty-Five

Another Sickles Affair

---

*"The town talk is still of the Sickle and Key affair.
Intelligent Washington, living in the hotels or resort-
ing to them, has not yet sprung a new topic: and
stupid Washington is of course agape...Never was a
place [more] mad for scandal than Washington."*
—The *New-York Tribune*

The American public refused to accept it: after two weeks of non-stop coverage and no new developments, the newspapers might possibly have said all that there was to say on the Sickles matter. To satisfy their readers, some reported on similar killings. As one newspaper wrote, every other day it seemed you could find the headline: "Another Sickles affair."

There was Arthur Holden of Saratoga, who shot the seducer of his daughter. And a newspaper publisher in Karachi, who saw his wife taking a stroll with her paramour. He found his double bar-reled shotgun, and killed them both.[1]

John Foster of Batavia, New York, had a live-in girlfriend who was still married to David Curry, who did not approve of this arrangement. Foster gathered two friends and assaulted Curry in public. Believing the matter settled, Foster was walking to work one day when Curry appeared, shooting him in the abdomen, kill-ing him.[2]

In Meriden, Connecticut, Orrin Prim was having an affair with John Williams's wife and decided to taunt him about it. Williams, a sixty-seven-year-old man, described as "peaceable" and "a good citizen," grabbed a butcher knife and ran it through Prim's heart. "Public feeling in Meriden," it was reported, "is much in favor of Williams."[3]

There was "A colored Sickles at Chicago." Dr. Covey fired four pistol shots "at his beloved pastor, Rev. D. G. Lott, while having a tete a tete with Mrs. Covey in his parlor," hitting nobody. "The lady declares that the pastor spake only of spiritual things, and that Covey's jealously had no reason in it."[4]

Alfred Hood, who had "been too intimate with another man's wife," was increasingly affected by coverage of Daniel Sickles. He convinced himself that the husband of his lover would kill him in some awful manner. Hood cut his own throat with a razor, nearly severing his head. It is unclear what worse fate he thought he risked by living.[5]

A young man and his mother were at a Philadelphia boarding house. A man at another table looked at the mother in between coffee sips. She threw her tumbler of water in his face. He returned the favor. Her son went to his room and returned with pistols "blaz[ing] away at the unlucky user of his eyes." None of the bullets found their mark. The *Pennsylvanian* reported: "Since the Key and Sickles affair, it is dangerous to look at a woman."[6]

A Connecticut woman decided that she had been insulted the night before by a man who had escorted her home. Her husband grabbed his guns and went to take vengeance. The gentleman in question, preferring not to die without knowing the cause, asked what he had done. The husband admitted he didn't know. They returned to his house and asked the woman, who said that when he helped her over a puddle, he had squeezed her hand a little hard. The husband, who had nearly killed the man, threw away his pistols. The escort "made up his mind that it is not safe business to gallant other men's wives so long as the Sickles mania prevails."[7]

Then there was the "honest Scotch shoemaker" who "found his wife and a perfidious neighbor as they should not be." He forced them to sign a confession and agree to pay for the divorce. Considering the high price paid by others in their position, they probably considered it a bargain.[8]

Chapter Twenty-Six

Deliberations of the Grand Jury

Monday, March 14, 1859

---

*"As Mr. Sickles has killed the District Attorney,
it will be necessary for the president to appoint
another to fill his place."*

—Albany Evening Journal

The *United States vs. Daniel Sickles* would take place at City Hall. The building was designed after a Greek temple, a "large and handsome edifice" with a "commanding position on Judiciary Square." It was built over a thirty-year period and completed in 1850, and it was home to the courts, the mayors and city councils,* and the US Attorney.[1]

Before Sickles could proceed to trial, he would have to be formally charged by the Grand Jury. The defense had struggled without effect to move the case along. They petitioned the Grand Jury to hear the matter ahead of others. They declined, opting to tackle their caseload in regular order. Sickles and his ilk may run the country, but they did not run the city of Washington. Defendants

---

* The District of Columbia consisted of the towns of Washington City, Georgetown, and Washington County.

like Lewis Bell, arraigned for "stealing a lot of pictures and picture frames from Charles Ellit," took priority.[2]

In fairness, some of the delay was Sickles's fault. Sickles had killed the man who would have otherwise prosecuted him. The president had to appoint a replacement. That replacement had to be confirmed by the senate.

Friends of Key were concerned that Buchanan would protect Sickles by picking someone weak. But they celebrated the selection of Robert Ould. *Leslie's* noted his "considerable reputation as a lawyer," reflecting "great credit upon Mr. Buchanan's administration."[3]

Ould had been educated for the Baptist ministry and "spoke with a clerical air." For sixteen years, his pulpit had been the courtroom and his congregants all jurors. He was "highly intelligent and well informed in the law, and full of perseverance." For his mastery of detail, Ould had been tasked with turning a mishmash of court cases into a coherent code of laws. And while Ould was the new US Attorney, he was an experienced prosecutor. Ould was frequently tapped to serve as temporary US Attorney in Key's absences.[4]

In his first day before the Grand Jury, Ould presented them with twelve witnesses. There was no telling how long it would take. One newspaper echoed the concerns of the defense: "If the trial were put off a couple of months, Mr. Sickles could not be acquitted. He has lost ground rapidly within the past fortnight, as facts in his previous history have become generally known."

Benjamin Perley Poore, a Washington reporter for five years, believed the "New York correspondents have done much to injure the position of Mr. Sickles in the opinion of the community here, from among which *the jury which will try him is to be selected*. Everyone is nauseated with their sycophantic attempts to elevate Mr. Sickles to the position of an injured hero, and to chronicle his very movements, as though the public cared what he eats, when he sleeps, or how often he 'takes a sponge bath.'" The "chief adulator" he wrote, is Reverend Hale, who is "delighted" at having his "name before the public."[5]

William Stuart had cultivated a source in the Grand Jury room. He reported that Sickles would most certainly be indicted. "But differences exist as to Mr. Butterworth." One of Key's family, Benjamin Ogle Tayloe, was on the panel and wanted to leave no stone unturned." He and another member had assumed "a dictatorial position" as public prosecutors, investigating every aspect of the case, which put them at odds with some of their fellow jurors.[6]

Stuart was himself subpoenaed to explain a paragraph from his initial story:

"Asking Mr. Butterworth, who was at his house, to follow Key and engage him in conversation, so that he would not get out of sight, he rushed up stairs for his pistols, and, quickly following, found Butterworth and Key together, at the corner of Sixteenth Street when the tragedy took place."[7]

Stuart explained that he was reporting what he had heard and had no firsthand information of the matter.

Eighteen days after the killing and three days from the start of their inquiry, the Grand Jury indicted Daniel Sickles for murder. It was now Ould's responsibility to draft an indictment—a short statement of the facts and law—and return it to the Grand Jury for final approval.[8]

Butterworth was cleared of any charges. The *Post* objected: "I do not care a straw which way the coroner's jury, or the grand jury, or the petit jury, or the Washington barkeepers, or the 'highest officers of the American government' may say on the matter. [T]o have witnessed such a scene as Butterworth acknowledges that he witnessed, between two men who were both his friends, and one of whom had consulted him on the subject of the quarrel…was in the last degree inhuman and dishonorable."[9]

It seemed the hard work was over. Ould had simply to prepare and present an indictment, consistent with the Grand Jury's findings.

But days went by.

Stuart reported: "A mystery seems to surround the Sickles indictment. The Grand Jury say they are waiting on the district attorney, and he says the delay is with the Jury."[10]

Delay to maximize the odds of conviction was widely thought to be the motive. Others speculated that Butterworth was still in the crosshairs and that they were looking at additional evidence.[11]

The Grand Jury was set to disband in two days, and it looked as though Ould would wait until the last minute.

On March 24, Sickles's defense team appeared in court, "extremely anxious that his trial should" proceed "at the earliest possible moment," and hoping to force the hand of the US Attorney.

The courtroom was filled with "scandal loving loafers," with no "other desire than the gratification of a morbid curiosity...trying to see what they could see." The *States* newspaper thought they would be "far more usefully employed devoting themselves to the care of their families and minding their own business."[12]

The case would be heard by Judge Thomas Crawford. Born in 1786, he was the son of a Revolutionary War officer and older than the Constitution. He had graduated from Princeton in 1804, represented Pennsylvania in Congress for two terms, and served as Indian Affairs Commissioner for Van Buren. President Polk appointed Crawford judge of the federal criminal court, and he had heard nearly every case in the District over the previous fourteen years.[13]

★ ★ ★

Erasmus Middleton, assistant clerk of the court, had an unpleasant task ahead. As he began, his mind flashed back to a happy memory: New Years' Day, 1859, one that opened with much cause for optimism. Barton Key came into the office and gave him "a large gold pen."

"Here's a New Year's gift for you."

"Thank you," said Middleton, placing it in his private drawer.

This memory played vividly in his mind as he opened the drawer and removed the pen and drafted the indictment of Daniel Sickles for the murder of Philp Barton Key.[14]

★ ★ ★

Ould returned to court that afternoon: "the Grand Jury has found an indictment against Mr. Sickles for murder."

Stanton demanded the earliest possible trial date. He claimed they were in danger of losing witnesses as well as members of the legal team, who had upcoming obligations. He claimed Sickles's right to a speedy trial was affected.

Crawford refused to intervene. In his time on the bench, he had interfered once in a trial date. That was an emergency. This was not, he said.[15]

"They are good lawyers," wrote the correspondent of the *London Morning Post*, "and close observers of public opinion, and they know that every day the trial is postponed" brought Sickles closer to being "convicted of murder, and probably hanged."[16]

The *Tribune* agreed: "Public opinion at first set strongly in favor of Mr. Sickles, but as more and more light has been shed upon the previous history of the parties, the current has changed."[17]

April 4 was a much later date than they had hoped. But at least it was a date.

Chapter Twenty-Seven

A Life for Sale

March 25, 1859

———

*"The trial will disclose an amount of scandal
far exceeding what has already been furnished
to the public."*

—*Boston Journal*

Key's C Street house was crowded once again. At ten in the morning, a McGuire & Company auctioneer took his place, surrounded "by an animated crowd of bidders," to sell off the estate of Philip Barton Key. Articles sold for a premium, both to curiosity seekers and to personal and family friends.[1]

The visitors were mostly women, walking up and down stairs and considering their bids. There was a small mantle clock, an ordinary bed, and a five-foot-tall miniature house for his daughter. In the closet was his Montgomery Guards uniform, brass horse pistols, a sword, a rifle, and his cap. Key, who had ventured into Lafayette Square defenseless, was quite well-armed at home.

The house was plainer than many of the guests expected, with the exception of some mahogany furniture upstairs. The walls of Key's bachelor residence were unadorned except for a single print on the wall—Fanny Elssler, the world famous ballerina. It seems strange, at first, for Key to have only one picture, and that of a ballerina. On closer inspection, however, the dark, thin, beauty in her gorgeous gown looked remarkably like Teresa Sickles.

The *States* newspaper had a name for it: *Sickliana*. There was a "greater rush for it by far than for the newest translation of the Bible or a rigmarole about the last ball or in fact anything else. With most persistent and indefatigable industry, people are hunting up items about this Sickles affair as if the fate of the nation depended on it." *Leslie's* agreed: "The people crave after information, and the newspapers seize hold of the slightest rumor to form a paragraph, which is eagerly devoured by millions of readers."[2]

Laura Jones, daughter of the Mayor of Georgetown, wrote in her diary of a popular new game played by her little brother and his friend. Her brother waved his handkerchief at the house, and the friend ran outside and pretended to shoot him.[3]

The Henry Clay Debating Club of Louisville, Kentucky, rented a local courtroom to settle the question "Was Sickles justifiable in Killing Key?" An ad in the *Louisville Courier* invited the public to attend, "the ladies particularly."[4]

Law students in Gallatin, Tennessee, were re-enacting the events of the case when the man playing Sickles accidentally shot his best friend, killing him. The student had to be stopped from committing suicide three times.[5]

Foreign correspondents fed the hysteria overseas. The *London Examiner* wrote: "Murder in America has not only its apologists but its admirers. We have long been struck with the theatrical turn which crime takes in the United States. When an American sets about a murder he prepares his part as for a scene in a drama."[6]

The French correspondent of the *New York Times* wrote: "The Sickles Tragedy is the prominent topic of discussion in the cafes of Paris. The French theory (and the correct one) is that the really guilty party in the sad affair is the writer of the anonymous note—the meddlesome informer—who is presumed to be a woman, jealous of Mrs. Sickles." He concluded "The society of Washington seems to have all the recklessness of Paris, without the refinement."[7]

Crime stories had been fodder for the penny press and its audience, but they had usually been limited to a few paragraphs. The murder of prostitute Helen Jewett in 1836 had foreshadowed Sickles's case. Jewett was asleep in her brothel when she was struck in the head three times with a hatchet and lit on fire. James Gordon Bennett went to the crime scene and wrote about it with a level of detail that hadn't been seen before.

Robert Robinson, Jewett's sometime paramour, was charged. For the first time, readers saw detailed accounts of witnesses and their testimony. Souvenir hunters had taken her charred bedframe or shavings from her furniture. Working class men wore white hats, called "Robinson cloaks" to show their belief in his innocence. The judge ordered the jury to disregard the testimony of other prostitutes, and the case against Robinson collapsed.[8]

The Massachusetts *Spy* detected the start of a new era in crime reporting. "No such stories of crime can leave us as they find us," they wrote. "While we listen to them and are stirred by their exciting details, we take impressions from them; they are felt in our blood and along our nerves, as well as in our thoughts and sympathies; they leave their traces everywhere, and add greatly to the influences whereby men become either better or worse. Therefore, such contact with great and scandalous crimes is a very serious matter. It is unfortunately the fashion of the present time to give very minute reports of all cases of exciting wickedness as soon as they get public attention; but the fashion is not a good one. It is sustained now by a popular taste for such things. Popular influence can change it, and we trust that the day is not distant when the change shall be effected." This was wishful thinking.[9]

Leslie's Illustrated advertised "a very large and accurate engraving occupying two pages of that paper," complete with pictures of the courtroom. Leslie promised "the greatest engraving ever published in this country" as well as "the most accurate and beautiful engraving ever issued in this country. This paper should be taken by every family."[10]

Chapter Twenty-Eight

For the Defense,
Part 2

---

*"The array of talent in the case would fill the
Court House to overflowing, even if the very deep
interest taken in it, and the high position of the
parties involved, did not."*

—Philadelphia Inquirer

A young woman stood on a crowded street in New York and desperately begged for money. "They are going to hang my brother," she said. Most passed without acknowledging her. Now and then, people gave her small bills, fives, and tens. When it equaled $250, she took the money to the law office of James Topham Brady on Broadway.

She "timidly approached his desk," knowing it was a fraction of his fee. "Mr. Brady, they are going to hang my brother, and you can save him. I've brought you this money. Please don't let my brother die!"

"They sha'nt hang your brother, my child," he said, taking her case and refusing her money and telling her to "Take it to your mother." Brady secured her brother's release but never asked for a fee. Days earlier, he had turned down a $2,500 retainer in another case. Brady's *pro bono* representation was the type of kindness that people associated with him from his earliest days.

Brady had been born in America, in accord with his father's ambitions. His parents came to New York from Ireland during the War of 1812 after "a narrow escape from a British privateer." Brady was born three years later.

Brady was remembered as a schoolboy for his encyclopedic knowledge and oversized head, as if he needed space for the things he was learning. As a trainee lawyer, he routinely stayed overnight in the office. At twenty years old, he tried his first case, a dead bang loser where his client had sued his insurance carrier for far more than he had lost. Brady stood before his first jury, trembling, as his vision faded to black. He steadied himself on the table and delivered an impressive argument. He lost; but he also gained a great deal of credit among those in attendance.

Brady's first case of note came a few months later when he defended a newsboy for selling papers on the Christian Sabbath. Although he failed—the law was clear—the Jewish community, who had taken great interest in the case, turned to him in their future legal difficulties. This was no less true among his own people. It was said that "every poor Irish man or woman in the city felt that he had a champion in him."

In court one day, the judge asked him to take on a client. "Mr. Brady, the next case is that of a man charged with murder. He has no counsel. Can you defend him?"

"Certainly." The scene repeated itself twice that week. Each time, he secured an acquittal.

A warmhearted, successful lawyer, Brady would have been an ideal husband. But his father's untimely death made him the head of a family with five unmarried sisters. "All the affection which I could have had for a wife went out to those sisters," he said. Meanwhile, his work in New York brought him to national attention, and Daniel Webster selected him as his junior counsel in the rubber tire case

Goodyear vs. Day. After months of preparation, Brady delivered a two-day opening statement. Webster told him their success would be due to this effort.

Many of Brady's clients stood accused of heinous acts. But his own gentle nature prevented him from hunting or fishing. Earlier in his career, Brady was appointed interim district attorney and had to prosecute boys for "borrowing" a boat to pick apples in New Jersey. Brady told the jury that he wanted a verdict of acquittal. "The boys did not intend to commit a crime, they only did what boys always will do, and what, perhaps, you and I have done. They only wanted a little fun and should not be punished for it."

On April 3, 1859, a mass of unfamiliar black curls on an oversized head appeared in the Washington train depot. Brady, known to people of all classes on the streets of New York, was a stranger in the capital. He made an odd pair with his companion John Graham, tall and built like a bear, another renowned New York attorney. Brady was one of Sickles's "earliest, and through life, one of his warmest friends."[1]

The defense met at the National Hotel. Sitting around the table, any one of them could make the case to take the lead. Edwin Stanton was a Washington lawyer with a national reputation; Ratcliffe, Magruder, and Chilton tried these kinds of cases, before jurors like these, in the same courtroom, and before Judge Crawford. Philip Philips, a new addition to the team, had been a member of the 33rd Congress from Alabama. Enjoying the excitement of the capital, he stayed to cultivate a law practice before the Supreme Court, with much success. Brady and Graham were the closest to Sickles and two of the best lawyers in New York, which was to say anywhere.

To make things especially difficult, their client was an excellent lawyer and would have ideas of his own. This confluence of egos and talent should have been a disaster. In the hands of lesser men, it would have been.

There was no shortage of work to be done in little time. Brady would handle witnesses. Stanton would focus on arguments of law. Graham would deliver the opening statement. Philips and the local lawyers would focus on "the organization of the jury." Together, they scoured newspaper coverage for interviews or testimony given at the coroner's inquest that could help or hurt their case.[2]

On the eve of trial, the *Herald* wrote: "The prosecution and defense are, up to this moment, ignorant of the mode of procedure that either will adopt. They stand like two combatants, fully armed, but not knowing where the attack will be made."[3]

★ ★ ★

The switch to New York and getting out of Washington and *that* house may have saved Teresa's life. Emanuel Hart, the former congressman who had accompanied her home, went with her for a stroll. In Washington, she was accustomed to long walks and plenty of exercise. But this was only the third time since arriving in New York that she had mustered the strength to go outside. Her body trembled, she felt her legs giving way, and her heart beating violently. She stared at the clock in her home, contemplating how life had changed: "One month ago this day, at this hour," of the things that "were going on in our once happy home."

Thomas Field, a New York politician who had visited Sickles in jail, brought Teresa a note from her husband. She wrote back to Sickles, thanking him for his "kind, good letter. Thank you many times for all your kind expressions and God bless you for the mercy and prayers you offer up for me." She also thanked him for the beautiful verses of poetry he had sent. "I will keep them always," she wrote. "That fearful Saturday night! If I could have foreseen the scenes of the following day I would have braved all dangers, all things, to have prevented them. No, dear Dan, I cannot say you ever denied me what was necessary, and you gave me many things I did not deserve. Everyone knows this." She offered to make him a pair of slippers. "Will you wear them for me? Or would you dislike to wear again anything that I have made? Can I say or do anything for you? Write when you can, and think and feel as leniently as possible of me and my unhappy position. God bless you for the two kisses you send me and with God's help and my own determination to be good, true and faithful to you and myself hereafter, those kisses shall never leave my lips while I am called wife and you husband. I swear it by Laura...God bless you, pray for me, and believe in the sincerity and gratitude of Teresa."[4]

ACT II

The Trial of
Daniel E. Sickles
for the Murder of
Philip Barton Key

Chapter Twenty-Nine

Twelve Dispassionate Men

———

*"The trial of Daniel E. Sickles for the killing
of Philip Barton Key has been set down by the criminal court at Washington for Monday next, the 4th
of April. It will be one of the celebrated causes
of the world."*

—The *New York Herald*

DAY ONE—Monday, April 4, 1859

———

*Every word of the testimony will be published and
read by hundreds of thousands, if not by millions, of
people, regularly every day during the trial, such is
the avidity with which curiosity seizes hold of such
things—nor less that curiosity in boudoirs than bar
rooms, it is mortifying to say.*

—*Philadelphia Inquirer*

The lawyers of Washington had the privilege of entering the courtroom early, where they took seats and discussed how they would handle the case.

Reporters were next, scurrying around the room in search of the best position. There were more journalists than seats. The reporter for the *Associated Press* couldn't find a place in the "dingy little room," much less "a desk or table." William Stuart thought it was "badly aired, looks damp and smells musty."[1]

Henry Watterson, the Philadelphia *Press* correspondent, described the lawyers: Stanton had an "expansive forehead, impending brows, and flowing beard." The prosecution and defense were seated at the same table. Ould was to Stanton's left. On his right "is a head [Brady's]—one that might be called bulbously massive—negligently covered with a profusion of black and silver curls…brightness and playfulness of the steel-blue eye shows the rapidity and vivacity, the force and verve of the mind that speaks through it." With that head on his small body, Watterson thought he looked like an exclamation point.[2]

A large contingent of police were the next to enter. Under the command of Chief Goddard, there were twelve daytime officers dressed in blue alongside eight night officers wearing gray. They were posted at every entrance to the courtroom. The remaining police force was managing an excited mob outside the courthouse.[3]

Judge Crawford took the bench at 10:15 a.m., "a venerable old gentleman in gold spectacles." Finally, the doors to City Hall were opened and the crowd flooded in like water through a broken dam. Some climbed in through the windows. The room soon reached capacity, and the doors were shut in the faces of a "grumbling and swearing" crowd. The spectators looked like "one mass of human heads, belonging to all classes and conditions." The fathers of Sickles and Teresa sat side by side, as did Key's brother-in-law and uncle.[4]

Reverend Haley accompanied Sickles to court and sat next to him.

The Reverend had testified in that room just four months earlier in the trial of Winant Streng. Streng, a "swarthy" Prussian immigrant, walked into the Washington Masonic Lodge and opened fire, killing one member. Haley had seen him entering as he was leaving and testified: "this was a person to be avoided," and he "walked away with unusual haste." It was learned at trial that Streng had twice met the president and was prepared to kill him if he had treated him harshly.[5]

In addition to family members of Sickles and Key, there were prominent members of Congress, "though the great majority of the dense crowd present are every day citizens and hotel loungers of Washington."[6]

Judge Crawford announced, "Case number 124, that of Mr. Sickles, is set for today. Is counsel ready to proceed?"

They were.

The panel of prospective jurors was ready. Everyone was ready, finally. Now they needed the defendant. Crawford ordered Sickles brought to the courtroom.

Sickles was more afraid of listening to evidence of Teresa's unfaithfulness than he was the possibility of being hanged. Marshals escorted him from the jail to the courthouse as the crowd stared. He entered the courtroom, still the center of attention, returning the acknowledgement of friends. Sickles took his place in the prisoner's box, which looked "a hen coop with a chair inside."[7]

Journalists scribbled down descriptions of the prisoner. Stuart thought he looked like any other spectator. Sickles was dressed immaculately in a dark coat, vest, and light pants, "[c]alm and self-possessed," "as easy as if he were sitting in his seat in the House of Representatives." But he was also "[p]ale and careworn," losing weight, his face lined with worry. "Confinement has made a visible effect in his general appearance."[8]

The audience pushed and jostled to get a look at him, like he was a caged animal. "Where is he?" they asked. Three people were ejected by marshals for the disruption. Sickles did not hide his annoyance.[9]

Robert Ould rose and introduced James Carlisle to the court, the man who would assist him as prosecutor. "This association," he said, "was extremely gratifying to him and he was sure it would also be agreeable to the court."

Carlisle had refused a spot on the defense team. He had studied at seminary and military academy before learning the law in the office of William Wirt, attorney general to John Quincy Adams and James Monroe. Carlisle had argued numerous Supreme Court cases and was the legal advisor to a number of diplomatic missions. He was described as "crammed with the tricks of the law, and gifted in the flow of language." Carlisle had defended Captain Drayton and served as co-counsel with Stanton on his first major courtroom victory. He was also a pallbearer for Barton Key.[10]

It was time to pick a jury.

The judge asked Joseph P. Brien, the first potential juror, "Have you at any time formed or expressed an opinion in relation to the guilty or innocence of the accused?"

"I have," he answered.

"You may retire," the judge said.

On it went. Charles Skippen had an opinion and could not "render a fair and impartial verdict." Joseph Savage had formed and expressed opinions after reading the newspaper. Daniel Ratcliffe, overseeing jury selection for the defense, studied the jury pool carefully, "reading the men instead of their names."[11]

Henry Hurdle cleared the initial barriers to serving when Ould asked him an unexpected question. "Are you worth $800?"

"I am not, sir."

"That I submit constitutes a disqualification." Ould "astonished and shocked everyone in attendance" with that statement. The District of Columbia applied Maryland law in cases originating in the part of the city that once belonged to Maryland. This had been meant as a placeholder until a code could be adopted, but every attempt brought about a fight over slavery, so many of the old Maryland rules remained in force. And under Maryland law at the time of DC's founding, there was a substantial property requirement to serve on a jury.[12]

As the *New York Journal of Commerce* put it, "It is gratifying to the really good citizens of Washington that public opinion in New York condemns Mr. Sickles for his recent act...that portion of the public excepted which hangs about the bar rooms and gambling houses, and which naturally regards little excitement." The prosecution's insistence on the property requirement was targeted at the latter.

The lawyers were searching for unbiased jurors in a case that had involved many members of a close-knit town. John Scrivener was written off for having had a conversation with an eyewitness. He would not be the last. Some potential jurors who made it through the gauntlet were struck by a peremptory challenge from one side or another; those challenges required no cause or explanation.

Rezin Arnold, a Washington County farmer, had not formed or expressed an opinion, had no bias or prejudice in favor of Sickles or against, had no objection to capital punishment, and was worth more than $800. He became the first member of the jury.[13]

Abraham Butler had formed and expressed opinions from rumor and conversation with others, was friends with some of the witnesses in the case but believed he could render a fair verdict. He added, however, that "every person who committed willful murder ought to be hung."

Carlisle fought admirably to seat him as a juror, but to no avail. The next three were similarly dismissed. Bennett Sewall had no opinion or prejudice but was "worth less than nothing," which turned out to be worth a laugh in the courtroom and disqualification.

George Kirk claimed a relationship to Sickles that would prevent him from reaching a fair and impartial verdict. When pressed, he said that he too was "a married man."

James Fullalove, Reuben Worthington, and Richard Simmons all had their minds made up. With that, the clerk announced that the panel had been exhausted.

Judge Crawford ordered the marshal to bring seventy-five prospective jurors, known as talesmen, into court the following morning. After all the anticipation and fanfare, the first day of the trial had ended after two hours with little to show for it. Five jurors were sworn. Four were challenged. Four were too poor. And twenty-one had already reached a decision.[14]

Before the judge could adjourn, Stanton rose to draw his attention to "a point of very great importance." The placement of the prisoner's box made it impossible to confer with Sickles. Judge Crawford replied that the box had always occupied that space but that it would be moved closer to the lawyers' table. Magruder argued that Sickles's life was at stake and that even Aaron Burr had been allowed to sit at the table with his lawyers at his trial for treason.

The judge said that he had never heard of a case where the prisoner in a murder trial could leave the box—neither in the United States nor in England, where the practice originated. While he was not disposed to deviate from this rule, he agreed to move the box near the counsel table so that Sickles could confer with his lawyers. Sickles was led by the marshals back to the jail, followed by a massive crowd.[15]

For now, Sickles was back in his cell. He had "A pile of books" on the windowsill. On his desk was a photograph of Laura and a drawing she had made for him, on which she had written: "Dear good, loving, kind papa." Sickles received letters from all over the country and passed the time sending replies. There always seemed to be visitors in his cell.[16]

Reverend Haley, ever-present and available for a quote, told reporters that he had bought Sickles *Lady of the Lake* to read. "My business is to keep his courage and his spirits up under the first terrible collapse from excitement. When he reads, when he becomes calm, then I will speak to him of religion."

Stuart, who had been observing his demeanor, thought that Sickles "is engaged in a continuous struggle with himself. His head and his heart are [in] a violent war. Thus far his head has triumphed," but he was "prey to sorrowful reflection."[17]

DAY TWO—Tuesday, April 5, 1859

An immense crowd in Philadelphia took to the streets to prevent the capture of a runaway slave named Daniel Webster. The Republicans swept elections in the state of Connecticut, furthering a political realignment where the North and South were controlled by separate parties. But on April 5, the headlines focused on the failed attempt to find a jury in the Sickles case.[18]

The crier opened the court at 10:20 a.m.: "Oyez, oyez, oyez...". Somehow, more people than yesterday had managed to squeeze into the courtroom.

Joseph Kelly, eleven years old, lived with his parents on 4th Street, between the jail and courthouse. Next door was a public school, with a sign labelled "School" on the front and "the S turned the wrong way."

He remembered a "Tall, soldierly figure, immaculately dressed, marching with head erect, glancing neither to left nor right, and as he went by our house on the opposite side of the street I had a good view of him each day. There was always a rabble crowing and running in the street but nothing could disturb the stern serenity of the man who was on trial for his life."[19]

Sickles was brought into the courtroom and placed in the prisoner's box, now located behind his lawyers and facing the judge. Stanton reviewed the list of potential jurors with Sickles.[20]

Twenty-one of the first twenty-two had made up their minds. The other was struck for being younger than twenty. William Harper had formed impressions from the newspaper that he didn't think added up to opinions. Close enough.

The court ran out of talesmen before 1:00 p.m. Three new jurors had been selected that day, for a total of eight out of 104 prospects.[21]

Deputy Marshal Phillips said that the jury pool in the city had been exhausted and that they would have to go out to the county. Crawford admonished the jurors not to discuss the case and permitted them to return home.[22]

The correspondent of the *London Daily News* expressed his surprise that having an opinion was cause for challenge. "[N]one but the most stupid and ignorant…who never read the newspapers, shall try him."[23]

DAY THREE—Wednesday, April 6, 1859

The *Star, Tribune,* and *Post* reported that, for the past "eight or ten days," the sympathies toward Sickles had dissipated. "The feeling was now strongly against him."[24]

In court that morning, Sickles nearly broke down crying when a friend came by to greet him. He turned his head away.[25]

One by one, the potential jurors came through: dry goods merchants, tailors, shoe dealers, plumbers, butter dealers, pump makers, well diggers, a druggist, and a hatter.

The first twelve talesmen were dismissed. Jesse Wilson said that he could render an impartial verdict but preferred not to sit on the jury. He found himself accepted and sworn. After a long list of biased talesman, and two who opposed the death penalty, Charles Kiltberger had the opposite problem, promising to hang Sickles "high as hell" if guilty.

Another "manifested a strong prejudice against Mr. Sickles." He was dismissed and walked through the crowd trying to exit the courtroom. He came near a man who stood up and approached him. "I heard you just now," he said, "say something harsh of the prisoner. But let me ask you if you had lost your wife, or had your daughter sacrificed, would you have been able to control your feelings and be governed by your reason?"

"I don't know. But who is asking me this question?"

"I am the father of Teresa Sickles."

The talesman was affected by this. He apologized for what he had said and admitted he may have done the same.[26]

Daniel Clark said that if approving of Sickles's action made him impartial, then he was impartial. He was dismissed to laughter.

As the third day of jury selection dragged on, there came some excitement that nearly brought the trial to a halt. Judge Crawford had large wooden panels on either side of him, apparently to protect against a draft of cold air. Without warning, one of these fell, landing just behind him. If he had been reclining in any way, he might have been killed. Stuart called them a threat to "the integrity of the judicial pericranium."[27]

Judge Crawford had been spared to rule on another fight over a potential juror's property. The man was worth more than eight hundred dollars, but his property was outside the District. Did it matter? The court ruled that it did not.

After three days and nearly two hundred potential jurors, they had found "the twelfth dispassionate man" in Washington. The jury would consist of four grocers, two farmers, a merchant, a furniture maker, a tinner, a coachmaker, a shoemaker, and a cabinet maker. The jury was "generally regarded as a good one," "composed of some of the most respectable men in the District of Columbia." New Yorkers Brady and Graham were not easily impressed but felt that they had never seen such a "fine collection of jurors."

Of the 180 potential jurors who had been called, many had their opinions, but less than a dozen expressed support for Sickles's acquittal.[28]

Judge Crawford sequestered the jury in the National Hotel. Since it was nearing the end of the day, he offered to delay swearing in the final juror. If he was not sworn, they could all return home for one last evening.

"Gentlemen of the jury, what is your desire about this?"

"We desire to be discharged," one of them, speaking for all of them, shouted to laughter. Stanton objected. He wanted the jury sworn and sequestered.

Overruled.[29]

Crawford was seated on the bench when one of the jurors approached him. "Can I say a word to you?" he asked.

"Not about this case."

The juror kept talking. "I answered the question put to me, but since I have been sworn, and been in the jury box, I have been reflecting on this thing. I am not quite satisfied with myself."

A reporter described him as under "extreme mental excitement." The judge refused to listen. "I cannot relieve you," he said. The juror turned and directed his attention to Chevalier Wikoff, who was walking out of the courtroom. Wikoff reminded him not to discuss the case.[30]

The Sickles trial would give birth to breaking news. As the *New York Herald* pointed out, "The improvement in telegraph operations is so marked, the popular demand for early news so urgent…that in a short time we shall probably give all the news outside of the city in the shape of telegraphic reports; and our correspondents, instead of dropping their communications into the Post Office, will deposit them with the telegraph operators, and we shall have their contents before the ink wherewith they were written is dry. It is fast coming to this, and it will be a great triumph for telegraphing, as well as a great boon to newspaper readers."[31]

Chapter Thirty

A Carnival of Blood

―

*"The trial of Mr. Sickles will doubtless elicit the
finest criminal pleading ever heard within the
walls of the City Hall."*

—Daily Union

DAY FOUR—Thursday, April 7, 1859

Philip Barton Key had vexed him in life. Now he haunted him in
death. As his deputy, Robert Ould had picked up slack and
stepped in as US Attorney during his sundry absences. Or, as Stuart
wrote less politely, Key was "indolent and unread to a degree
almost beyond belief" and had "committed the conduct of nearly
all of official business to Mr. Ould." Now Key was gone for good,
and Ould was once again in his chair—this time in the most
watched trial in history.

The courtroom was hot, smelled, and was somehow more
crowded than any previous day by people willing to stand for five
hours. The jury walked down Pennsylvania Avenue in a double file
line, led by two bailiffs, "attracting as much attention as a military
company without music."[1]

John Graham complained that his correspondence with Sickles
had been tampered with at the post office. Letters had been opened

in transit or never reached their destination. He could complain all he wanted. Postal workers were not immune from Sickles mania.[2]

Judge Crawford told the court about the juror who had talked to him after yesterday's adjournment. "I think it right to mention this publicly in case counsel may think proper to move about it." The problem was that Crawford did not remember who it was. "So little impression did the man's appearance make on me, that I cannot recognize him now."[3]

William Moore identified himself as the unmemorable juror. "I was impressed with the responsibility that rested on me, and felt a kind of shrinking from the duty" by his attempts to leave.

"I hope you were," Crawford said.

"It made me feel unpleasant, but this morning I can say to the court that I feel perfectly satisfied on my own mind."

"Very well," Crawford said. "I am glad to hear it."

The twelve jurors were called by name and answered. The Clerk asked Sickles to stand up in his box. "Daniel E. Sickles, look on the jurors while the indictment is being read."[4]

The clerk read the findings of the Grand Jury before the court: " ... Daniel E. Sickles, in his right hand, then and there had and held, then and there feloniously, willfully and of his malice aforethought, did discharge and shoot off, to, against and upon the said Philip Barton Key...did strike and wound him...the said Philip Barton Key, then and there instantly died...[Sickles] of his malice aforethought, did kill and murder, against the form of the statute in such case made and provided, and against the peace and government of the United States."

When the clerk finished reading, he asked Sickles: "Are you guilty or not guilty?"

Sickles looked the jury "full in the face." "Not guilty," he said, "in a clear, firm tone."[5]

Ould began his opening statement. He was a "fine, square built, athletic man," "one of the finest looking men in the District," with small gray eyes, a broad forehead, and straight black hair. He looked "like a friend to be honorably trusted" and was known for his "ability, vigor, and legal experience."[6]

"May it please your honor and gentlemen of the jury," Ould began, "the indictment which has just been read to you charges Daniel E. Sickles, the prisoner at the bar, with the willful murder of Philip Barton Key.

"In the soft gush of that Sabbath sunlight, at an hour midway between morning and evening did he commit this act...when the church bells were lingering in the air, the deceased all unconscious of the tremendous woe [ahead]."

Sickles "had come to that carnival of blood fully prepared," a "walking magazine," with different kinds of guns, a "temporary armory" beneath his "convenient overcoat on an inconveniently warm day." The defenseless Key plead for his life, which "might have moved other men" but "fell upon ears of stone" in this instance.

"[F]rom the first act in this tragedy down to its full fruition...through each and every successive scene of horror not only [was] the deceased unarmed, but that the prisoner at the bar knew such was the fact; that he must have known it when the first shot was fired at the corner; that he must surely have known it when, subsequently, the exclamations of the deceased were ringing in the air; and that, if possible, more certainly still he must have known it when he stood bravely over his victim, revolver in hand, seeking to scatter the brains of one who had already been mortally wounded in three vital parts, and whose eyes were being covered with the film of death."

This was murder, "no matter what may have been the antecedent provocations in the case...four or five shots were fired, or attempted to be fired," punctuated by "[e]arnest, perhaps frantic entreaties such as a man would make for his life," for "the little ones that he had left clustering around his hearthstone.

"Murder, gentlemen of the jury, as you will find the definition accepted by almost all the civilized world, is the unlawful killing of a human being with malice aforethought."

This law has "come down to us consecrated by time...springing like an arch...over the vast chasm which separates the remote past from the present.

"Whenever those principles are perverted, whenever they are warped for the purpose of shielding a criminal, whether he be humble or powerful, a blow is struck at both humanity and justice. The jury that sends its deliverance to the offender, whose stains are not washed off by the evidence of the trial, is itself morally derelict to the high obligations which humanity alone imposes on it.

"Innovation, even in its widest moments, has never yet suggested the propriety of allowing revenge, as either a justification or even a palliation of the crime of murder. Human society could exist upon no such basis.

"The common law has the most sacred regard for human rights. So sacred that even the rankest criminal who has assumed unto himself the functions of judge, jury, and executioner, is himself given by that law the privileges of a fair and impartial trial. It gives today, to Daniel E. Sickles, the prisoner at the bar, not only what he denied his victim—an impartial jury, and an upright judge—but, until he is proven guilty, clothes him in the spotless robes of innocence.

"[P]roclaim to the four quarters of the now listening world that there is virtue yet left in a jury, no matter how high the position or lofty the pretensions of the offender."

Ould had spoken for around forty minutes with the judge, jury, and audience listening with "breathless attention." The *Post* called it "eloquent and effective." The *Star* thought it "was one of the most masterly legal efforts ever listened to in this District. Clear, concise, temperate, and conclusive, it carried conviction to the minds of all who heard it."

Judge Crawford turned next toward the defense for their opening. Brady reserved their statement for the conclusion of the prosecution's case. The public, anxious to know Sickles' defense, would have to wait a little longer.

Ould called James Reed, a buyer and seller of wood and coal, to the stand. He had been walking near Madison Place when he "heard loud talking." He turned to see two men "four to six feet apart. One of the men raised his arm gradually and steadily" with a pistol pointed "at the other man, who was trying to avoid the aim. He fired, and the parties moved forward some twenty feet." Then "the man shot at retreated, the other following him, and the former running 'round a tree crying 'murder, murder...don't shoot me.'"

The second shot didn't seem to have any effect. At the same time, the man being shot threw something at the man with the pistol, hitting him and falling at his feet. Another shot was fired, "and the man shot at twisted round on the pavement and fell," crying out "Murder!" He landed on his side with his elbow facing the shooter. The man on the ground was shot once again as he cried out "Don't shoot!" Reed counted two misfires after the final shot.

Brady would handle cross-examination. He was "studiously polite," even to witnesses trying to hang his client, as well as to the judge and opposing counsel.

Did he see the features of either man, Brady asked, "so as to recognize them?"

Reed had not.

Had he seen other witnesses to the first and second shots?

Reed didn't think that anyone on Pennsylvania Avenue could have seen what happened. He believed it had lasted one and a half to two minutes, but he wasn't sure.

On redirect questioning by Ould, Reed testified that the shot sending the man to the ground was fired from five or six steps, while the last shot, and the two misfires, were fired from two or three feet away.

Philip Van Wyck, a clerk in the Treasury Department, was on the north side of Pennsylvania Avenue. He saw two men talking and then maneuvering around the street, saw and heard shots fired, and lost sight of them behind a house. He ran toward the scene, and as he came closer, the two men came back into view. One man lay on the pavement motionless while the other stood between him and the fence of the Gurley House, on the northeast corner of Madison Place and Pennsylvania Avenue. Van Wyck saw Daniel Sickles point the gun at the head of the man on the ground and attempt to fire. He saw also Samuel Butterworth resting on the railing of the house.

On cross examination, Van Wyck said that he was fifty yards away when the first shot was fired and that two minutes had elapsed until the final misfire. He saw a single barrel pistol on the ground, stocked to the end of the muzzle.

Edward Delafield was the third witness. He was on the south side of Pennsylvania Avenue in front of the White House and walking toward Madison Place. He saw Sickles walk south on Madison Place and address a man on the corner. Delafield thought nothing of it until he heard a pistol shot. He saw both men move into the street, heard Key beg for his life and saw him retreat behind the tree. Sickles followed, and Key reached out from behind the tree and grabbed his hand. "Sickles threw him off and fired." Delafield saw Key fall to the ground. Sickles shot again, followed by his attempted *coup de grâce*.

Joseph Dudrow heard the first shot from Pennsylvania Avenue while headed west and corroborated previous testimony.

Richard Downer was on 15th Street and New York Avenue, close enough to hear shots, and ran toward the sound. He was about to turn a corner to see when he heard a snap and decided "that he was near enough." When the shooting had finished, he turned the corner and saw Key "lying on the pavement." He saw Sickles with a revolver in his hand and heard him ask, "Is the damned scoundrel dead?" Or maybe it was "damned rascal." Nearly a half hour later, Downer saw a Derringer pistol in the street. It was unloaded, and an exploded cap was on the nipple. He picked it up and turned it over to the coroner.

Cyrus McCormick, inventor of the mechanical reaper, was the next witness. Stanton had done brisk business defending inventors against his patent claims. McCormick was in Washington again fighting a patent lawsuit, living in the third house from the corner on Madison Place. He was on the second floor when he heard the first shot and, rushing to the window, saw the remainder. Over the years, Stanton had brutalized him on the stand. McCormick was grateful not to be cross-examined.

Thomas Martin, a clerk in the Treasury Department, had left the Club House and was heading toward H Street to the north when he heard a gunshot. "Sickles had apparently just fired a pistol. Butterworth was leaning against the railing. Sickles and Key had moved out towards the middle of the street, and then came back towards the pavement." Martin ran back toward them, darting into the Club House to announce that Sickles was shooting Key. He returned to the street to see Sickles pointing a gun at Key's head and the final misfire.

Martin testified that he placed himself "between Key and Sickles, took hold of Key, and looked up inquisitively into the face of Mr. Sickles."

"He has dishonored my bed," he replied. Or maybe "violated my bed."

Ould interjected. "No matter about that, sir." Ould was careful not to open the door to evidence of the affair. Sickles was on trial, not Key.

"The witness had a right to continue his narrative unmolested," Brady said.

The judge ruled that having been "sworn to tell the whole truth and nothing but the truth, it was his duty to tell everything he knew in regard to the transaction."

Martin continued. He placed his hand over Key's heart "and found that it was still pulsating" and his lungs were still working. Martin asked whether he had anything to say, perhaps to his children. There was no response.

Francis Doyle, the next witness, had been inside the Club House during the shooting. He ran outside in response to Martin's alert. Doyle put his hand on Sickles's shoulder "and begged him not to fire." Sickles turned on him and said, "He has defiled my bed." Or maybe "dishonored."

Abel Usher, a clerk in the Navy Department, was in the Club House along with Doyle. "Murder!" was Key's last word.

Edward Tidball, the last witness of the day, had also come from the Club House. He testified that Sickles was wearing a long brown overcoat, light pantaloons, and hat.

Eleven witnesses had taken the stand. Their recollections differed, but they were in accord on what mattered: Sickles was the aggressor, firing numerous shots, and Key, unarmed, begged for his life.[7]

Watterson contrasted the styles of Brady and Stanton: Brady "submits gracefully when the judge is wrong on small matters" and was "decidedly the most popular counsel for the defense." Stanton was as forceful as Brady was graceful. "There is no ceremoniousness about him...he comes up to the point with a sledge hammer of earnestness which stands out in contrast to his colleague's extreme politeness."

As the trial neared the end of its first week, it continued to set historic standards for news: a daily average of 15,000 words had been telegraphed to New York and Boston alone. "Such an amount of telegraphic transmission never was heard of in Europe and is unprecedented in this country," wrote one paper. The Associated Press was spending $1,000 a day to distribute news of the trial.[8]

Chapter Thirty-One

The Implements of Death

*"This dreadful affair is the theme of conversation
in every social community in the country. No event
of a similar kind in our remembrance has excited so
much comment."*

—Louisville *Daily Courier*

DAY FIVE—Friday, April 8, 1859

Coroner Thomas Woodward was the first witness. He produced the Derringer pistol that he had been handed the day of the shooting.

In Key's pockets, he'd found a handkerchief, the case for the binoculars he had thrown at Sickles, and two brass door keys "about three inches long." He held them up. Every neck in the courtroom stretched forward.[1]

Woodward testified to Key's wounds. "One ball had entered his side; another the thigh, near the great artery; and there was a bruise on the right side; also, a slight wound on the hand."

Woodward then unfolded a bundle, holding up a blood-stained white shirt and gray striped pantaloons. "There is where the ball entered the right thigh," he pointed. "The place is stiffened and stained with blood."

He continued. "This sir, is the vest. There is the hole made by the ball, on the left side."

"Is there any other mark in the vest?"

"Yes. Here is another hole on the right side."

The bloody vest was handed to the jury.

Woodward then produced Key's overcoat. It was tweed with a brownish hue. He held up the coat to the light so that it could shine through the bullet hole. A reporter thought he resembled "an old clothing auctioneer in a dingy shamble in Chatham Street."[2]

"I do not see the materiality of this examination," Brady objected.

"We are through with this witness," Ould replied.

Dr. Coolidge was the Army surgeon who had been the first to examine Key at the Club House. Key had been wounded on the left side, between the tenth and eleventh ribs, he said. Two inches below the groin was another wound, passing through the thigh and exiting "in the groove of the buttock and the thigh."

The wound to the chest was fatal. At least a quart of blood had filled the cavity. Coolidge had examined Key's heart, and it was healthy.

Ould asked: "From the course and direction of the ball, please state what was the position of the descendant at the time the shot was fired."

"The course of pistol balls is at times very tortuous and difficult to trace, but my opinion" is "that the body must have been in a semi-recumbent posture. In other words, that Mr. Key must have been lying on his right side, the body turned a little over to the right, and the shoulders a little higher than the hips." The spleen and liver had also been damaged.

Brady asked Sickles to stand. Was the prisoner about the same height as Mr. Key? Coolidge thought he was. "If Mr. Key was falling, and his body was in the same position that the witness assumed," the result would be the same. Coolidge agreed that Key could have been falling at the time of the shot.[3]

Ould handed the witness a pistol ball. Was this the one he had removed from Key?

"To the best of my knowledge and belief, it is. It has the mark made on it, in my presence."

"To what particular classification of pistols does that ball commonly belong?"

Brady objected. A doctor is not an "expert in the manufacture of firearms."

"Certainly if he is a physician in the army. If not, he cannot discharge his duty."

"I think he can discharge his duty without discharging his firearm," Brady said to laughs.

Dr. Coolidge continued. "This is the ball we extracted from the right side. It is the only ball we found. The ball in the groin passed through."

There was then an in-court comparison between the ball cut out of Key and the Derringer found at the scene. It was too large and did not fit. That meant there was another, missing gun that had fired that ball into Key.

James Reed was recalled to the stand. Ould wanted to head off any attempts to claim that the Derringer belonged to Key. "You stated yesterday that when you saw these parties at the corner that you saw a pistol in the hand of the party at the south. Was any pistol in the hands of the other party?"

"No, sir. Nothing in his hand."[4]

Charles Wilder was the final witness for the prosecution. He was with the body of Key until the mayor took charge.

Ould moved to admit the Derringer pistol and ball into evidence.

"On what ground do you offer these as evidence?" Brady asked.

"Because they are the implements of death."

After some wrangling, Judge Crawford admitted the ball, since it had been removed from Key, and the Derringer found nearby. "Whether the prisoner used the pistol or not is a matter for the jury to decide."

The prosecution rested.

Chapter Thirty-Two

The Atonement of John Graham

—

*"Great excitement at the City Hall the case of Mr.
Sickles takes up all of every man's time of talking this
thing and that thing some think he deserves to be
hung for his murder."*

—diary of Lee Aldrich

DAY SIX—Saturday, April 9, 1859

It was a "low drinking shop" and late at night. A sailor was singing a song. John Austin, president of the Empire Club gang, entered with a group of friends.

Timothy Shea, one of the bartenders, asked, "Won't you take a chair?" Austin declined. Shea repeated himself twice. Then he ordered: sit down and listen to the song. A chair was thrown at the bar. The bartender threw back a decanter.

Austin and his friends were pushed out of the bar. One of them returned and fired a pistol shot that found its mark in Timothy Shea's chest, killing him.[1]

John Graham's first publicized case was in defense of John Austin. He had studied law with his father, and when he died, he completed it with his brother, David. They would try the Austin case together. The trial was a sordid affair, with one of the Shea brothers brought from "the Tombs," the infamous city jail, to testify. The jury, who brought beds to the deliberation room at 10:00 p.m., reached a verdict a little over an hour later. Not guilty.[2]

John Graham entered Columbia at age eleven and was valedictorian at fifteen. He'd made a big mark in the Austin trial. Flush with success, he disregarded the advice of older men and took on a libel case against the *Herald*. No other lawyer would pick a fight with the city's largest newspaper. James Gordon Bennett would remind them why the following year, when Graham was nominated for District Attorney. "Day after day [Bennett] made violent personal attacks on [Graham's] character," even after the election, "exulting in his defeat." It was a "merciless savagery without parallel."[3]

The same could also be said of their next encounter. Bennett and his wife were on Broadway. She went into a shoe store while he remained on the street. Graham, seeing his antagonist, swung a fist at Bennett, a glancing blow that knocked his hat out of shape. The second punch landed on his ear and sent him to the pavement. Graham then grabbed and beat him with a rawhide cowskin.[4]

While electoral failure stung, it was a success that haunted Graham the most. In a rare appearance on behalf of the state, he won an appellate ruling that voluntary drunkenness was not a defense to a crime. But behind the published opinion was a real person: James Rogers, "a grossly ignorant lad." After being sentenced to death for a stabbing, he said: "I've nothing to say—don't know that I did it, and if I did it, I don't know why I did it." Rogers became a *cause celebre* among those who understood that he was mentally deficient. The governor was mobbed on a visit to New York by people urging a pardon. But three months before Sickles's arrest, James Rogers was administered the last rites of the Roman Catholic Church and hanged at the Tombs before an audience of a hundred people. Graham was overwhelmed with guilt for his role in bringing this about. For the rest of his life, he would defend many men without charge, "to clear my conscience of the burden of sending Rogers to the gallows."

The first would be Daniel Sickles.[5]

The defense team had tasked him with the opening statement. Some thought brevity was advisable. Not Graham—he had many things to say and would take the time he needed to say them.[6]

Graham told the jury that he was a friend of Daniel Sickles, a "companion of his sunshine," now participating "in the gloom of his present affliction." It had been a "few weeks since the body of a human being was found in the throes of death in one of the streets of your city…the body of a confirmed and habitual adulterer."

His words were greeted with "solemn silence and attention."

Ould had argued that the killing was especially wrong for having occurred on Sunday. Graham responded that it was Key, and not Sickles, who had violated the Sabbath. "On a day too sacred to be profaned by worldly toil—on which [Key] was forbidden to moisten his brow with the sweat to honest labor—on a day when he should have risen above the grossness of his nature" and "sent his aspirations heavenward…we find him besieging with the most evil intentions that castle where for their security and repose the law had placed the wife and children of his neighbor.

"Had the deceased observed the solemn precept, 'Remember the Sabbath day to keep it holy,' he might at this day have formed one of the living. The injured father and husband rushes on him in the moment of his guilt, and under the influence of a frenzy executes on him a judgment which was as just as it was summary.

"You are here to fix the price of the marriage bed. You are here to say in what estimation that sacred couch is held by an honest and intelligent American jury. You are favored citizens. You live in…the city of our federal government, a city consecrated to liberty above all others, but not of the liberty of the libertine.

"You may feel a pity, in reviewing this occurrence, for the life that has been taken. You may regret the necessity which constrained that event. But while you pity the dead, remember also that you should extend commiseration to the living. That life, taken away as it was, may prove to be your and my gain. You know not how soon the wife or daughter of some one of you would have been...marked by the same eyes that destroyed the marriage relations of the defendant.

"An interference with the marriage relations must strike every reflecting mind as the greatest wrong that can be committed on a human being. It has been well said that affliction, shame, poverty and captivity are preferable."

Graham compared Sickles to Othello, who said that if Heaven had tried him with affliction and rained "all kinds of sores and shames on my bare head," "poverty to the very lips," or taken his "utmost hopes," he could have "found in some place of my soul a drop of patience." But "the fountain that my children and all my descendants flow from, has rejected" him, "and polluted herself.

"You are here to decide whether the defender of the marriage bed is a murderer—whether he is to be put on the same footing with" Cain.

"If between the act which has placed the defendant in his present condition" and the act of a common murderer "you can trace any similarity, it will be for you to institute and perfect the comparison. It is not in my power."

Graham dismissed the relevancy of all the evidence that had been presented. "It is perfectly immaterial how death was inflicted—whether by one or three shots, whether the man was killed standing up or lying down. The question is what was the influence of the provocation on the mind of the man who slew him? What was the mental condition of the defendant at the time he took the life of the deceased?

"Our legal system does not reach every case. There are certain wrongs which are not punished, and therefore the only law in such events is that traced in the human bosom by the finger of God—the law of human nature and instinct. When the law does not protect us, we are thrown on our own instincts, and have the right to defend ourselves from wrong.

"In this District you have provided no protection against adultery. The inevitable result is, that you are thrown upon the principle of self-defense to protect yourselves and your own. The law tells you...you may take the life of the burglar, but it still permits your house to [be] polluted by the tread of the adulterer.

"If a man come into your house against your will and lie on your bed, that is a trespass, and you can put him out by force. And yet if he lies down by your wife, and takes from her that which cannot be restored, according to the hypothetic position of the prosecution, he is not entitled to any redress at all.

"Frailty," he said, "thy name is 'woman.' A man who obtains the affections of another man's wife is as guilty as him who deflowers her by ravishment."

Adultery, he pointed out, had been an offense under English law since the thirteenth statute of Edward I. But under Maryland law, "adultery is not an offense." Only four states—Massachusetts, Virginia, Ohio, and Pennsylvania—had made it a crime. With no recourse to criminal courts and civil remedies unsatisfying, this was an area that the law simply did not reach.

By your verdict in this case, gentlemen of the jury, "you will strike terror into the heart of the adulterer" or "embolden him in his course.

"It is a well settled legal principle, that every man's house is his castle." Even "the humblest hut is as much a fortress for the protection of a man's family as a fortress for defensive purposes.

"One of the aggravated features of this case was that Mr. Key entered the abode of Mr. Sickles as a friend. We will show that they stood almost as close as do those two human beings, the Siamese twins, who now stand connected by a link which renders them indissoluble. The hearts of these two men have beaten almost against each other."

When "Mr. Sickles invited Mr. Key into his house, and Mr. Key entered for the purpose of accomplishing the downfall of his wife, he was as much a trespasser as if he entered it without an invitation.

"I submit" that "Philip Barton Key seduced the wife of Daniel E. Sickles" and "in a transport of frenzy," Sickles "sent him to his long account.

"I believe in the maxim, *De mortuis nil nisi bonum*." [Speak not of the dead except to mention them favorably.] He returned to Shakespeare, quoting Marc Antony's funeral oration of Julius Caesar: "'the evil that men do lives after them; the good is oft interred with their bones.' I would leave him where he slumbers, but as he is a fact in the case, and his conduct is a fact in the case, it is necessary that it should be reviewed" by the living.

"Had Mr. Sickles any worse foe on earth than Philip Barton Key? Had Key come to him and sunk his stiletto in his bosom, he would have been merciful to him. He wraps himself in the habiliments of friendship, and under that garb, supposing that he is masked, commits the most frightful, and at the same time the most sneaking of all crimes.

"It is strange that though adultery is twice forbidden in the Decalogue, no human law has caught up and carried out the spirit of the divine law. What is the reason of that? Do you suppose that society means that adultery should go unpunished? No. It throws you on the law of your heart...go by them and you reflect the will of Heaven, and when you execute them you execute the judgment of Heaven.

"Is not that enough to madden any man's brain who thinks upon it?" The District Attorney prosecutes thieves and burglars yet refuses "to protect Daniel E. Sickles's house against the greatest malefactor that walked the face of the earth, himself keeping the burglar out in order that the adulterer might pass in.

"The question which I present to your mind is this: [when] a man receives provocation which excites in him an amount of frenzy which he cannot control," is he "responsible for what he does under the influence of that frenzy? It is folly to punish a man for what he cannot help doing, if you concede that the transport is such that he cannot control it. You cannot make him criminally responsible for what he does under the influence of that transport.

"We mean to say, not that Mr. Sickles labored under insanity in consequence of an established mental permanent disease, but that the condition of his mind at the time of the commission of the act in question was such as would render him legally unaccountable, as much so as if the state of his mind had been produced by a mental disease.

"Under the old law, the doctrine of insanity was based on a narrow foundation."

Sickles "did not act in cold blood. If he did, he is more or less than human. He knew when he met with Mr. Key on the afternoon in question that Mr. Key was at his house to make an assignation with his wife. He knew that Mr. Key had hired a house but a few blocks from his own mansion where in the indulgence of his beastliness he polluted the body of his wife. He knew that Mr. Key, by the aid of a park, and a Club House, and an opera glass [binoculars], could at any distance from his castle easily tell whether it was safe for him to approach. This thing was well considered.

"Mr. Key hired this house in a part of the city where he knew no witnesses could come against him." From his place at the Club House, he could look through his opera glass "into the very center of Mr. Sickles's family circle."

When he saw Key, Sickles was "laboring under such a state of frenzy as deprived him of accountability for his act."

Graham had spoken for nearly five hours with no signs of fatigue. The same could not be said for Judge Crawford, who now adjourned. Sickles listened to the whole effort with his head bowed in his hands.[7]

The jurors were not permitted newspapers—only the Bible and some religious works. "It is said they may be seen any afternoon on the balcony of the National Hotel, gathered around one of their number who is reading the Bible aloud to them."[8]

William Stuart made light of the fact that the *Herald* never referred to Graham by name, calling him "counsel for the defense." After their "personal difficulty on Broadway," the *Herald* edited their reports "so as to prevent its readers from knowing that there is such a man as Mr. Graham in existence!"

That night, a saddler in Madison, Indiana, decided to satisfy his curiosity regarding his wife. He told his family that he would leave that evening for Cincinnati. Instead, he returned home at 9:00 p.m., finding his neighbor in his bed. He shot him with a revolver, left the house, and turned himself in to police.[9]

Chapter Thirty-Three

The Queen Against Daniel M'Naghten

Marcus Aurelius reigned over an empire of sixty-five million people from modern-day England to Egypt and from Tukey to Morocco. The emperor was the supreme judicial authority. Marcus saw justice as a core function of his office: he dramatically expanded the days for hearing appeals to 230. Parties could take all the time they needed to make their case. Marcus would devote the time necessary to resolve it justly.

The Emperor was presented with a homicide committed by a mentally ill man. He responded: "If you have ascertained that Aelius Priscus is so insane that he is permanently mad and thus he was incapable of reasoning when he killed his mother, and did not kill her with the pretense of being mad, you need not concern yourself with the question how he should be punished, as insanity itself is punishment enough."[1]

Marcus, writing in the second century AD, was well ahead of his time.

On May 15, 1800, King George III entered his royal box at Drury Lane Theatre. He acknowledged the audience with a bow, ensuring the assassin's bullet passed over, rather than through him. It was nothing personal: James Hadfield believed the death of George III would bring about the Second Coming of Christ.

Hadfield would have been hanged in a week had he fired on an ordinary Crown subject. But an attack on the king was high treason, a charge that guaranteed him the use of two lawyers. They argued the "wild beast" test was inadequate, as Hadfield's act had clearly proceeded from insanity, produced by a head wound in battle against the French. Hadfield was found not guilty by reason of insanity, but the case failed to establish a lasting English precedent.

★ ★ ★

"I was driven to desperation by persecution...they follow me...they persecute me wherever I go, and have entirely destroyed my peace of mind." So thought Daniel M'Naghten, a Scottish woodworker, who arrived at Number 10 Downing Street to kill Prime Minister Robert Peel, the leader of the grand conspiracy against him. Confusing Edward Drummond, his secretary, for the target, M'Naghten opened fire, hitting him in the back. Drummond believed he was fine and had the bullet removed.

Five days later he was dead.

M'Naghten was clearly mentally insane. The existing insanity defense, which would only work if the defendant were as a "wild beast," was inadequate, the court decided. M'Naghten was clearly insane, though he went about his business as a sane person would. The judge was so convinced of M'Naghten's insanity that he ordered him released. The public went into a panic, wondering if they were now at the mercy of insane murderers. The House of Lords responded by summoning the trial judges: what is the standard for a successful insanity plea? They answered: "(1) Did the defendant know what he was doing when he committed the crime? Or (2) Did the defendant understand that his actions were wrong?"

The M'Naghton Test, as it came to be known, was quickly and widely adopted in the United States.[2]

Chapter Thirty-Four

The Libertine Punished

DAY SEVEN—Monday, April 11, 1859

Graham resumed his opening argument. Key "was the prosecuting officer of this District," Graham said, who "came into this court and hunted down...the mere worms that crawl upon the face of the earth, while the full grown man of crime, such as he himself was, was permitted to stalk through your community." Teresa Sickles was a woman "young enough to be his daughter." He did not seem to know or care that Sickles and Key were born a year apart.

> It is for you to say what must have been the frenzy of Mr. Sickles at the time he encountered Mr. Key, under the circumstances leading to his death.
>
> You are here at the seat of our federal government. You are overshadowed by the halo of the name of Washington. Let the recollection of that name inspire you with fitting and becoming thoughts. Be reluctant and loath to

incorporate in your verdict a principle which, if it be the principle on which you act, will have a more demoralizing effect than any other principle that could be sustained or acted upon by an intelligent jury.

Graham "resumed his seat amid suppressed indications of applause and was complimented by many of those who were within reach of him."

The court took a brief recess.

The *Tribune* liked "the breadth and frankness of this opening. Mr. Key was an adulterer—therefore, he should have been killed. He had seduced Mrs. Sickles—therefore, Mr. Sickles did right in killing him." The *Daily Confederation* of Montgomery, Alabama, thought it "the most brilliant and forcible forensic effort ever made in Washington."[1]

The Philadelphia *Inquirer* was less impressed. Observers would doubt they were watching "one of the most brilliant lights of the bar. His premises are partial and false, and his deductions, if admitted, would justify every jealous woman, or suspicious man, in committing murder in obedience to the dictates of their passions."[2]

The *Post* pointed to its contradictory nature: on one hand, "slaying an adulterer is a perfectly justifiable deed...right and praiseworthy." On the other, "Sickles was so frenzied by the wrong he had received that he was no longer responsible for what he did. The inevitable conclusion would seem to be...that Sickles is only capable of doing right when he is out of his head."[3]

After the opening, Brady moved to place a series of letters into evidence. It was the correspondence between Sickles, Key, Jonah Hoover, Marshal Bacon, and Stephen Beekman. Ould objected that the letters were a year old and had no bearing on the case.

Brady responded that Ould had told the jury that Sickles had no purpose other "than remorseless revenge." As it stands, the jury knows nothing "as to their former personal relations. We do not propose offering the testimony to prove the adulterous act on the part of Mr. Key, but to show the friendly relations between the deceased and the accused." This correspondence shows "that their relations were of a friendly character."

Nothing in the letters expressed "either a kindly or a hostile feeling," Ould said.

"The jury will determine that," Brady said. "The letter commences 'Dear Sir' and ends with 'respectfully and truly yours.'" The letters are also admissible to prove that Sickles believed his relationship with Key to be "of an innocent and honorable character."

Carlisle weighed in: "An assassination is no less an assassination because the deep motive or passion which led to it—whether it be gold, or ambition, or vengeance."

Phillips, the former Alabama congressman on the defense team, argued that proof of the friendship contradicts the claim of malice, a required element of murder. "This is but one link of the chain of circumstances to show the friendship which existed between the parties prior to the date of the tragedy, and which continued down to within a few days of the commission of the act."

Crawford was ready to rule. "The law undoubtedly is that when a man is on trial for murder, previous expressions of good will and acts of kindness toward the deceased may be proved." These letters, however, are "simply courteous, and had no bearing on the issue. The letters are not evidence."

Brady called the first witness for the defense. William Badger was the agent of the Philadelphia Navy Yard. He had known Sickles since his return from London; and he had known Key for the same amount of time.

"Do you know what the relations between Key and Sickles were in regard to friendship or association?" Brady asked.

"Their relations were, as far as my knowledge extended, of the most intimate character."

"Did you know the wife of Mr. Sickles?"

"I knew her very well indeed."

On February 10, Badger had been at a dinner party at Sickles's house and had sat at the table with Sickles, Teresa, and Key.

"What other persons were there as guests?"

Carlisle objected.

Brady wanted to show that the Pendletons, Key's sister and brother-in-law, were also there.

Carlisle thought this irrelevant and "those who had already suffered too much in this matter should not be unnecessarily brought into this inquiry."

Brady lamented the suffering of the Pendletons, but to leave them out would be a disservice to a man on trial for his life. The friendship between Key and Sickles was relevant to prove the effect on Sickles' mind "when he learned of Mr. Key's perfidy. He must have thought, as Julius Caesar thought as he fell at the foot of Pompey's statue, exclaiming, as the blood dropped from the point of his friend's poignard, 'Et tu Brute!'"

The judge sustained Carlisle's objection. "Mr. Key's being there is evidence to the jury of an act of kindness on the part of Mr. Sickles towards him. But I do not see, and cannot perceive, how the presence of his sister or his sister's husband there can go to prove the same thing."

The next witness for the defense was Congressman John Haskin.

"How would you characterize the relations between Mr. Key and Mr. Sickles, as to the degree of intimacy?"

"Very much like the degree of intimacy existing between myself and Mr. Sickles," Haskin said.

"Did you visit frequently at the house of Mr. Sickles?"

Yes; "My lady visited there, too."

"Did you meet Mr. Key there?"

"I did."

"Was he frequently there?"

"He was. I last saw him at the Opera, when Piccolomini performed."

★ ★ ★

In the days before Daniel Sickles opened the most popular show in town, Washington was "badly infected" with "Piccolomini fever." The Tuscan noblewoman and worldwide opera star earned $4,000 a month, more than a member of Congress made in a year, and spurned marriage offers from royals throughout Europe. As the *Evening Star* put it, "She would rather be a great artist than the first lady in the land."[4]

Piccolomini arrived in the capital by way of Philadelphia, where a newspaper reported that she "much resembled that very charming and interesting young lady, Mrs. Daniel E. Sickles, of New York." The reporter who wrote the article thought that such comparisons were a greater compliment to Piccolomini.

On February 7, she performed as Norina in *Don Pasquale*. Sickles arrived late, detained by business in the House, and scanned the darkened theater for his wife. She was seated with Emanuel Hart and Mrs. Badger. He saw Key seated elsewhere. "A look of recognition passed between them. They bid each other the time of day."

The audience first saw Norina in her room, laying on her side, reading aloud from a romance novel:

She but glanced at that proud knight. And his heart was pierced to the core. Straightaway he knelt before her, and declared... "I am your cavalier." With one glance at her beauty, he tasted paradise.

He swore a vow on all the stars. He swore he would never give a thought to any other.

Norina then dressed herself, singing of her magical virtues:

I too know the magic power of a glance. I too know how to make hearts smolder. I too know the effect of a flashing smile. I know a thousand tricks in the game of love. And all the snares to trap a man's heart.

Norina marries Don Pasquale, but her true love is Ernesto. In the final act, Ernesto stands in the park outside the home of Don Pasquale and sings for Norina to come outside and see him:

Oh, my dearest. Why aren't you already mine? If I should die, how you would weep! But you could not restore me to life. Your faithful lover is torn by desire.

Did Teresa and Key dare to exchange a look?
Ernesto continued his serenade:

My cruel darling, would you have me die?

Norina sneaks outside, and he covers her in his coat. The secret lovers embrace. They sing to one another in unison:

Tell me again that you love me. Tell me again that you're mine. When you call me your treasure, life is twice as precious. Your voice is so dear. It soothes my anguished heart.

How safe I feel when I am near you. But how I worry when
we're apart.

Norina and Ernesto kiss at last. They are interrupted by the
sounds of an angry Don Pasquale as he thunders out of the house.
Ernesto spirits off before he can be seen. Don Pasquale demands to
know, Where's the philanderer who was just here?

I'll find him, he says.

Key watched the stage through his opera glass. In twenty days'
time, he would throw it in a futile effort to survive the wrath of his
lover's husband.

It is unknown whether Sickles, Teresa, or Key attended the next
night's performance of *Don Giovanni, Il dissolute punito* ("The
Libertine Punished"). They would have made every effort on that
rainy night, to see an opera written by Teresa's grandfather, Lorenzo
Da Ponte, in whose home they had met. If so, she would have spent
another night with her life uncomfortably mirrored on the stage.

In the final act of *Don Giovanni*, the unrepentant libertine is
confronted by the vengeful spirit of a man, in the form of the statue,
whose house he defiled. Justice is served when the statue drags Don
Giovanni into the fires of Hell.[5]

★ ★ ★

Daniel Dougherty, a Philadelphia lawyer, was the next witness
for the defense. Dougherty had long been a friend of Sickles and had
visited him and Teresa in Washington and New York.

"What was the last time you saw Mr. Key?"

The day before his death, Dougherty answered. Around noon.
Dougherty was headed to the Sickles's house to say goodbye on his
way out of town. He ran into Key, who walked with him up

Pennsylvania Avenue. Dougherty assumed they were headed to the same place. But on Madison Lane, Key made an abrupt turn and headed for the Club House. Dougherty passed a considerable amount of time with Sickles. On leaving, he was surprised to encounter Key in Lafayette Square, headed from the Club House toward the Sickles home. They passed in front of the Jackson statue and exchanged goodbyes.[6]

Brady then made a strange maneuver. He asked Carlisle to admit that Key had been the lawyer for Sickles in a legal matter concerning his lease of the Ewell Mansion. Carlisle said, yes; in September or October of 1858, he had had three interviews with Key.[7]

★ ★ ★

The night before the trial began, Simon Hanscombe of the Boston *Atlas and Daily Bee* entered the jail, hoping to get an interview with the defendant.

He judged Sickles "one of the coolest men living. The deliberate manner in which he approached Key, not knowing whether the latter was armed or not, and notified him that he must prepare to die, giving Key, whom Sickles had a right to suppose was armed, a chance to draw upon him, is an evidence of this. Not less cool was the manner in which he described to the writer, in his cell in Washington, the manner in which he perpetrated the bloody deed."

Smoking a cigar, Sickles "detailed with precision the manner in which he approached Key, what he said to him, how Key received the awful warning, that he drew his first Derringer and fired, and how Key reeled and cried 'Don't kill me!' and then in a desperate struggle for life rushed upon Sickles and grasped his arm, how he threw him off and then drew his second Derringer and fired again, how Key cried 'murder!' and staggered against a tree, that he drew a revolver and tried to fire that, but the nipple caught and he came near losing his third shot but luck favored him and the revolver worked and he fired a third ball."

Sickles said he "was about to fire again, but observing by his eyes that Key was dying he desisted and left with Butterworth."

The reporter sat uncomfortably as this "was related with as much ease and apparent coolness as though he was describing the shooting of a deer instead of a human being."

"He dishonored me," Sickles explained. "And we could not both live on the same planet."[8]

The story appeared in the *Atlas and Daily Bee* on the second day of trial. It was one of thousands of articles on the case to appear that day, and, in a smaller Boston newspaper, it did not attract much attention. And its full significance did not become clear until John Graham's opening statement, raising the defense of temporary insanity. But Sickles' cool rendition of a planned, premeditated attack in which he used three guns sharply contradicted the arguments being put forward to save his life.

The article made its way to the desk of Robert Ould. It was hearsay and not admissible by itself. But he prepared a subpoena for its author compelling the reporter's testimony at trial.

Chapter Thirty-Five

A Thrilling Scene

DAY EIGHT—Tuesday, April 12, 1859

The *Albany Journal* reported that so many prominent Democrats had come to support Sickles the trial became a warmup for next year's presidential convention. In the courtroom, elected officials and party leaders compared notes on the possible candidates, with Stephen Douglas appearing to be the favorite.[1]

The first witness of the day was John McElhone, a reporter for the *Congressional Globe*. "When I saw" Sickles and Key "together they always had toward each other the language and appearance of good friends. Mr. Key frequently expressed his friendship for Mr. Sickles."

Former US Marshal Jonah Hoover was the next to testify. "Key was my most intimate and cherished friend for ten years or more," he said. Shortly after Buchanan's inauguration, Hoover had introduced Key to his killer. During that time, in "March 1857, Mr. and Mrs. Sickles" spent "two or three weeks as guests."

"Did you know at the time it occurred of a correspondence between Mr. Key and Mr. Sickles?"

"I was privy to it, and to everything relating to it. Everything."

On February 23, Hoover said he opened the door to his home. Key was standing there. With Laura Sickles. Laura remained at the Hoover residence for "two or three hours" until Key returned for her.

Sickles managed to keep a brave face. Key had dropped Laura off so that he could be with her mother. And Hoover, whom he had considered a friend, not only knew what was happening but appeared complicit.

Police Chief Goddard took the stand and held up Key's opera glass. It was handed to me in the jail at the time of the commitment of Mr. Sickles, he testified.

Stanton demonstrated for the jury that the opera glass fit in the case that had been found on Key.

Reverend Smith Pyne was the pastor of St. John's in Lafayette Square, known as "The President's Church," as every chief executive since Madison had worshiped there. On the night before the shooting, Pyne was riding in a carriage through Lafayette Square with his son. They were headed to the White House and saw Sickles walking quickly in the opposite direction. "I was struck by his appearance and called my son's attention to it."

"What was it?"

"I thought there was a wildness about Mr. Sickles's appearance on that occasion; he seemed to be like a man who was in some great trouble of some kind or other." He had a "Mingled defiant air"—a "desolate air."

Governor Robert Walker, who had arrived at the Sickles house after the killing, was the next witness. He testified to Sickles's excited manner, "strange and unusual behavior," and a change in his voice. Sickles had thrown himself suddenly on the sofa, convulsing, screaming, sobbing and spazzing violently. He was worried about the dishonor brought to his family, particularly to his daughter.

Walker continued his description. "He was in a state of frenzy and I feared if it continued he would become permanently insane." There were high pitched "Screams of the most frightful character," "unearthly" and "appalling," something between a "sob and a moan."

Listening to this testimony, Sickles fell forward, his face leaning on the shoulder of a nearby friend. "At length his habitual self-command gave way, and he burst into a passion of sobs and tears which rendered him completely helpless, and the man who had hitherto preserved a demeanor apparently too calm, impassive and frigid, was torn with an excess of agonized emotion."

Stanton rose: "If your honor please, may the prisoner be removed for a few moments."

"Certainly," said Crawford, looking at Sickles.

Sickles was "so utterly exhausted and overcome that his physical powers failed him, and he was unable to rise." Emanuel Hart and another friend helped him out of the room as he sobbed like a child. "It was the most affecting scene I ever witnessed," Stuart wrote, "and will be remembered when time shall have dried the tears that will be shed over the grave of many a spectator."

When he returned, his countenance reflected "extreme mental suffering" and a "desolateness of his whole appearance."

Another reporter called it a "thrilling scene...when the wounds of Mr. Sickles were opened afresh. There was hardly a dry eye in court and certainly not a heart remained unaffected by it."[2]

Thomas Meagher was a late addition to the defense team. In Ireland, he had led a rebellion with no military experience, no money, and few guns. Refusing to admit high treason, he found himself in a Tasmanian penal colony. Meagher escaped, hiding for ten days on an uninhabited island. He sailed to Brazil and on to New York. Fame preceded him in his new country. Newspapers had covered his trial and daring getaway, resolutions had been passed in his defense, songs had been written in his honor, and Irish civic associations had adopted his name with pride. He was invited to more events than he could ever attend. Meagher was admitted as a lawyer in 1856 but had never tried a significant case. His role was to sit at the defense table and draw the sympathy or jurors or reporters who admired him. But Sickles was his friend, and he hoped to contribute something more substantive.[3]

This outburst gave him an idea. He started writing.

Carlisle asked Walker: "Do you recollect that Sickles grew calm and said he was ready to go with the magistrate?"

"I do. When I say calm, I mean comparatively calm." Walker had stayed with him for some time in jail because of his concerns.

Francis Mohun was next. He'd known Sickles since before he was sworn into congress. He saw him on February 27 near sundown. "His whole appearance, though I cannot exactly describe how it affected me, did affect me very seriously at the time. I thought there was some very high excitement operating on his mind at the time. I heard the next day of this occurrence. I said I thought he was crazy or insane."

Ould cross-examined Mohun. "If you had not heard of this occurrence, would his appearance have made that impression on you?"

"It might not. But his wild appearance excited my attention then. He was walking quite rapidly at the time, more rapidly than I ever observed him before. There seemed to be a strange movement about his person and head. I confess that I heard rumors about the city which perhaps made me observe him the more closely."

Bridget Duffy was next. "I live in Mr. Sickles's house in the capacity of nurse and lady's maid, and partly chambermaid. We arrived in Washington from New York between Christmas and New Year's."

Stuart thought she gave "her testimony with marked precision. She is not only an intelligent but a well-educated woman—most unusually so for one of her class in life."[4]

Sickles came home the night before the killing between five and six. "I heard loud talking between Mr. and Mrs. Sickles. Their door was partly open."

Brady had a piece of paper handed to Bridget. "That's my hand-write," she said. "I signed at Mrs. Sickles request."

"Do you know Mrs. Sickles's handwriting?"

"Yes."

"Is that hers?"

"To the best of my belief it is. I saw her write a paper, which I signed my name to. I did so at her request. Mr. and Mrs. Sickles were, I believe, then in their own room. I heard Mr. Sickles cry. Also Mrs. Sickles."

Teresa's confession was then offered into evidence.

Ould objected.

Brady said that it was "offered as a communication to Mr. Sickles, affecting his mind, and producing or continuing the excitement under which he labored."

Crawford "read over the papers slowly but attentively."

It was hearsay, Ould said, and not evidence of Sickles's mind. And communications between husbands and wives are not admissible.

Brady responded: "It helped to constitute the irresistible pressure under which he acted. How far that confession would act on the prisoner's mind would be a matter for the jury to decide. In the case of *Jarboe*, decided in this court, had not the prisoner acted on the statement of his sister, and was not that hearsay evidence as much as this?" And "if the husband chose to waive that privilege and permit his wife to open her mouth, on what principle of law is he to be denied that right?

"Who lighted the flame in the breast of the husband we now propose to show. The materials are always there. They are in your honor's bosom. They are in every man's bosom. And only require the application of the torch to burst into a complete conflagration."

Judge Crawford said, "It is now within ten minutes of the hour of adjournment." They would revisit the issue in the morning.

On the same day, a crowd of thirty thousand gathered in Baltimore to watch four executions. John Cyphus, "a colored man, about 30 years of age," had killed "for an offense such as that of Mr. Key." Cyphus thanked God that he could state his innocence. Whether he meant that he was not the killer or that a man who kills his wife's lover commits no crime, the newspaper did not grant him the space to say.[5]

As the *Tribune* noted, if the scene had been "Whitechapel or the New York quays" and the crime between a laborer or a sailor, it "would have been dismissed in a single contemptuous paragraph. The morbid sympathy which attends the murderer is a melancholy feature in American morals." The *States* agreed: other killings were "ignored because neither [the killer or victim] belonged to the 'upper ten.'"[6]

The *Alexandria Gazette* hoped that the two-penny wood cuts and illustrations of the Sickles trial and the Baltimore executions would "over-do the business and nauseate even the appetite of those from whom they cater."[7]

That night, George Sickles, Daniel's father, was surprised at his hotel by a group of twenty women. Their ostensible leader, a sixty-year-old woman, said, "We demand [Sickles's] discharge on behalf of our sex. Let him be convicted, and the libertine obtains new license. Let him be vindicated, and virtue requires new guarantees."[8]

Chapter Thirty-Six

The Confession

DAY NINE—Wednesday, April 13, 1859

The day opened with Carlisle opposing the admission of Teresa's confession. It was irrelevant, he argued, for the possible effect it might have had on Sickles. "In all cases the question is not whether the prisoner drank liquor enough to make him drunk, but whether, in point of fact he was drunk."

Watching the two sides fight reminded William Stuart of a battle. Brady was "like a 24-pounder gun in the center of a park of flying artillery." Carlisle was a "Minie rifle—quick, clear of aim, sure of hitting his mark," and "a deadly logician."[1]

As the lawyers argued, Stuart looked over at the confession on the counsel table. "I was extremely struck by the beauty of the handwriting," he wrote, "and its clearness and firmness. The orthography is perfect, and the whole document, in its mere external features, bears the impression of a mind perfectly collected and a hand unshaken by emotion." He wondered whether there had been multiple drafts, or if she had maintained her composure in the face of an angry husband.[2]

The judge took a brief recess and returned with his ruling. "Declarations of a wife or husband, for or against each other, stand on the same footing as though it was testimony given on the stand. Suppose the wife of the defendant were in court at this moment, could she be put upon the stand? Could she be heard? Certainly not. It would violate well-established principles and rules to admit it. It would have a most injurious effect upon the relations of husband and wife in destroying their confidential identity. The proposition is therefore rejected."

Sickles's lawyers had asked, begged him from the beginning to release the confession. It was proof of the affair. It had been going on over a year; they were intimate in Sickles's own house; Key had dropped Sickles's daughter off so that they could be together. Without the confession, they might never be able to prove the affair. It could save his life.

Sickles was adamant. He would not further his wife's humiliation. And, if it were made public, Laura would read it someday. No; he would take his chances.[3]

But Judge Crawford had ruled the confession inadmissible. There was one last chance, however. If the confession were published, the jurors, though sequestered, might hear about it.

The courtroom was abuzz. Someone had a copy of the confession. The *Star* reporter had never seen "more nervous anxiety manifested" in reporters to get a story to their editors. Sickles was desperate to stop it from getting out. But he couldn't leave the prisoner's box, much less the courtroom. Sickles sent someone to the telegraph office to stop the transmission. But Teresa's words were miles away. The *Post* accused Sickles of leaking the confession. William Stuart set the record straight. Sickles had the confession in his hands since it was written. He could have released it at any point.[4]

The coverage was about to enter an entirely new level of scandal. The newspapers, when they had charged full-speed into the case, committing column inches and complete coverage to their readers, had no idea where the case was going. Was it time, they wondered, to pump the brakes, starting with the confession?

"The appearance of a foul confession of shame by Mrs. Sickles, in this afternoon's *Star*, is the subject of much comment," wrote the *Boston Journal*, and it is a matter of wonder how any woman would thus chronicle her fall."[5]

The *Post* printed a redacted version of the confession: "it is altogether too disgusting to be laid before our readers." The *Times* accused the *Post* of "cheap virtue…suppressing in the evening what it very well knew that everybody had seen in the morning."[6]

The *Cincinnati Gazette* refused to print the confession. The *Lafayette Daily Journal* pointed out that the testimony was just as salacious. The *London Morning Post*, which did not publish verbatim coverage of the trial, printed the confession word for word.

The *Evening Bulletin* was prosecuted by the state of California for obscenity for publishing the confession. The owners were fined one hundred dollars each.

Laura Crawford Jones wrote in her diary: "Mrs. Sickles's confession is in the papers tonight, it is shocking! Such grossness in such a young woman. Only 23! I think she must have been a great fool as well as a very low minded, ungrateful creature."[7]

Verina Davis, wife of Jefferson, wrote her husband about the "Everlasting Sickles trial." "Have you seen her confession? Filth-filth—beastliness in its most bestial form." One of her friends joked that she herself might have done the things confessed, but she should *never have told it*."[8]

Octavia Ridgley was the next witness. She entered court with a double veil of blue and black but removed it at the request of the lawyers. "A blonde with sparking blue eyes," every man was looking at her. She was a guest of the Sickles beginning on the Thursday before the killing. "After we returned from the hop I noticed a change in his manner. The change was more particularly observable on Friday." It was "a wild, distracted look, especially on Saturday."

"Octavia was on the verge of fainting. She took a drink of water, which seemed to make things right."[9]

On Saturday night, she went to Teresa's room where she saw her writing. Teresa asked her to sign her name to the paper. They spent the night in the same room. Octavia in the bed. Teresa on the floor with her head leaning on a chair.

In the morning, she dressed and ate breakfast alone. Daniel Sickles "was very much agitated. While sitting at the breakfast table I heard sobbing. He was going up stairs. I could hear him all over the house," uttering "unearthly," "fearful groans" that "seemed to come from his very feet." She last saw him on Sunday, as he lay on the bed with Butterworth by his side.

Bridget Duffy was recalled to the stand. Watterson described her in the *Press* as a "Pretty, intelligent looking, black-haired Irish woman, of some twenty-five years," who "gave her evidence with great clearness and self-possession."

She returned from church shortly before 11:00 a.m. George Wooldridge was in the study. Bridget went upstairs to clean Sickles's room when he entered, tearing at his hair and calling on God to witness his troubles, crying and sobbing. She heard the door open and Butterworth come up the stairs, saying, "Where is Mr. Sickles?"[10]

She saw Key sometime after 11:00 a.m. He entered Lafayette Square as if coming from the Club House. She saw him "take out a handkerchief and wave it, as he passed, three or four times."

The Sickles dog came and greeted him familiarly.

"You're positive of that?" Carlisle asked.

"Sure," she answered, "spiritedly and indignantly," "and you don't think I would lie?" The courtroom laughed.

"Don't fire up so, Bridget," Carlisle said with a smile.

"He does not mean anything by it," Brady assured her.

She repeated her testimony about the dog.

Carlisle asked, "The waving of the handkerchief was one continuous act or whirl?"

"It was not a continuous whirl," she responded. "It was so-so-so," demonstrating the act.

"About as fast as you would turn the handle of a coffee-mill?"

"I am not in the habit of turning coffee mills."

Deputy Marshal Phillips tried to stop the laughter. "Silence, silence, gentlemen, in court."

Carlisle attempted to restate her testimony.

"I did not say any such thing," Bridget said.

"Repeat what you have said."

"I have repeated it twice already, and that ought to be sufficient. The dog fawned on Mr. Key."

"How came you to take particular notice of where the dog was when Mr. Key whirled his handkerchief last?"

"Because I saw the dog at the house. I cannot exactly say the certain spot where the dog was at the fourth whirl." She did not see Sickles leave the house and did not hear the shots. When he returned, Sickles went upstairs with Teresa for three or four minutes. She "did not see him sobbing or crying."

William Mann, a lawyer from Buffalo, was called to the stand. He was traveling in Washington and saw Key on the day of his death.

"State where you saw him," Brady said, "and the circumstances connected with it."

"I saw him in the square, opposite the President's house, where the Jackson monument is. I came up towards the monument and met

Mr. Key walking along. I passed the time of day with him; stated to the person with me who he was. We saw him leaving the park by the southwest corner."

"What did you see him do?"

"I saw him whirling a handkerchief as he went along. He had the handkerchief first in his two hands, this way, and he drew it out and waved it." He illustrated this backward and forward.

Thomas Miller was then called. He had been in the Club House with Key's body. Brady asked if there were any items removed from his body other than that which had been placed into evidence.

"A gentleman present examined some of the pockets and removed some scraps of paper, or folded papers, which seemed to be of very little importance."

"We do not ask their importance," Brady said.

"There was also an old card case, with one or two visiting cards. These were handed to me. I did not examine them, but I put them into an envelope and directed them to Hon. Mr. Pendleton."

Judge Crawford announced that he was indisposed from "the oppressive atmosphere of the courtroom." They adjourned at quarter till three.

Chapter Thirty-Seven

Give Vent to Your Tears

"The Sickles trial is the only topic of conversation just now. Mother and Papa sympathize with Sickles, [my brother] with Key, and I feel sorry for them all."
—diary of Laura Crawford Jones

DAY TEN—Thursday, April 14, 1859

For the first time since the trial began, Congressman George Pendleton and Key's brother appeared in the courtroom.[1]

The prosecution opened by announcing that they were prepared, if Teresa's confession had been admitted, to produce a guest registry from Barnum's Hotel in Baltimore. A January entry shows that Sickles stayed there, and ten rows below in a different handwriting was the name "Mrs. Daniel E. Sickles."[2] The signature would belong to a woman other than Teresa.

George Wooldridge was called to the stand. He testified encountering Sickles on the Saturday before the murder in the House of Representatives, "affected and distressed." He arrived the morning of the killing and found Sickles in his library, eyes "bloodshot and red. There was a strange manner about him. He would go upstairs and then come down stairs again. Then he would talk about matters and go upstairs again. Every time he came into the room where I was, he pressed his hands to his temples," leaned on the secretary desk, "and sob."

"Give vent to your tears," Wooldridge told his friend, "as they will relieve you."

"Did you see Mr. Key that Sunday?" Brady asked.

"I did, twice."

"Where and when?"

"The first time between ten and eleven o'clock" in Lafayette Square. He saw him again around a quarter to two o'clock, "directly in front of the library window of Mr. Sickles's house. There was a lady and gentleman with him then."

"Did you observe Mr. Key do anything while passing?"

"I saw him take a handkerchief out of his pocket and wave it three times. While doing so his eyes were towards the upper window of Mr. Sickles's house." Sickles entered the library "very excited." Butterworth "endeavored to calm him. That is the last I saw of him until he came into the house with the police officers," and Mayor Barrett, Chief Goddard, Walker, "and some other gentlemen. I never want to see another day as that."

Brady asked whether he had communicated anything to Sickles when he saw him at the Capitol on Saturday.

Ould objected on the same grounds as before. Only the effect on Sickles was relevant. Not the trigger.

Stanton demanded the rights for Sickles that would be given a slave in North Carolina, referencing a murder trial there.

"I could let my argument and conduct in this case go before the court and before the world in contrast with the disreputable rant which this counsel had exhibited," Ould said, pointing to Stanton. He mocked the oversized defense team and their various roles: "There seemed to be divisions assigned to counsel for the defense—to some, high tragedy, to some, comedy, to some, the part of walking gentlemen, and one gentleman appeared to fill the office of clerical supe, to set the theological part of the house in order." A "supe" was a meaningless extra in a play, and the "clerical supe" was a clear reference to the ever-present Reverend Haley. "One of the counsel," Ould continued, "had carried out the part...of the bully and the bruiser."

Stanton looked "thunderbolts at him, and "sprang to his feet" with such a "rapid and violent...utterance that the reporters laid down their pencils in despair. They combined the rush of an avalanche with the impetuosity of a cyclone."[3]

Stanton replied that Ould's version of the law "would send my client to the gallows by those who are malignantly seeking for his blood. I have not the honor of his acquaintance, and after his language just uttered, do not desire it." Stanton was interrupted by commotion in the audience. He continued when the police had restored order. "I cannot reply to the counsel's remarks. I defy them. I scorn them. I don't fear them." The courtroom lost order again. They couldn't be expected to behave better than the lawyers.

Carlisle responded for the prosecution. The evidence offered "was not competent to prove insanity by the declarations or communications of other parties, but by the acts and declarations of the prisoner himself. Whatever communication this witness, like Iago, poured into the ear of his friend was not important."

"I appeal to the hearts of other men, Stanton said.

Ould replied. "There are a great variety of human hearts in the world."

"Yes, sir, and some of them very bad ones."

"And I am happy to say that mine does not contain many things which seem to exist in the hearts of some other people, though like all other human hearts, I suppose it is filled with much that would be better out of it."

"It would be better were something else in it."

Judge Crawford intervened, finally. "Really, gentlemen, this thing must be interrupted."

Crawford ruled against the defense.

Stanton persisted. "Will your honor be good enough to explain a little further, so that we can understand how to meet your Honor's views on that point. Your honor will recollect that we are trying to get in evidence to save the prisoner's life."

Brady interjected. We offer to prove that this witness had communicated to Sickles that his wife had gone to a home with Mr. Key on the Wednesday before his death "for the exclusive purpose of having there adulterous intercourse with her."

The judge sided with the prosecution.

John Cuyler, a plasterer, was the next witness. He knew Key for three or four years. He saw "Key in the vicinity of the house the week before his death."

Carlisle objected. What did this have to do with Sickles's mind on the day of the killing?

"It is now too late to shut the door to that kind of evidence," the judge ruled.

"We want to know whether Mr. Key waved the handkerchief to excite the admiration of the dog, or anything else," Brady said to laughter.

Cuyler entered the corner gate of Lafayette Square and saw Key enter through the center gate. Key sat on the iron bench beneath the Jackson statue. Cuyler thought his behavior was curious: he hid behind General Jackson and watched. Key rested his head on his left hand and pulled out his pocket handkerchief, waving it at the Sickles home. The courtroom laughed at his imitation. When Cuyler's curiosity had worn out, Key was still sitting on the bench. "I have often seen him loitering back and forth in the square. For two months he had been attracting my attention."

Stanton asked, "Was that when the members of congress were at the Capitol?"

"Yes."

Carlisle objected. "Argumentative."

"That's all," Stanton said.

"The inquiry whether that was before or after congress was in session is not proper," Crawford ruled.[4]

"I think it is important as to the time," Stanton said. "The signals must have been made when Mr. Sickles was out of his house."

"I can clearly see what you mean by it," said Judge Crawford.

Jeremiah Boyd saw Key on the morning of his death. He was coming from Reverend Pyne's church and saw Key standing in front of the Club House, looking toward the Sickles home.

Charles Bacon saw Key on Wednesday, February 23, in Lafayette Square. He stood near the Jackson statue twirling his handkerchief between ten and eleven in the morning. "Some hours after" he saw Teresa, Octavia, and another man, between three and four o'clock.

S. S. Parker saw Key on the Sunday a week before his shooting. Teresa was on the platform of her residence, her hand over the shoulder of a little girl, apparently trying to keep her from falling over the steps." Key emerged from the southwest gate of Lafayette Square, hat in hand. He "bowed to Mrs. Sickles, and twice waved his handkerchief."

"I ask whether when you saw him a second time, your attention was not directed to him by a remark made when you first saw him?" Stanton asked.

"It was."

"Was that remark in reference to Mr. Sickles killing him?"

The witness answered, as Carlisle tried to object.

"It was."

The objection was sustained. What Key had said about Sickles killing him would not become part of the record.

William Rapley was the next witness. "The Thursday preceding [Key's] death I saw him in front of Green's, the cabinetmaker's, with a letter in his hand. Mrs. Sickles and the child were with him. She left him and went out into the shop, and when she came out they walked together up the Avenue, he was reading the letter."

Neither Rapley nor his friend came close enough to read the letter, but its substance had been reported: "Unless he desisted, Mr. Sickles would detect him and that in such an event the consequences would be serious."[5]

Frederick Wilson, Rapley's friend, said to him that he was going to cross the street and try "to get a good look at them." The courtroom laughed at Wilson's nosiness.

Stanton held up the "R. P. G." letter, sent to Sickles that same evening, for Rapley to compare. "The paper I saw in Mr. Key's hand appeared to be about that size of paper."

Wilson was the next to testify. He crossed the street and stood fifty to seventy-five feet away. Key, Teresa, and Laura walked up the avenue past him. Wilson rejoined Rapley across the street. "In about fifteen minutes afterwards they came back on the south side. Just as they passed me he put the letter in the envelope and they walked on down the avenue."

"What was the color of the envelope?"

"It was a yellow envelope, something like this," he said, referring to the envelope containing the "R. P. G." letter.

Stanton held up a copy of the anonymous letter to Sickles. He confirmed that it was the same size.

"Why did you cross over to get a good look at them?" Stanton asked.

"I saw Mr. Key" near the Sickles house "a great number of times. Nearly every day."

"He appeared to be making a business of it?"

"Yes sir." Laughter. "Between the hours of twelve and one I usually found him there. It appeared to be quite a regular business."

Amidst more laughter, the judge ended the questioning.

Brady called Thomas Brown to the stand. "I reside in the city of New York. In pursuance of instructions from you, I obtained a certain lock."

Brady handed Brown a sealed package. He opened it and produced a door lock.

Carlisle objected. What was the point of this?

Brady said he wanted it identified to be introduced as evidence later.

Brown testified that he had received it from Mr. Wagner on Pennsylvania Avenue, who took it from the door of 383 Fifteenth Street.

Jacob Wagner was next to testify. Wagner was a locksmith who verified that he had given the lock to Brown. "I took it off a house on Fifteenth Street, No. 383. It was John Gray, the black man's house." Several other men, including Congressman Pendleton, were there. "This was about a week after Key's death."

"What was said on that occasion?" Stanton asked.

Objection!

Stanton "proposed to show that the lock was taken off for the purpose of destroying evidence."

Ould withdrew his objection.

Stanton "wanted to know whether it was the persons engaged in the prosecution who tried to destroy this evidence."

Carlisle demanded to know whether Stanton made insinuations that it was him.

"None in the world. God forbid I should believe you would do it."

The Judge intervened. This "is an exceedingly grave case, and must be conducted with a great deal more regard to dignity and order and decorum than has been observed hitherto. I cannot permit this."

"I ask the witness what I asked him before," Stanton said.

"But it must be done in an orderly manner," said the Judge.

Stanton returned his attention to the witness. "What was said about this lock at the lock and who said it?"

John Gray directed its removal, Jacob Wagner said.

"Were the other persons present at the time?"

"No, sir."

"What time was it?"

"About eleven o'clock."

"How long were you engaged in taking it off?"

"Ten minutes."

"What door?"

"The front door."

"Was there another lock put on that door?"

"There was."

Chapter Thirty-Eight

An Intense and Sudden Excitement

John Seeley was a painter who lived near the Gray house. "I witnessed the taking off the lock. Saw opening of the back door and heard the order given to take the lock off the front door, because, as I thought, the key had been lost. Mr. Charles Lee Jones and Mr. Pendleton were present. One of them directed the locksmith to remove the lock off the front door.

Louis Poole was next. He was also a neighbor. He was present when the lock was taken off. "Mr. Pendleton ordered the old lock to be taken from the door and replaced by a new one."

Woodward, the coroner, was recalled as a witness. "Had you in your possession, at any time, any papers, cards, memorandums, or anything of that kind belonging to Mr. Key?"

"No. Last Monday in court, a gentleman asked me if I was aware that Dr. Miller had taken some papers out of Mr. Key's pocket. That was the first I heard of it."

The next witness was Reverend C. H. A. Bulkley of Westminster, Connecticut. "I have known Mr. Sickles since 1838. We were associated together in the New York University."

"Do you know the liability of Mr. Sickles to intense and sudden excitement?" Brady asked.

"Yes, sir."

Carlisle objected. Proof of excitability is inadmissible unless going to the extent of insanity.

Brady explained: "Some men are lunatics for a few days, some for years, and some are incurably insane. The physiological and psychological constitution of a man, as bearing on a tendency to insanity, is a fair matter of evidence."

Carlisle withdrew his objection.

"State what you know of the tendency of Mr. Sickles's mind to become disordered on being subject to great emotion."

It was 1840, observed Bulkley. Professor Da Ponte the younger, Sickles's mentor and friend, had died suddenly. As his body was lowered into an open grave, Sickles "broke out into a spasm of passionate grief and most frantic energy. He raved, and tore up and down the graveyard shrieking, and I might even say yelling, so much so that it was impossible for us who were his friends to mollify him in any measure by words. We were obliged to take hold of him, and by friendly force restrain him, and thus ultimately we took him out of the cemetery, the demonstration that he made might be called one of frantic grief."

"Is the statement now made by you one that was sought by the prisoner's counsel, or are you here in consequence of a voluntary communication from you?"

"It has not been solicited at all." Bulkley continued, "I suppose we would have called ourselves young men then. I cannot say how long this frantic grief lasted. Somewhere between five and ten minutes. I saw no trace of it the day following." This grief "was the most remarkable one I ever saw. I have been in the ministry for several years, and have never seen anything like it. We were apprehensive of some further violence to himself, and that his mind would entirely give way."

Major Hopkins took the stand. He worked as a coachman for Colonel Freeman, on H Street between Fifteenth and Sixteenth Streets. The week of the shooting, he saw Key walk back and forth "five or six times. Mrs. Sickles came out and joined him on the corner of H Street and Madison Place. I saw them go up Fifteenth Street and lost sight of them on the steps of John Gray's house."

Carlisle cross-examined. "As a matter of curiosity, is Major your Christian name or title?"

"My name."

"That explains why the Major drives the Colonel's carriage. Do you know Mrs. Sickles well? What's her size?"

"She is not very large nor very small, but of middle height, light hair, a little stout. I cannot say how tall she is."

"How tall are you?"

"About five feet seven inches."

"Is she as tall as you?"

"I guess not."

"Is she five feet two?"

"I can't say, I never measured her." The marshals had to quiet the "excessive laughter."

"I saw her with her veil up," he continued, "and distinctly recognized her. She had on a black dress and dark cloak, bordered with red and white."

Carlisle put the witness on the defensive as to his exact vantage point and what could be observed from there and then excused him.

Nancy Brown was the next witness. For years, she had been the conduit of all information in the neighborhood north of Lafayette

Square. Now, it was her turn to take center stage in the biggest story
in the country. Nancy claimed not to hear the oath. She moved close
to the clerk and had him repeat it. Nancy lived two doors down from
No. 383, she testified. Her husband is the president's gardener and
she recognized Mr. Key. "I saw him on the Wednesday before he was
shot."

"Where did you see him?" Brady asked.

"Going into a house on Fifteenth street, the next but one to where
I live."

Carlisle attempted to cut off the testimony. "They were sliding
along in the direction of giving evidence of adultery." Did your Honor
mean to admit evidence of adultery between Key and the prisoner's
wife? If so, the state "would have evidence to offer on the same subject." Nancy Brown's moment of fame, it seemed, would have to wait.

"I will say a few words, politely, I hope, in response to the prosecution." Brady said. The evidence is offered "to prove an adulterous
intercourse and connection carried on between Mr. Key and Mrs.
Sickles by a standing agreement between them, dating further back
than the hiring of this house on Fifteenth Street. "When a man and
a woman go habitually to a house for the purpose of adultery, they
are living in adultery all the time, and it was not necessary for the
husband to wait for the disgusting exhibition of his own dishonor to
slay the gorged and satiated and brutal adulterer."

After testimony on the handkerchief, "no one could look on any
part of this case without seeing this tainted banner floating in the
atmosphere. They had shown that with that banner in his hand, and
with the key of that house of prostitution in his pocket, the deceased
was hovering around the house of Mr. Sickles when the outraged
husband met and slew him." The deceased was killed in the act,
Brady said.

"As I understand this proposition," the judge said, "it brings up the question of admission of proof of adulterous intercourse."

The court took a brief recess. When they resumed, Carlisle objected to any evidence of adultery, warning of dire consequences arising from a dangerous new precedent. Rest on the ancient roads of the law, Carlisle said, rather than "new and devious paths." He cited legal treatises on homicide: "If time had elapsed for passion to subside, the killing is murder." Evidence of the affair is irrelevant. If he had caught them in the act, he could make a case for the lesser charge of manslaughter. But he did not.

Carlisle cited the case of *Queen against Fisher*, where a father murdered a man who had corrupted his son. The court ruled "that there would be exceedingly wild work taking place in the world if every man were allowed to be the judge of his own wrongs." Only "an instant provocation" could justify manslaughter.

Fisher was convicted of manslaughter, Brady replied.

"That is true." But the facts showed a scuffle that proceeded the killing, giving the jury what it needed to spare the father his life. "As a humble member of this community, as one who expected his bones to rest on this soil, and the bones of his children, and his children's children to rest in the same hallowed soil," he would regret living to see the day "that such a doctrine should be proclaimed by the authority of the jury box."

Carlisle then moved on to the case of *Jarboe*. There, "the deceased had drawn from his person a loaded weapon, which fell at his feet." That is not the case here. "If a woman leaves her husband's house and goes to live with her paramour in open adultery, might the injured husband at any time he thought proper go and slay that adulterer?" The handkerchief, the key, the house, what did it prove? "Did that knowledge justify murder? Why, not at all."

"I beg your pardon," Brady said. "Nobody has stated that in my hearing. The proposition is that just before Mr. Sickles left his house that Sunday, he had discovered these facts and had also witnessed the waving of the flag."

"It was only competent to inquire into the question of insanity itself," Carlisle said, "not into the cause of that insanity."

There was an argument over whether Sickles could have sought legal recourse. Adultery is a misdemeanor, Carlisle said, and some have been punished for it.

Magruder asked, "under the statute of Maryland, the punishment for that crime was not a fine of a hundred pounds of tobacco?"

Carlisle didn't know.

"Then the only satisfaction an injured husband could have would be a chew of tobacco." There was laughter in the court.

Carlisle said that he would conduct the case in truth, justice, and that if he departed from his duty, he trusted his life would not be spared.

Brady said, "Certainly we don't want Mr. Carlisle to die."

"We are growing so fond of each other, sir," Carlisle replied, "that I am afraid it will prevent us from doing our duty."

Phillips joined the fray. "The evidence we propose to offer is on four points: justification [that a man is justified in killing the lover of his wife], provocation [that the crime should be no worse than manslaughter], insanity, and explaining the defendant's words at the time of the homicide ("You have defiled my bed!"), which had been introduced by the prosecution's witnesses.[1]

The hour of adjournment arrived.

DAY TWELVE—Saturday, April 16, 1859

Phillips resumed his argument to introduce evidence of the affair. If the evidence is admissible for any reason, he said, then it must be admitted. The indictment accuses Sickles of murder, not just a killing. Murder requires malice. Malice can be rebutted by showing that the killing was in passion. "As the law declares adultery to be the greatest of all provocations," it would be absurd to allow evidence of their friendship while excluding evidence of the affair. He was not urging the invention of new law but the application of existing law to new facts. "What were the rules of evidence made for, but the elucidation of the truth?

"It is said by my learned friend that malice may be presumed out of the act of killing. Granted. But this is only a presumption, and like other presumptions, may be rebutted by evidence showing the fast friendship of the parties, which would exclude malice. It may be shown that the killing rose from passion excited by just provocation."

Phillips then referred to Commonwealth against Bell, "where a judge held that passion arising from sufficient provocation is evidence of the absence of malice."

The state is arguing that seeing a wife in the act of adultery can produce sufficient provocation to lessen the sentence of murder, but "if he did not see it, then the adultery, however heinous, and under whatever state of aggravation the mind can conceive, forms not the slightest provocation in the eye of the law for the act, and the gentleman in giving his construction of the word 'finding,' which is the word in most of the books, interprets it to mean 'see with his eyes the act of adultery.'

"The knowledge of the adultery of Mrs. Sickles was the propelling power, and was part of the res gestae." *Res gestae* was an ancient rule that allowed evidence that would otherwise be excluded in order to tell the complete story.

Sickles "was the witness of his wife's shame, and in imagination could carry himself to that period of time when on her bed she surrendered herself to the debasing lusts of Mr. Key. He became satisfied of the fact the night before; his feelings were hovering and culminating through the night; he had no sleep, this victim of grief; there was everything to drive his excitement forward to the maddening point, and every moment he heard the story of his wife's shame and saw the infamy before him. Why deny the effect of this waving on the mind of the prisoner?

"Now, why the eye? We have the eye, the ear, and the touch, all of them are mere messengers of the mind, in which knowledge is obtained." He told the story of a former client, a stevedore returned from sea, who entered his home in the darkness, felt around the room for his bed, and where there was supposed to be an empty space, he "felt a man. He drew his knife—the knife of a stevedore—long and broad bladed, and stabbed him repeated blows, till he fell from the bed to the floor, dead.

"Where then is the reason for the argument that no provocation of this kind is worth anything in a court of justice except it be presented to the eye?"

The time for adjournment arrived before Philips got his answer.

Chapter Thirty-Nine

"John B. Haskin, Salad and Champagne"

DAY THIRTEEN—Monday, April 18, 1859

Newspapers across the country had charged ahead with turn-of-the-screw coverage of the trial. The *Independent Democrat* of Concord, New Hampshire begged "to be excused. We have already given the principal facts of the murder, and the alleged prosecution. If Sickles shall be acquitted or convicted, we shall give the result." While "many, perhaps most of the papers" were "regaling their readers" with the gory details, they pledged to return to real news.[1]

The *New York Times* and the *New York Post* continued their war of words. "Like the green grocer who gloried in having once been kicked by the King of France, the *Evening Post* of this city prefers superlative disgrace to comparative obscurity." With "unflinching malignity...this obstinate little journal persists in pursuing a political opponent and a personal enemy under the cowardly pretext of a concern for public justice."[2]

★ ★ ★

The court had now heard hours of argument on whether adultery was evidence. Ould had the final word, challenging the defense to a single case where it had been admitted. If he had asked a few minutes later, there would have been a ready answer.

Finally, Judge Crawford ruled: "I am of opinion that the evidence is admissible."

Stuart thought the silence that followed was "almost painful." The trial of Daniel Sickles was soon to take a dark and unpredictable turn.[3]

Nancy Brown was recalled to the stand and examined by Daniel Ratcliffe. She recognized Key as the man entering the front door of No. 383. She also claimed to know that Teresa was the woman who came in through the back. Brown had last seen them on the Wednesday before the shooting. They remained inside an hour.

She told the story of how Key had come through her neighborhood last October, asking about the Gray house and whether it was for rent, and how she had helped him, telling who to ask to find out where John Gray was living.

Key "came about three weeks after that, and tied his horse to my tree. I asked him whether he did not know that that was against the law?" The courtroom laughed at the neighborhood scold lecturing the US Attorney.

"I suppose that is not evidence," Ould said.

"I asked him not to tie his horse there again."

"That's not evidence," Ould said. "Stop, Mrs. Brown."

"I was only telling you what it was. He said, 'I won't tie it there any more.' He said, 'I rented this house for a friend of mine and want to see how it is situated. He then untied his horse and went away. I never spoke to him anymore."

"Did you notice anything Mr. Key had with him?"

"I noticed on that Wednesday he had on a shawl when he went in. It was on his left arm. But had none when he came out. This was on the Wednesday before he was shot. When he first came to the house, we laughed when we saw the smoke come out of the chimney. He went down to the yard and got wood to make a fire. Saw a white string tied to the upstairs shutters, so that when the wind blowed it would swing."

"Have you seen the shawl since?"

"I saw the shawl, but you know there are many alike, I don't like to swear to this one."

Ratcliffe asked for an officer to have the shawl brought in.

"I don't want to tell a lie," Brown said. She looked at the shawl with the gray and red border. "This looks like it. He had it folded on his left arm."

"How was Mrs. S. dressed?"

"She had on a little small plaid silk dress, which she wore open, and she had a black Raglan—a cloak, you know, as I call it—fringed with bugles, and a black velvet shawl with lace."

Brady asked the next question. "You say Mr. Key told you he hired the house for a senator or member [of congress]. Did anybody occupy it except for Mr. Key and the lady?"

"Never saw anybody go in but theirselves. I am sure I did not."

John Graham asked about an incident where Key and Teresa left the house but turned in a different direction after seeing two policemen on K Street.

Stanton asked the court to excuse Sickles for the balance of Nancy Brown's testimony. The state did not object. An officer escorted him from the courtroom.

"Did you see them come back that day?" Graham asked.

"It is not likely they returned that day. Not likely, gentlemen. I did not watch more after that. I knew they were not so foolish. After they seed the police, not likely after that."

Ould asked where she lived. "Next door but one to John Gray's," she answered. Brady introduced evidence of a map from the surveyor's office pinpointing the location.

"How do you know it was Mrs. Sickles?"

"Because I inquired and was told. I asked different people, and they all told me it was her, and when I saw her at her own house, I knew it was the same person. [Officer] Mann who called for me to go and see Mrs. Sickles, and there I identified her as the person whom I used to see go to that house. The shawl was shown to me the next week, week after the death of Mr. Key."

"How do you know that [Key] made the fire?"

"Because there was nobody else to make the fire and because I saw him to go down and fetch the wood."

The courtroom was thoroughly entertained by her testimony, and the judge tried to maintain order. "There is no cause for laughter," he said.

Brown continued. "Saw the string out of the window three or four times. If I had looked oftener I might have seen it oftener."

"How did you come to notice it?"

"Because I knew it was the signal, of course."

"You did not know whether he was there by himself?"

"I should think he was not when I saw the signal flying."

And with that, Nancy Brown's turn on the national stage came to an end, much to her chagrin and that of the audience.

But Brady had an exciting follow-up: a demonstration for the jury. Brady held the lock that had been removed from No. 383 and used one of the keys found on Key's body to open and close it.

Policeman Charles Mann followed. He had gone to No. 383 with Magruder and Ratcliffe on the day after the killing. They found Teresa's shawl inside the house and brought it to Nancy Brown to be identified. They then took her to the Ewell House, where she confirmed that Teresa was the woman who had been meeting Key at No. 383.

Ratcliffe took the stand and testified that Officer Mann had let them into 383.

"That is all," Brady said.

Congressman John Haskin was called to the stand. Sickles approached him on the floor of the House of Representatives, days after the Beekman affair, with a favor to ask. He had been called to New York on business. Would you and your wife drop in on Teresa occasionally and see if she needed anything?

The next day, Haskin and his wife were headed to Georgetown to buy shoes. They passed the White House, and Haskin was reminded of his promise.

He pulled his carriage in front of the Ewell House, and he and his wife stepped down. To minimize delay, they rushed up the stairs and went inside without knocking.

"On entering the little library, I found Mrs. Sickles and Mr. Key seated at a round table with a large bowl of salad. She was mixing it. There was a [half-empty] bottle of champagne and glasses on the table. I excused myself for the abrupt entrance."

"Mrs. Sickles got up, blushed, and invited us to take a glass of wine with her. After sitting there for a moment, I hastened away with my wife. On entering the carriage, or immediately after, my wife said that 'Mrs. Sickles is a bad woman.'"

"Did you have any conversation with Mr. Key at that time in that room?"

"Very little. I think Mrs. Sickles on that occasion introduced my wife to Mr. Key."

"Did your lady ever visit there afterwards?"

"No, sir."

"Did you see Mr. Key and Mrs. S. any time after that?"

"Yes."

"Where?"

"Shortly after that, I met Mr. Key and Mrs. Sickles in the cemetery. Saw them at the theater once or twice. And once or twice on the avenue."

Haskin never told Sickles what he had seen.

Carlisle asked the witness: "She was mixing the salad for him?"

"There was a large bowl containing salad with a large wooden thing to fix it," Haskin said, trying to demonstrate what he meant. "She was using the wooden thing." The courtroom laughed at the Congressman's attempt at fake salad mixing.[4]

★ ★ ★

"*She is a bad woman*," said Abraham Lincoln, cracking himself up, and others around him. That line of testimony "tickled Lincoln's fancy," and fellow lawyers on the Eighth Circuit of Illinois "heard him tell it over and over again."[5]

Lincoln, like many attorneys, enjoyed following the Sickles trial. It gave them a chance to think about what they would do with such a case. For his part, Lincoln was in Champagne County for the spring term of the Circuit Court, fighting over groceries. Lincoln represented the county against the city of West Urbana, who was taxing groceries, monies the county believed rightfully belonged to them. The court ruled for West Urbana.

In the middle of the week, Lincoln handled six eviction cases. But on Thursday, he had a homicide case of his own. A drunken Samuel Dehaven came into Tom Patterson's store to buy a hatchet. Dehaven had exhausted his credit, and so Patterson refused. Dehaven left, then decide to return and menace Patterson with one of his own spades. Dehaven threw a two-pound scale weight at his head, killing him.

Community sentiment ran strongly against Patterson. Dehaven, notoriously drunk and violent, was *their* reprobate and Patterson a relative newcomer. The trial had been delayed while Lincoln ran for US senate. Defeated by Stephen Douglas, he found himself in the Champagne County Courthouse defending Dehaven. He was found guilty of manslaughter and sentenced to three years. When president, Lincoln lobbied the governor successfully for a pardon.[6]

Chapter Forty

"Revelations Respecting the Intercourse Between Key and Mrs. Sickles"

*"Of what crime has Sickles been guilty?
Of making a Skeleton Key."*
—Cleveland *Plain Dealer*

DAY FOURTEEN—Tuesday, April 19, 1859

France and Austria were at war in Italy. But as one newspaper pointed out, "something else is upon our minds, our counters, our book tables, work tables, tea tables, chairs, sofas, window seats, door steps, in our heads, pockets, and every nook and cranny where a newspaper can hide himself...The Sickles Trial! Even politics holds its head downcast before the overshadowing importance of the great theme, which is discussed, they say, 'in every place where men—and women too, meet.' People who 'never read an improving book,' or have 'one moment per day for self-cultivation'...find hours to pore over the closely printed columns of the city daily that publishes the evidence in such cases."[1]

★ ★ ★

Officer James Mann testified to the contents of No. 383 on the day after the shooting. He produced a gentleman's gloves and a comb taken from the scene. There were cigarettes also, he testified, but he did not preserve them.[2]

Sickles was excused from the courtroom in anticipation of upcoming testimony.

John Thompson was a young Scotsman who had driven the Sickles coach from November 16, 1857 to February 4, 1859.

Shortly after taking the job, he noticed they were seeing an awful lot of Mr. Key. Mrs. Sickles would leave her house alone around noon and return before dinner. They would see him in the street: "Good morning, Madam," he would say, with a salute. They would see him at the daily receptions around the capital: the President's, the Donaldsons', the Gwyns', and the Slidells'. Sometimes Key would get in the coach. The command was the same: "Drive through the back streets." Key always exited the coach before they returned to the house.

"I knew him only once to come home with Mrs. Sickles, that was in April or May of last year. He went into the house and when he came out I could not say. I have known Mr. Key to come to the house while Mr. Sickles was absent in New York. He always came at dusk. I knew him to be there every night almost. Sometimes I knew him to remain until late at night. At other times I did not know how long he would remain." He and Mrs. Sickles always remained in the study with the door shut. One night he arrived at 7:00 p.m. and didn't leave until at least 1:00 a.m. "I think that was May of 1858."

"Did anything particular occur to which your attention was called?"

"Yes, sir."

Relate it to the jury, said Brady.

Thompson was headed to bed at 1:00 a.m. He saw Bridget Duffy at the head of the stairs. Both had heard the hall bell ring.

Teresa and Key both poked their heads out of the study and into the hall. No amount of discretion could cover up for accidentally ringing the hall bell. But they were relieved to see nobody there. They shut the hall door and locked it again, walked through the study into the parlor, and locked that door for good measure.

Now Thompson and Bridget were curious. Thompson testified: "I stood a little while and heard them making this noise on the sofa for about two or three minutes. I mentioned to [Bridget] that they were making a noise." Thompson made what he thought was "a little joke," which sent Bridget running away. "She would not hearken to me as it was not language suitable for her to hear."

Thompson listened for two or three minutes. "I knew they was'nt at no good work. I had been out that night and came in at 12 o'clock. I knew they were and it was the conversation among us all that—"

"Never mind that," Ould said.

Teresa took the carriage to the Congressional Cemetery two or three times, and two or three times to the burying ground at George-town. Key would meet them wherever they went.

"The first time I saw [Key] was in April 1858, from that time to the 1st of July never a week passed without my seeing him."

Key "always visited at night when Mr. Sickles was away," whether it was to New York, Philadelphia, or Baltimore. "By the time I returned from the train station to drop of Mr. Sickles, Key would already be at the house."

George Emerson had a butcher stall in Centre Market, "an unsightly, unsanitary, and overgrown sprawl, row after endless row of fruit, vegetable, and meat vendors, and marketers, that pushed outside the building to the streets around it and still could barely contain all the market activity it supported." Key and Teresa came together on the Thursday before his death. Teresa came earlier than expected, between 8:00 and 9:00 a.m., rather than her usual time of between 10:00 and 11:00 a.m.[3]

She came to the bench and gave me the order, he explained. "She asked me how much it came to and handed her wallet to Mr. Key, saying, 'Pay Mr. Emerson.' He took a ten-dollar gold piece out and handed it to me and I gave the change. Key had regularly come to market with Teresa last session. But not as often as this session."

John Cooney moved to Washington early in 1859. He was delighted to find himself as the Sickles's coachman after a month of searching. On his second day, he drove Teresa down Pennsylvania Avenue. She rang the bell, signaling him to stop. Key boarded the coach. Cooney thought nothing of it. But then he started seeing Key "pretty much every day," picking him up in the back streets. He always entered and exited the coach away from her house. Sometimes, they met at the greenhouse or the bookstore.

In the late afternoon of Thursday, February 24, Teresa drove around from one reception to another with Octavia Ridgeley. Cooney noticed that Key arrived at all the same receptions, either a little before or a little after. Their last event of the day was at Rose O'Neal Greenhow's. She was a popular widow and the aunt of Mrs. Stephen Douglas. From there, Teresa and Octavia headed home to her reception for Mrs. James Gordon Bennett.

Wooldridge was recalled to the stand and identified the R. P. G. letter and envelope that Sickles had presented him. It was read aloud and handed to the jury. *With deep regret I inclose to your address a few lines ...*

Brady wanted to question Wooldridge as to what Sickles had said before leaving the house to kill Key.

Ould objected. I do "not see how this could, on any ground, be received as evidence."

Magruder handled the argument for the defense. It was "offered as bearing on the prisoner's state of mine."

Judge Crawford ruled that a defendant's declarations are generally not admissible in his favor. However, "the acts and declarations of a man alleged to be insane are the best possible evidence of insanity. And if these declarations are offered for that purpose, I do not feel at liberty to reject them."

Brady returned to his questioning of Wooldridge. What did Sickles say to Key's waving of the handkerchief on the day of the shooting?

He said, "that fellow, who had just passed my door, has made signals to my wife."

Did you make inquiries as to the truth of the R. P. G. letter?

"Yes, sir." Wooldridge detailed his investigation of Friday and Saturday, Sickles's reaction, and the events inside his house on Sunday.

On cross-examination, Wooldridge said that he did not know Sickles had left the house and that he was wearing an overcoat when he returned. From where he was sitting, he could see anyone leaving the house by the front stairs. Butterworth was the only person he saw. To pass the time, Woolridge set his crutches aside and went to pick up a nearby stereoscope, a device for viewing three dimensional images. By the time he came back to his chair, he saw people running outside. Sickles must have left through the basement door.

A New York correspondent reported that the city was unusually quiet, as it seemed everyone was at the Sickles trial as an observer or witness.

Chapter Forty-One

"Conclusion of the Evidence for the Defense"

"If anything could reconcile the relatives of that unfortunate individual [Key] to his hasty depar-ture, it would undoubtedly be the reflection that he thereby escaped the intolerable nuisance of seeing in the newspapers every day the report of the everlast-ing Sickles case."

—New London *Daily Chronicle* (Connecticut)

"You know?"

—Felix McCluskey of Brooklyn

DAY FIFTEEN—Wednesday, April 20, 1859

The *Albany Evening Journal* printed an apology to their readers for not properly sanitizing their coverage of the Sickles trial. They promised that, if they couldn't clean up future editions before deadline, they would discontinue coverage. "We do not intend that our columns shall contain any paragraph which may not be read in the family circle." The *Boston Recorder* thought the "publication of the trial must have a bad moral effect upon the community."[1]

Felix McCluskey of Brooklyn testified to his attempts, mostly unsuccessful, to insert himself in the story. He arrived on the scene after the shooting and followed the crowd to the attorney general's. He knocked on the door and handed the attorney general his calling card. McCluskey waited for ten to fifteen minutes until Sickles, Butterworth, and the rest walked right past him to a carriage and rode to Sickles's house. Undeterred, McCluskey then walked into Sickles's house.

He saw Sickles looking "like a man frightened to death...with his hair over his face. I thought he would kill every man, woman, and child in the house." McCluskey saw Sickles climb the steps to tell Teresa. "I thought, even, that if he went upstairs he might injure his wife." McCluskey wanted the world to know that he took a few steps forward, ready to act. Sickles "stayed upstairs only a few minutes, for if he had stayed longer I know I would have gone up." His opinion was that Sickles "was not responsible for anything he did. Mr. Black looked scared and excited too."

"Do you think the attorney general is crazy too?"

"No, sir."

Sickles departed for jail less than an hour after he arrived.

"While I was in the entry, I heard this confusion, you know? I thought it was Mr. Sickles crying, you know? Everybody was excited, you know? Mr. Walker appeared to be taken aback, you know?"

Then the question everyone was wondering: who are you and why were you there?

"I went there," McCluskey said, "in the capacity of a citizen, you know? I heard that somebody had shot somebody in cold blood."

Charles G. Bacon brought a certificate from the surveyor's office. Madison place, the street between Lafayette Park and the homes on the eastern edge of Lafayette Square, is 90 feet wide, the same as Jackson and Seventeenth Street. The park is 419 feet north to south and 725 feet across, not counting Jackson and Madison places. This was entered into evidence.

John McDonald, "a smart young Irishman," was called. He had served as a groom and footman to the Sickles since February 10. As part of his job, he accompanied John Cooney when he was driving the coach. On Thursday, February 24, they traveled from one reception to another and seemed to see Key wherever they went. As they were leaving the last event, a reception at Rose O'Neal Greenhow's, Key sat with his hip on her carriage and his legs out. He sat in that position, looking straight in Mrs. Sickles's face.

"Are you going to the hop at Willard's?" Key asked.

"If Dan will allow me," she said.

"I expect to meet you there."

"Your eyes look bad."

"I don't feel well," Key said.

Key entered the carriage and she told them to drive to 11th street. They stopped and let Key out on K between 15th and 16th. From there, they stopped at Gautier's, the confectioner. Teresa went in and came out as fast as she could. "Drive home rapidly," she said. She arrived at her own party, just in time.

The defense rested.

Ould rose with a startling offer. The prosecution was prepared to waive all objections to evidence of an affair, including Teresa's confession.

Brady asked for time to consider. We "will imitate the example we are told prevailed with some of the aborigines of the country, whenever propositions were made in the spirit of peace, never to give an answer immediately." Brady added that "Any publicity which [her confession] has found anywhere is not in the slightest degree attributable to [Sickles], but was in direct opposition to his expressed and consistent wish."

"We are not responsible for its publication in any sense, form, or shape." Ould declared.

"There is no pretense that you had," Brady responded.

"The paper was never in our possession, except for a single moment," Ould added.

Brady knew exactly who was responsible for its publication. The only thing keeping Sickles alive was the possibility that the jury would believe the stories about adultery and use them as an excuse to acquit him. Sickles could dig in all he liked. But Brady was not going to risk his friend's neck over this. He directed Thomas Meagher to copy the letter. Meagher handed the copy, page by page, to Reverend Haley, who passed it on to the press. Sickles never had any idea.[2]

Graham complained that the offer was late and came "after we had disbanded our witnesses and sent them to the four winds of Heaven. The effect of this offer is to embarrass the defense."

The judge gave leave to the state to introduce rebuttal evidence while the lawyers for Sickles talked it over.

"It is not intended as a continuing offer, but one which must be accepted or rejected tomorrow morning." Carlisle said.

The *Evening Press* of Providence thought this a brilliant maneuver, now that evidence of adultery was in. They thought the confession was damning against Sickles: look at the legalese of the confession. It looked like a cool-headed lawyer creating a paper trail for a murder.[3]

The United States began its rebuttal evidence, with Congressman George Pendleton as its first witness. "I am the brother-in-law of [the] deceased." A week after the killing, he went to No. 383. He suggested a locksmith because the front and back doors were locked. Gray sent for one. Nothing of Key's was found in the house.

"I called Gray and gave him half a dollar for his trouble of going for a locksmith. I never gave a direction or made a suggestion to the locksmith as to removing that lock at that time, or to anybody else. I did not see anyone taking off the lock. If it was, it was without my knowledge."

Pendleton received the items that had been taken from Key's body on the day of his death. There was the case to the opera glass, two brass keys, a set of small keys, a pocket book in which were fourteen dollars and some cents, and a pair of kid gloves."

A week later he "received an envelope containing one or more papers, with a card from Dr. Stone, saying he was requested by Dr. Miller to deliver them, but that he was prevented from doing so sooner by professional engagements."

Brady said, "May I ask you the character of your feelings? Was it not one which naturally excited strong emotions?"

"I was very much pained at Mr. Key's death."

"Do you remember this slip of paper?" Brady asked, showing him one of the letters.

"I have seen it since I returned to Washington last week. I am certain I delivered all the papers I received from Dr. Stone to Mr. Howard [Another of Key's brothers in law]. I believe nothing is lost."

"When did you first learn that the lock had been removed?'

"I heard it in court," Pendleton answered, "the other day a remark was made by one of the counsel for the defense with regard to the suppression of evidence. I desire to say before I leave the stand, in the most positive and circumstantial manner, that I gave no intimation or direction, nor made any suggestion as to the removal of the lock, nor did I hear it had been removed until I heard it in court. And I say further, that any intimation or charge that any suppression of important or unimportant evidence had been by my participation or knowledge, by whomsoever made it, I may be permitted to say, infamously false." The audience applauded.

Colonel Charles Jones was the next witness. He'd gone with Pendleton to No. 383 and suggested breaking down the doors.

Pendleton thought it would be more dignified to gain access by a locksmith. Nothing of Key's was found in the house.

"You are a member of the bar?" Brady asked.

"I am, sir."

"You have been assisting the prosecution ever since the trial commenced?"

"I am going to answer your question, but I want to understand though—"

"I don't mean to complain of what you have done. I ask whether you have not assisted the prosecution in this case."

Jones said that he had "handed two or three" cases to Carlisle, who was already aware of them.

"I intend to treat you with all proper respect, but as to furnishing Brother Carlisle with authorities, that is unnecessary. You have, Mr. Jones, taken in this case—"

"The very deepest interest." Jones interrupted. "Shall I tell you why?"

"Not at all."

Carlisle interjected. "You were an intimate friend of Mr. Key."

"From early youth to the time of his death," said Jones.

"I never object to a man standing by the memory of his friend as long as he deserves to be respected." Brady said. With that, he withdrew.

Chapter Forty-Two

"Curious Anonymous Letters Received by the Counsel and Jury"

"The proceedings in the Sickles case today were interesting rather than important."

—*New York Herald*

DAY SIXTEEN—Thursday, April 21, 1859

A carriage of ladies from the countryside arrived to see the trial. No females, they were told, "other than witnesses, had visited the trial room." After "making some inquiries as to the 'handsome prisoner,'" they had lunch instead, of "a fare more wholesome, if not quite so highly seasoned, as that of the trial."[1]

The *Vermont Chronicle* asked: "When will reform come" to government? "Never till men of moral worth wake up and unite in the name of the people, of humanity and justice, sternly demand that no immoral man shall have public promotion." Until then, "Brooks may assault who he pleases in the senate chamber, Key seduces his neighbor's wife, and Sickles murder his fellow under the wing of the United States Capitol." Wicked men did not arrive in office by some foreign power. "We, the people have done it."[2]

Day sixteen began with a mystery. A letter bearing a New York postmark had been sent to one of the jurors. "The letter was filled with abuse of the prisoner," wrote the *Herald*.[3]

"It proceeds from the very worst motives," said the judge. "It is an impertinent, improper, and unwonted interference with a court of justice." The juror "knows nothing about it or the writer," the judge said.

Brady "remarked that the manuscript was similar to that of the anonymous letter to Mr. Sickles." The letters were compared. It was agreed by the lawyers that they came from the same hand.

"It is a matter of extreme regret that the author of the letter is not known," said Judge Crawford, speaking for everyone. In addition to its condemnation of Sickles, it contained slander against his lawyers.

"It is agreed on all hands," said Carlisle, "that it is an atrocious interference with the course of justice. If its author were known, he would deserve to be prosecuted for an act as high as a misdemeanor. But as it is written from a distance, and there is no probability of its author being known, it is not worth preservation."

"Only with the view of punishing the author," said an agitated Judge Crawford. "With all the rigor that could be applied to the case."

Of all the claims in the letter, Brady said, "There is but one thing stated [in] relation to which I have any personal knowledge, and that is an atrocious falsehood. If that is a fair criterion of the whole letter, it shows how much its statements are worth."

Ratcliffe suggested: "Your honor might preserve it for some day and perhaps the author may be found out. I think that may be advantageous."

★ ★ ★

Some day, perhaps. But not yet. R. P. G. is the unseen hand that set this story in motion, and it will never be complete until he or she is known.

I partnered with a board certified forensic document examiner who came to an interesting conclusion. R. P. G. may have preferred to stay anonymous, but they did not attempt to disguise their handwriting. The handwriting is consistent from beginning to end, whereas a person attempting to hide their true handwriting would lapse into familiar and subconscious "tells." This leaves two possibilities: they didn't care about getting caught or they were confident of not getting caught. We can safely eliminate the former. The letter was anonymous. R. P. G. refused to answer Sickles's ads asking for a meeting. It's clear he or she did not want to be identified. This means that the writer was not someone close to him, as Sickles could identify the handwriting of someone who was.

William Swanberg, an early biographer of Sickles, wrote that Rose O'Neal Greenhow was suspected of being R. P. G. After Greenhow was exposed and revealed as a Confederate spy, one who may have made the difference at the Battle of Bull Run, she was an easy mark. Plus, they share the same first and last initials. But her handwriting positively excludes her from being R. P. G. Handwriting samples of Butterworth and Wikoff were examined and they too were excluded.

Even when newspapers were starved for Sickles content, the identity of R. P. G. was subject to limited speculation. Under the headline "Hell hath no fury like a woman scorned," the *New York Times* wrote: "There is a lady here who knows a certain widow in Washington, to whom Mr. Key had for some time been quite devoted who has been made miserable, for a twelvemonth, by the pangs of jealousy. Did *she* play the part of Iago in the bloody drama? Perhaps."[4]

If the goal was to break them apart, the letter to Key makes sense but the letter to Sickles does not. Sickles would almost certainly divorce his wife, thus freeing her to be with Key, or harm Key, which would limit his ability to be with the writer. Warning Key increased the chances of his being armed, which may have led to him killing

Sickles. In that case, he would either be free to be with Teresa or incarcerated.

What if the writer was a Washington woman with a different motivation: to dethrone Teresa Sickles from her place in society? Teresa's sweet and welcoming nature may not have been enough to deter someone motivated by social jealousy. But Teresa's public ruin had been accomplished well before Day 16 of the trial, when the third anonymous letter was received.[5]

In fact, the letter writer is probably not a woman at all. Both Henry Watterson of the Philadelphia *Press* and James Shepherd Pike of the *New York Tribune* interviewed different witnesses who saw the Man in the Shawl observing Key and Teresa on Wednesday, February 23. Sickles and Key received their letters the following day. It is reasonable to conclude that the Man in the Shawl is the letter writer. Pike believed he was, as did the people he interviewed, but he did not reveal his name.

Stephen Beekman makes the most sense of the possible suspects. He had stalked Key and Teresa once before. Beekman had moved back to New York, but DC was easily accessible. Beekman was in love with Teresa: pitting Sickles and Key against one another makes sense. If he was lucky, they would kill each other, or one would kill the other and go to jail. It follows that he would tell Sickles of the affair and warn Key to be on his guard. If Beekman were R. P. G., it would explain the New York postmark of the letter sent during trial. But would I ever get a handwriting sample to prove it? As it turns out, Beekman served in the Civil War, and a letter was found in the papers of his regiment at the National Archives. But he too was not R. P. G. Or at least not the writer of the letter. A scribe could have been used to cover their tracks—but it would have to be the same scribe on all three letters.

But it is just as likely there was a second man who stalked Key and Teresa and who wrote a letter informing her husband, a letter warning

Key, and then a letter from New York during trial encouraging Sickles's conviction. As Iago told Othello, "what you know, you know."

★ ★ ★

Brady responded to the proposition of the day before: to allow the confession as well as all evidence of adultery. "We do not accept it. The case of the accused is closed and the prosecution must therefore pursue such course on their part as they may deem advisable."

Francis Doyle, one of the Club House members who had responded to the shooting, was recalled to the stand.

"Mr. Doyle, state what was the appearance of Mr. Sickles at that time."

"When I came up to Mr. Sickles, he turned round almost immediately. I thought his manner was self-possessed. More than his speech indicated. There was more excitement in the expression than in the manner."

"I don't know to what extent you have given yourself to the study of men," Brady said. "Have you ever been in a lunatic asylum?"

The witness was hurt by the question. "No, sir," and expressed his hope that the judge would cut this off.

"He does not mean as an inmate," Ould said, "but as a visitor."

Everyone laughed, including Doyle, who now understood.

"Have you ever spoken to a person unmistakably insane?"

He had not.

Doyle testified that Key's overcoat stayed in the dining room at the Club House for a week.

Officer Jacob King was the next witness. "Did you observe the manner and expression of Mr. Sickles at the time of Mr. Key's death?"

"I did."

"State what it was."

"I thought he was exceedingly cool, as far as I could judge. As soon as we got up to him, he desisted, turned round, and made the remark I have already sworn to. I did not see any indication of great excitement that I am aware of."

"Were you familiar with Mr. Sickles's countenance before that?" Brady asked.

"Had seen him I suppose fifty times."

Tidball, another of the Club House group, was recalled to the stand. "My attention at the time of the homicide was directed more to Mr. Sickles's manner than anything else. I thought it was rather cool and deliberate. His face was somewhat pale, of course."

"Have you ever visited a lunatic asylum?" Brady asked.

"Not that I recollect."

"Talked with an insane person?"

"I do not recollect that I have."

Charles Howard, one of Key's brothers in law, was given a letter removed from Key's body four or five days after the murder. It was written in cipher, but he believed he had cracked the code. It was not complicated: one letter of the alphabet was exchanged for another. The judge carefully read the translation.

"What is it to rebut?" Brady asked.

"Not to rebut anything," Carlisle said. "It was brought out by the defense."

"Then we ought to offer it in evidence," Brady said, "not you."

Carlisle pointed out that the defense had referred to items removed from Key's body at the time of his death, and that they now planned on explaining the content of one of those items.

Brady pointed out that while many people had access to Key's body and that more than one individual had taken items from his person, the prosecution had access to all of them even before the indictment was handed down. "What had disappeared from the person of Mr. Key and what appeared was left in a state of the greatest confusion and doubt."

Crawford excluded the cipher letter and translation from evidence. It was reported that the cipher was a coded love letter from Teresa to Key.[6]

Officer William Daw was next to testify: "I heard no unusual sounds. Nothing like shrieks or moans. Mr. Sickles invited us to take some brandy just before starting for the jail. Offered to everyone there. Nobody drank but Mr. Sickles and Mr. Butterworth."

Officer James Suit was next. Did you hear Sickles make any "unusual noises" at his house before leaving for jail?

"No, sir."

John McBlair took the stand. Sickles's neighbor in Lafayette Square was present at the house after the shooting and traveled with him to jail. He "heard no unusual noises." He spoke with Sickles after he came downstairs, right after telling Teresa that he had killed Key. "Mr. Sickles was extremely calm. I thought it the calmness of desperation. He appeared to be suffering internally and to be endeavoring to restrain his feelings I thought him and still think him to be a man of remarkable powers of endurance or he never would have been able to withstand the relentless persecution extended to him."

Ould asked: "Is it not a fact about Mr. Sickles that this appearance of calmness attends him even when under the strongest excitement?"

"I have always found him calm."

"He is a man of great command over his feelings?"

"I do not know that he has a great command over his feelings. He has great command externally."

Brady asked, "Your attention had been drawn to Mr. Key's maneuvers about that house?"

"Yes," McBlair answered. "For twelve months."

The mayor of Washington was the next witness. "There was a very brief examination [of Sickles] at the jail. His manner was composed under the circumstances." He did not see any "exhibition of grief."

The judge concluded the day by seeking the jury's thoughts on whether to meet the next day, Good Friday.

We have a solemn duty to perform, said one juror.

"The better the day, the better the deed," Graham quipped.

Chapter Forty-Three

"The Case Drawing to a Close"

*"This disgusting, demoralizing farce is still contin-
ued in Washington."*
—The *Wooster Republican*

DAY SEVENTEEN—Good Friday, April 22, 1859

It had been nearly two months since Sickles mania overtook the
nation. Yet Frederick Douglas's newspaper published one of its
first stories on the matter, one that "affects us but slightly."

For the many cheering on Sickles, "A million and a half of
defenseless women are given up to the vile lusts of not only one
seducer, but any number of lecherous libertines who may present
themselves." Enslaved women, even ones who were married, were
routinely forced to have sex against their will. It is a "diabolical
wickedness which is ever and always being inflicted upon our suffering people. Is there a God that judgeth in the earth and will He
not visit upon this nation a penalty adequate to the sin?"[1]

The Albany *Evening Journal* recognized this as well. "Had
their skin only been tinged with a shade of African blood," there
"would have been no Sickles case to try...no crime to atone
for...no sin to repent for...no wrong to avenge," and in the eyes

of slaveholding Washington, Key's actions would be "eminently fitting and proper."[2]

★ ★ ★

Day seventeen began with Charles Winder, a Washington lawyer, attempting to call himself as a witness.

"It is out of the usual course," said the judge, "and I do not see how it can be done unless you are put on the stand as a witness."

Carlisle said, "Mr. Winder himself feels some desire on the subject. There is none on our part."

Judge Crawford seemed to hope someone would object. "Explanations have become so frequent as to be annoying. That is not the object of testimony at all." But seeing no objections, Winder succeeded in taking the stand.

He wanted to correct Doyle's testimony. Doyle "was utterly mistaken in saying that I had told him these papers were found on the person of Mr. Key at the time of the Coroner's inquest. What happened afterwards I do not know."

"I think that fully meets all that was said in respect to you," Brady said.

"I desire distinctly to say that at the time the search was made of Mr. Key's person, during the coroner's inquest, there was not a scrap of paper found."

"No one says there was," Judge Crawford said.

"Mr. Doyle says I said there was," Winder replied.[3]

Joseph Dudrow was recalled as the prosecution's witness. "I did not think Mr. Sickles was any more excited than any other man would be in a fight or anything of that kind. When the last shot was fired, I was thirty-five or forty feet from him."

Edward Delafield thought Sickles was "Cool. After he shot Mr. Key, he walked away quietly. He put the pistol in his pocket afterward. I saw nothing strange in his manner before he met Mr. Key," and "I thought from his firing such a number of shots that he was rather cool."

"From that I should think he was rather hot," Brady said.

Francis Smith was a reporter for the *Congressional Globe*. He was examined by Carlisle. Sickles had delivered speeches in the House on the Friday before the killing, around 5:00 p.m., and the following day around 4:00 p.m.

Carlisle read aloud from Sickles's remarks and introduced the original transcripts made by the *Globe*. It was standard practice for members of congress to be allowed to revise their statements before the newspaper was printed. The originals of the Friday and Saturday before the killing reveal that Sickles had taken the time to read them and had made edits.

Brady, Graham, and Ould went to the bench and whispered. The prosecution had brought the proprietor of Barnum's Hotel, Baltimore, to testify that Sickles and a woman other than Teresa came in as guests, arguing that the door had been opened.

"For very obvious reasons, the court will do no more than merely state his opinions on this point. And that opinion is that the evidence is not admissible." The defense team huddled.

Brady said: "The gentlemen of the jury have been from their homes and families for now nearly three weeks, and those of us who reside away from Washington have certainly a strong inclination to see our homes, however agreeable our stay here is made by the kindness and hospitality of many of the citizens of this District. We are very anxious, therefore, to have the case finished."

"We will accede to it most cheerfully," Ould said, "and with the greatest gratification on our part." The prosecution would conclude their testimony tomorrow.[4]

Chapter Forty-Four

"The Testimony Closed"

———

"There is a graveyard smell about the whole affair."
—The *Plattsburgh Republican*

DAY EIGHTEEN—Saturday, April 23, 1859

The *Milwaukee Sentinel* reported an enterprising man of that city had set forth for Washington to acquire Key's handkerchief. Pieces would sell for one dollar per thread, and he was accepting pre-orders.[1]

There was a vicious gale outside, the end of a cold and raw week.[2]

Colonel William Schouler was present, having been subpoenaed to appear as a witness. He was the publisher of the *Boston Atlas and Bee*, which had printed Sickles's confession.

Senator Stephen Douglas entered the courtroom and sat at the counsel table next to Sickles's lawyers. Presidential candidates needed publicity, and there was little to be had outside this courtroom. Now he would figure prominently in tomorrow's newspapers across the country.[3]

Richard Brodhead, former US Senator from Pennsylvania, took the stand. He and his friend Haldemar, a newspaper editor in Harrisburg, were visiting Washington. They called at the home of the attorney general and were seated in the back parlor. Sickles arrived a moment later. Brodhead introduced his friend. Sickles and Haldemar began a mundane discussion of Pennsylvania politics.

"You were unfortunate in crossing the street," Brodhead said, referencing Sickles's muddy boots. With more context, he may have been less vigilant over his host's carpet.

Sickles looked at his boots and agreed. Yes, he had been unfortunate in crossing the street. He went outside and cleaned his boots. Soon after he returned, they heard the attorney general descending the staircase. Sickles arose, leaving the room to speak to him privately. Black entered the parlor "very much excited."

"What's the matter?" Broadhead asked.

It was then that they learned that Sickles had come straight from shooting the US attorney. "Is it a bailable offense?" Brodhead asked.

"I do not know," Sickles said. "But if all the facts were known, it would be. For God knows I would be justified." Butterworth soon arrived, having returned to Lafayette Square to retrieve Key's opera glass.

Someone asked whether Key was dead. "Yes," Butterworth answered.

"One wretch less in the world," Sickles muttered. Sickles and Butterworth left in a carriage with the police. Brodhead and Haldemar remained.

The senator would be the final witness.

"You are closed on both sides?" the judge asked.

"Yes," Brady said.

The jury had now heard every witness and seen all the evidence. They had heard from the inventor of the mechanical reaper, a maid, a coachman, and members of the House and Senate. They had examined anonymous letters and a pistol ball cut out of a man and a bloody vest with a hole in it.

Now Judge Crawford would instruct them on how to apply that evidence to the law in order to reach a verdict. Before he could do that, both sides would submit proposed instructions and argue them.

Carlisle began for the United States. "If the homicide were willful and intentional, and was induced by the belief of the prisoner that the deceased had criminal intercourse with the prisoner's wife, nevertheless it was murder."

Nor was evidence of previous adultery a provocation that could reduce the charge to manslaughter. "All authorities confine" such evidence "to the case of instant killing."

There had never been a case that held adultery was a justification for homicide. The defense had argued that "every man was the judge, when he finds himself aggrieved, whether the law of the land gives him adequate relief," and if not, he may "rely on his natural rights." Carlisle believed this argument, that there is a government of laws that you may ignore at your convenience, "was its own refutation."

"It was also argued that human law must be in accordance with Divine law." Conceding this "for the sake of argument," the Divine law never "authorized the taking of a human life for any wrong, by the person wronged. The Divine law did not make adultery as great a crime as murder." He reminded the court of Jesus's words to the Pharisees on the adulteress: Let him that is without sin cast the first stone.

"What could be more shocking, what so irreconcilable with the existence of peace and good government than the doctrine that he who is grievously wronged is to take into his own hands the knife, and to execute summary judgment against the offender? Society could not exist with such a doctrine. If it were established here, in the capital of the nation, the land would present one great scene of violence and confusion—because the principle would not be confined to the single crime of adultery, but would extend to all other wrongs for which the law did not give the offended party adequate reparation."

Further, "the defense of insanity is a specific defense, and must be proved affirmatively and beyond doubt. It had been laid down by all authorities, and decided by the twelve judges of England, in M'Naughten's case, that the defense of insanity must be proven to the satisfaction of the jury."

With that, Carlisle turned the floor over to the defense.

Stanton began: "The event which had brought the jury and the prisoner at the bar into solemn relations, and made the court and counsel participators in this momentous trial, was the death of Mr. Key at the hand of Mr. Sickles, on Sunday, the 27th of February. The occasion of this event was an adulterous intrigue between Mr. Key and the wife of Mr. Sickles. The law rising on the case must depend on the relations each held to the other at the time the occurrence took place."

Congress has defined two classes of homicide: murder and manslaughter. Stanton said that three defenses would excuse these crimes. Self-defense, defense of your home, and a third, "arising from the social relation—the law holding family chastity and the sanctity of the marriage bed, the matron's honor and the virgin's purity, to be more valuable and estimable in law than the property or of life of any man." This "principle never came before a judicial tribunal in a form more impressive than now. Here, in the capital of the nation, the social and political metropolis of thirty millions of people, a man of mature age, the head of a family, a member of the learned profession, a high officer of government, entrusted with the administration of the law, and who for years at this Bar has demanded judgment of fine, imprisonment and death against other men for offense against law, has himself been slain in open day in a public place, because he took advantage of a sojourner in this city. Received into his family, he debauched his house, violated the bed of his host, and dishonored his family."

Stanton asked Judge Crawford to instruct the jury first that Sickles was justified under these circumstances, and second, he "is free from legal responsibility by reason of the state of the prisoner's mind."

"Eternal discord and violence would ensue if man's chief object of affection were secured to him by no legal tie. No man could enjoy any happiness or pursue any vocation if he could not enjoy his wife free form the assaults of the adulterer."

Key, he argued, was killed in the act of adultery, just as if Sickles had found him in Teresa's arms. He has "provided a place for the express purpose of committing adultery with another man's wife" and was using "preconcerted signals to entice" Teresa from her "husband's house, to besiege her in the streets, to accompany him to that vile den," "spy glass in hand," "lying in wait around a husband's house." It was "the most appalling" act of adultery "recorded in the annals of shame."

Key had "grown so bold as to take the child of the injured husband, his little daughter, by the hand, to separate her from her mother, to take the child to the house of a mutual friend while he leads the mother to the guilty den, in order there to enjoy her…surpassing all that has ever been written of cold, villainous, remorseless lust.

"The death of Key was a cheap sacrifice to save one mother from the horrible fate, which on that Sabbath day, hung over this prisoner's wife and the mother of his child. You may also plant on the best and surest foundations the principles of law which secure the peace of the home, the security of the family, and the relations of husband and wife, which have been in the most horrid manner violated in this case."

Stanton deferred the remaining points to Brady.

Chapter Forty-Five

"Address of
Mr. James T. Brady
for the Defence"

DAY NINETEEN—Monday, April 25, 1859

The doors of the courtroom were "besieged" by "a large number of persons" for a full fifteen minutes after Judge Crawford opened court.

Brady picked up where Stanton had left off. "The whole world, your Honor, has its eye on this case, and although there may seem to be egotism involved in the remark which I make, I cannot help saying, because I am here in the discharge of my duty, that, when all of us shall have passed away, and when each shall have taken his chamber in the silent halls of death, and while some of us would have been totally forgotten but for this unfortunate incident, the name of everyone associated with this trial, from your Honor who presides in the first position of dignity to the humblest witness that was called on the stand will endure so long as the earth shall exist.

"The whole world, I say, is watching the course of these proceedings, and the nature of the judgment, and I believe I know what kind of a pulsation stirs the heart of the world. I think I know, if the earth could be resolved into an animate creature, could have a heart, and a soul, and a tongue, how it would rise up in the infinity of space and pronounce its judgment on the features of this transaction."

Brady refused to drop the self-defense argument. "In view of the facts of that collision, that pistol [found in the street] belonged to Key and as used by him in that encounter, this is made conclusive.

"Did not Mr. Sickles accuse him of having dishonored his house and may not Mr. Key have replied, 'I have, and you can make the best of it,' and this reply may have been accompanied by profanity. Who can say anything I have stated is inconsistent with the testimony adduced? The bullet which killed Mr. Key came out of the revolver. What then became of the bullet from the Derringer, which was found to be exploded?"

The waving of a handkerchief, Brady argued, a white cloth, was the symbol of purity and peace and truce. "I hope I may be pardoned by my learned brethren for this remark, in passing, made not in anger, but sorrow, with all the feelings which belong to me. It would have been well if Mr. Key had attached as much importance to the dignity of a banner as did his distinguished sire, and had always within him a fresh recollection of those lines which identified him with the flag of our country wherever seen on earth. If he had remembered that the star-spangled banner has been raised everywhere, in the wilds of Africa, and on the mountain high, by the adventurous traveler, he would never have chosen that foul substitute for its beautiful folds. He would never have forgotten these two lines:

And thus be it ever when freeman shall stand.
Between their loved homes and the war's desolation!

"If his noble father inculcated in lines imperishable the duty of the American people to protect their homes against the invasion of a foe, how does it become less a solemn duty of the American citizen to protect his home against the invasion of the traitor, who, stealing into his embraces under the pretext of friendship, inflicts a deadly wound on his happiness, and aims also a blow at his honor?

"All the emotions of his nature charged into one single impulse. Every throb of his heart brought distinctly before him the great sense of his injuries. Every drop of his blood carried with it a sense of his shame, an inextinguishable agony about the loss of his wife" and "the dishonor to come upon his child. A realization that the promise of his youth must be forever destroyed. That the future, which opened to him so full of brilliancy, had been enshrouded perhaps in eternal gloom by one who, instead of drawing the curtain over it, should have invoked from the good God his greatest effulgence in the path of his friend."

Brady cited the testimony of Reverend Pyne and Francis Mohun, who saw Sickles's vacant eyes, his altered "countenance," and "some great affliction, some great change affecting his whole nature.

"What are the incidents of the Saturday night? In feverish earnestness he paces that chamber of suffering more ferocious than the caged and starved tiger, thinking through the whole night of nothing but these reflections to which I have alluded, and which darkened the past, the present, and the future.

"Think how, on that Sunday morning, he made this exhibition to which the witnesses have referred, when he saw Mr. Key with his opera glass for inspection or for spying, with his handkerchief to make the adulterous signal, and with the keys in his pocket of the house in Fifteenth Street, to which he was about to take Mrs. Sickles at that moment, if he could obtain her person."

The "realization of all these facts" were "pressing down with terrific weight on his mind, heart, and soul, thus meeting Mr. Key and understanding thoroughly the vile purpose of his heart, was not to shoot him, I ask my learned brother to tell me what he was to do. I would like to ask all assembled humanity what he was to do. To bid him good morning, to pass him silently by, to avert his eye?

"Daniel E. Sickles, a man of unblenching and unvaried courage, as I know from the past associations of our lives, let Philip Barton Key believe that he could not only seduce his wife, but cow him? If he had done anything more or less than became a man, under these circumstances, whatever may have been the intimacy of our past relations, I would have been willing to see him die the most ignominious death before I would venture to raise anything in his behalf, but a prayer to Heaven for the salvation which after death might come.

"He did meet him. He met him under the influence of intense provocation fresh upon him.

"Hear it, men of the universe! Hear it, men of the United States! It is claimed that a man is not permitted by law to do anything for the protection and vindication of his honor." He "can have the greatest affront put upon his right," and "have the relations between himself and his wife violated...made valueless to him by the ruthless hand of the adulterer—he can have his name made a byword and a reproach, and can have his wife reduced to a thing of shame, and cannot raise his hand to prevent all this—he can have what more?

"Look, your Honor, at Daniel E. Sickles, look at Teresa, that was his wife. Look at the woman whom I knew in her girlhood, in her innocence, and for him, in the past as now, I pray the good and merciful interposition of Heaven to make her future life a source of happiness, and of no more anguish than is inevitable."

Teresa may have consented to the affair, but that was immaterial. "The consent of a child five years of age to taking articles out of her father's house no more avails the thief.

"In the share I have taken of this case, I have been permitted to avail myself of the great services of the gentlemen around this table, and in the address I have made, I have endeavored to speak their sentiments, thoughts, and opinions. I am sorry, indeed, if under their instructions I have been led into anything erroneous."

Meagher, who had wanted to serve as more than an ornament for the defense, had taken detailed notes during Sickles's courtroom breakdown. Now Brady read from those notes, reminding the court that it had witnessed a small sample of the "distraction, bitter woe, the wild desolation, the frenzy, the despair, the strange, unutterable, unearthly agony in which he found Daniel E. Sickles on the afternoon of that memorable Sunday, the 27th of February."

The words of Meagher describe "the tempest that had been so long pent up, a scene which, from the memories of those who witnessed it, never will be, never can be, blotted out." Sickles, who had "borne himself with a heroic calmness, [was] suddenly overcome and racked with a relentless grief, struck down as though he were himself the motherless and houseless child for whom he wept."

To the jury, citizens of the city of Washington, "Mr. Sickles commits his life, his character, all that is to elevate or keep him in existence."

Brady took his seat. There was some applause. He sat and covered his face, "sensibly affected."

Now Robert Ould would conclude for the United States. The prosecution, he said, "stands now on a position the same as taken by the other side, to wit: denouncing the offense of adultery. The question, however, is not of adultery, but one of murder, and whatever vice and criminality may attach to adultery does not relieve the other and higher offense of murder from the condemnation which the law passes upon it."

Adultery "is an offense which cries aloud from heaven for condemnation, and to man for his reprobation."

But "[t]here has never been a civilized nation, never a code of laws, human or divine, where the sacredness of human life did not, first and foremost, receive all the sanctions which human society itself could gather around it."

Does taking a life not also strike at the family relationship? "If so, then the right of punishment not only belongs to the injured husband himself, but to any person, no matter how much a stranger to the husband, who might become a witness of the adultery."

According to Blackstone's treatises on English law, "If a man takes another in the act of adultery with his wife and kills him directly upon the spot, though this was allowed by the laws of Solon, and likewise by the Roman civil law if the adulterer was found in the husband's own house, and also among the ancient Goths, yet in England it is not absolutely ranked in the case of justifiable homicide."

No "code had received the approbation of any civilized people wherein the adulterer was allowed to be pursued after the fact and slain. It had not been shown to exist anywhere."

Ould was busy proving this assertion when three o'clock arrived.

Chapter Forty-Six

Recalled to Life

DAY TWENTY—Tuesday, April 26, 1859

O uld began where he had left off the day before.

The law in *Manning's* case reduced the crime from murder to manslaughter when the seducer was caught in the act. "From that time to this the law had never gone further. It would be very unwise for courts of justice to relax that rule. It would overturn the principles of common law in regard to murder, and would establish the principle that a man could kill another from motives of revenge."

In *Jarboe's* case, Judge Crawford had considered whether the seduction of his sister amounted to provocation or justification, "and his Honor had decided that it amounted to neither." The parties were not caught in the act of adultery. But even if they were, it would mean that Sickles was guilty of manslaughter.

"Society could not exist on any such basis and human civilization would be an impossibility. Standing here," he said, "not as a public prosecutor, but as a private citizen, I, on the part of the people of this District, denounce the doctrine that the protection of the wife's or daughter's virtue is to be bound in the husband's or brother's revolver.

"Stronger than bars and bolts, the flash of woman's virtue is as quick as God's lightning and as sure. Far more effectual is it for silencing seducers or revelers in licentiousness than Derringer or revolver. Every pure woman necessarily, and by the gift of God in Christian communities carries that weapon along with her.

"There is no seducer, no villain, I care not from whence he comes, or how he may have trained himself in the arts of seduction, who can resist the showing of that weapon for one solitary instant. I thank God that the matrons and maids of our land have a surer protection than the pistol or the bowie knife. Sad, indeed, would be their fate if it were not so. The very moment you bring the law of force for the purpose of protecting female honor, that moment you sacrifice female honor. If it is to be protected by the sword, the knife and the pistol, it is unworthy of protection."

Speaking of weapons, "Not a solitary witness" saw anything in Key's hand. Multiple witnesses had seen Sickles armed.

"I would to God, that Philip Barton Key could be put upon the stand, perhaps much that is now dark, much that is now covered with gloom, much that is now not understood, could be made plain as if by the flashing of the sunbeam.

"The only party who could array facts in his defense, or in his behalf, has been silenced in death, and the testimony which might have been adduced for the purpose of vindicating his character is unknown and unheard."

Now Judge Crawford would instruct the jury. A profound silence fell over the courtroom as he began. "The Court is asked to give the jury certain instructions." He began by rejecting the defense argument that the killing was justified. If the jury believed that Sickles killed Key, even if under the belief that Key "had adulterous intercourse with the said wife," then "such willful and intentional killing...is murder. But such killing cannot be found to have been willful and intentional in the sense of this instruction if it shall have been proven to the satisfaction of the jury, upon the whole evidence aforesaid, that the prisoner was in fact insane at the time of such killing."[1]

The judge granted the second and third instructions for the prosecution together: shooting the victim "implies malice in law, and is murder," and "the burden of rebutting the presumption of malice...rests on the prisoner."

Fourth, "every person is presumed to be of sound mind until the contrary is proved." The "burden of rebutting this presumption rests on the prisoner."

Fifth, if the jury believes that Sickles killed Key while attempting to signal his wife inviting an act of adultery, "such provocation does not justify the act" or reduce "such killing from murder to manslaughter." Crawford had again sided with the prosecution, rejecting the defense's expansive definition of what it meant to catch the parties "in the act."

Now the court turned to the instructions requested by the defense. He agreed that it was for the jury to decide whether Sickles had the mental state to be found guilty. "The law does not require that the insanity which absolves from crime should exist for any definite period, but only that it exist at the moment when the act occurred with which the accused stands charged."[2]

The case now rested with the jury.

Jurors talked amongst themselves with every eye in the courtroom watching. Would they render their verdict then and there? No, they were not in agreement. Supporters of the prosecution claimed loudly that Sickles would be hanged.

People tried to lift Sickles's spirts. "Thy will, not mine, be done," he said.[3]

Ten minutes before two, the jury left the room. When they did, it was as though a weight had been lifted from everyone. The audience rose to their feet, "seemed to think themselves at liberty to talk as much as they pleased," and shared opinions and impressions.

Many seized the opportunity to talk to Sickles. Reverend Sunderland of the Fourth Presbyterian church took Sickles by the hand. "Sir, I have come to express to you my heartfelt sympathy, and to say that if the voice of the people of this city could speak at this moment your acquittal would be instantaneous. In case, however, an adverse verdict should be rendered, be assured that you have hearts around you, and mine not the least warm of them, to sustain you in your affliction." Sickles was "much moved," and "expressed his thanks as well as his emotions would permit him."

Time went by. The "noise and confusion grew greater." Judge Crawford, "in a good natured manner," said that "under the circumstances he could not expect the audience to keep silence, he hoped there would be a slight regard exhibited for the place where they were."

But soon all eyes were on the clock. The advance of every minute hand was "set down as fresh proof presumptive of a disagreement."

A policeman entered the courtroom and brought back chairs for the jury. Then they asked for a fire to be made.

"I am prepared for the worst," Sickles said. William Stuart saw on his face a "perfectly unaffected calmness and self-possession." His friends, on the other hand, were visibly anxious.

In the jury room, a juror withdrew from the table and knelt in a corner, asking for divine guidance. As the deliberations continued, he went in the corner and prayed again. He returned to the table with his mind made up.

The door to the jury room opened. The courtroom felt like an electric shock through it. "Make room for the jury," the deputy marshal called out. One by one, the jurors took their seats in the box.

"Here they come," people said. The crowd, unable to wait another second to know the verdict, stared at their faces, hoping for a clue.

People stood up on benches and tables and whatever was around them.

"Down in front," "Get off the benches," "Sit down," Silence in court," "Order, order." But order would not return until the judge called the jurors by name. Then, "a pin might be heard to drop in the suddenly stilled court." The jury was standing.

The clerk addressed the prisoner. "Daniel E. Sickles, stand up and look to the jury."

Sickles did so.

"How say you, gentlemen, have you agreed to your verdict?"

"We have." It was Rezin Arnold, the foreman.

"How say you? Do you find the prisoner at the bar guilty or not guilty?"

A "loud, wild thrilling, tumultuous hurrah sent up by the spectators, cheer after cheer resounded in the court room, and it was taken up by the multitude on the outside and repeated."

"Not guilty."

What followed was minutes of "unparalleled uproar," hundreds yelling "as though gone mad, others wept," as people leapt into the prisoner's box to embrace Sickles.[4]

Hats and handkerchiefs were waved, Stanton did "a jig like David before the ark," Brady "became pale, nervous, and agitated," Phillips covered his face with his hands and wept. Graham was "passive and undemonstrative." Magruder, Ratcliffe, and Chilton joined the rush on the prisoner's box to congratulate their client. Meagher patted strangers on the back, asking, "Is it not glorious?"

"I thought it would be so," said Ould. Carlisle, who had declined the biggest case of his career to vindicate his friend, took leave of the scene as fast as he could.[5]

Only two people were unmoved: Judge Crawford and Sickles himself, "though doubtless a volcano of feeling straggled within."[6]

Stanton tried to gain the attention of the court. "I move that Mr. Sickles is discharged from custody."

Judge Crawford reminded him to "wait till the verdict is recorded."

"Of course, your honor," Stanton replied. "You must excuse excitement on this occasion."

The clerk said, "Your record is, gentlemen, that you find Daniel E. Sickles 'not guilty.'"

The jury nodded.

"And say you all."

They nodded again.

Stanton was "boiling over with excitement." "In the name of Mr. Sickles and of his counsel," he said, "I desire to return thanks to the jury. I now move that Mr. Sickles be discharged from custody," Stanton said.

"The court so orders."

Marshal Selden tried to tamp down the celebration. "Come to order gentlemen, come to order. This is a place where there should be no noise." Nobody cared. The marshal had lost control of the courtroom.

Two of Sickles's Tammany friends escorted him on a slow march through the crowd and their "earnest, loud, and frankly expressed" congratulations.

The madness continued outside. The police were powerless to stop it. Sickles declined requests for a speech.

A small fleet of carriages were lined up, hoping for the honor of taking Sickles away. Some of the crowd tried to disconnect the horses from his carriage in order to draw it themselves, but "the movement was detected in time and prevented." Finally, they managed to pull away. Hundreds of people "of all classes" followed.

From the second the verdict was read, the shouts within were heard by the crowd of thousands outside, and the news "spread like wildfire." All business in the capital came to a stop. In the dining room at Willard's Hotel, guests stood up "and gave repeated hurrahs."

Sickles arrived at the home of his friend John McBlair, his neighbor on Lafayette Square and the current occupant of the Decatur House. His jailor had accompanied him. With the entire world clamoring for a private sentiment from Sickles, he turned to his jailor and took him by the hand. "I would wish, if I could, to make it known how grateful I feel for all the affectionate and considerate kindness that has made my prison a second home."

McBlair's house could not be secured. Hundreds flowed in for hours, shaking hands with Sickles, congratulating him. An "old fruit-man from the neighborhood of Georgetown" showed up with "his choicest stock" of oranges: "Mr. Sickles, I am a poor man, but I have a wife and child at home, whom I love, and I, if you will take this poor gift, as a token of how I honor a man who has taught me how to defend them, will be made most happy." Other merchants and tradesmen did the same.

The crowd, looking to participate in some way at the end of this great drama, came up with the idea of burning down the house where Key and Teresa had carried on their affair, forgetting or disregarding the fact that it had been a rental. Thankfully for John Gray, they did not.

A delegation of jurors came to see Brady at the National Hotel. One of them, John McDermott, said: "I want you, sir, to tell the people of New York, that the citizens of Washington are not behind those of any other part of the country in devotion to the family altar."

Juror Henry Knight played the fiddle. We were worried about you, Brady said, because you're a member of the Know Nothing Party, "but if we had known that [you] played the fiddle we might have made our minds easy, for no fiddler was ever known to find a conviction for murder."

Rezin Arnold, the foreman, said that "his only fear had been that his health might not last him throughout the trial, and that he hoped that his latest posterity would honor his memory, from his having served on this jury."

Juror William Hopkins said that if it had been his wife, he'd have "brought a howitzer to bear" on Key, rather than a Derringer.

A crowd arrived at the National Hotel to serenade the defense team. They returned their thanks, and Chilton asked that they defer their intention to serenade Sickles, who "wished to retire to rest undisturbed." The crowd then serenaded Reverend Haley and the jury. Accompanied by the Marine Corps Band, the serenaders also went to the prosecution. Washington was a single "scene of rejoicing."

One of the jurors said: we rendered our "verdict on the principle that, in the absence of any adequate punishment by law for adultery, the man who violates the honor and desolates the home of his neighbor, does so at the peril of his life, and if he falls by the outraged husband's hands, he deserves his doom." They "have made it from this hour a principle of American law." He could not have imagined how right he was.

Schouler, of the *Boston Atlas and Bee*, had been subpoenaed to come to Washington to testify as to the interview with Sickles, where he had coolly described how he had done it. But it was an era without bylines, and it had been his colleague, Simon Hanscombe, who did the interview and wrote the article. Ould had not realized this until testimony closed. Brady was thankful for the near miss.[7]

The following day, the New York lawyers boarded a train for home. They wanted it known that they were impressed by the "extraordinary power, brilliancy, legal knowledge, and eloquence" of Stanton. William Stuart, in seeing them off, wrote that they had "stood at some sacrifice, and with much devotion, around their friend like a wall of fire." Stuart had made enough money from covering the trial to return to New York and put on another production.[8]

Brady had just won the biggest trial in American history. He was asked: "Have you any special end or aim in this life to accomplish? Anything which, when done, you will say, 'I've gained my ends and will stand aside for younger men'?"

He considered his response in silence. "Nothing for tomorrow, nothing for the future. I am thankful only that I have been allowed to live for today."[9]

The cover of *Harper's* announcing the verdict featured a sketch of an angel opening a heavy cell door as a haggard prisoner steps forward into freedom. It was an illustration for the first installment of a new work by Charles Dickens—*A Tale of Two Cities*—and above it stood the name of part one: "Recalled to life." *Harper's* congratulated its subscribers: "Such an opportunity is rarely enjoyed by the readers of any periodical."

The opening words were as true in the spring of 1859 as the period to which they referred: "It was the best of times, it was the worst of times ... "

Chapter Forty-Seven

An Appropriate Finale to the Sickles Tragedy

—

"The long agony of the Sickles trial is over."
—The *New York Times*

Sickles refused visitors and lay "in a state of great prostration" at the Decatur House. He wasn't the only one who needed a rest: "The disagreeable trial in the criminal court of this district has been brought to an end," wrote Judge Crawford. "Thank God this trial is now matter of history." [1, 2]

Fifteen years earlier, the American public doubted the value of the telegraph, unable to imagine news so important that they would need to hear it immediately. The Sickles trial demonstrated the full "power of the printing instrument." The American Telegraph Company wired 2,000 to 2,500 words per hour, a feat unperformed "since the first wire was stretched." Over 16,000 words a day were sent to New York alone. The Associated Press alone telegraphed a total of 152,140 words at a cost of $3,682.29.

Joseph Gordon Bennet, a media pioneer of the previous two decades, recognized that a new era had begun: "The time is not far distant when the correspondents of this journal, at all points, will be instructed, as they are now in some cases, to drop their letters not in the post office but the telegraph office—when all the news now transmitted to the New York *Herald* by mail will be flashed along the magnetic lines from the most distant parts of the country—when space and time will be compassed by science until they are almost known no more.

"The public mind even now craves with so ardent a longing for the earliest intelligence of all interesting events, and the conductors of the press are so ready to appease the craving appetite of the people, that, as in the case of the Sickles trial, the echoes of that shout which welcomed the verdict in the court room at Washington had not died out ere the scene was presented to the eyes of our citizens in the columns of the New York daily press. And this is but the beginning of the end."[3]

Meanwhile, Sickles had a life to lead. A month after his acquittal, he was back in court, this time as a lawyer representing the Board of Supervisors.[4]

The pistol entered at trial, used to shoot Key, went unclaimed. It was sold to the police officer who had recovered it at the crime scene, and it was then resold as a souvenir for $25.[5]

Reverend Haley, who from the first moments of the story had cast himself as a main character, was presented with a Bible in a ceremony at the National Hotel for his ministry to Daniel Sickles. He responded with a discourse on the importance of visiting those in prison.

"Has he ever visited the prison before or since the Sickles trial?" asked the *Baltimore Sun*.[6,7]

The Sickles were an almost daily sight on the Bloomingdale Road in a splendid carriage drawn by two gray horses. When the weather was nice, they went sailing on the Hudson. On the river, there were no unkind stares or comments.[8,9]

The *New York Times* reported that "the most resolute of avengers has approved himself also the most relenting of husbands" and was now living with his wife. "This of course is a purely personal and private matter, with which the public have nothing to do." Some of Sickles's friends who stood behind him at the trial wanted newspapers to know that they were not responsible.

The *Herald* reported that the Sickles's had decided "to live together again in peace and mutual affection, burying the past in the grave of oblivion." It "is said their love is greater than ever. There is an immense rejoicing among their friends, who have written letters of warm congratulations."[10]

Alabama's *Daily Confederation* wrote: Man "can tread the lowliest haunts of vice and infamy, and still the right hand of fellowship is extended. He was lost but now is found. But poor woman, like Teresa Sickles, when she sins, when she acknowledges her sin, when she is willing to be turned loose on the cold charities of the world—but simply asks forgiveness from one—that same mankind is insulted."[11]

Sickles broke the silence he maintained through twenty days of trial. His letter to the New York *Herald* was publicized across the country:

> Through the course of sad events, which during the last few months have brought so much affliction upon my family, I have been silent. No amount of misrepresentation affecting myself only could induce me now to open my lips. Nor could I deem it worthwhile under any circumstances to notice what has been or can be said in journals never regarded as the sources or exponents of public opinion, for in these it is too often obvious that only unworthy motives prompt the most vindictive assaults upon the private life of citizens holding public stations. But the editorial comments in the Herald of yesterday, although censorious, (of which

I do not complain whilst I read them with regret) differ so widely in tone and temper from the mass of nonsense and calumny which has lately been written concerning a recent event in my domestic relations, that I cannot allow a mistake, into which you have been led by inaccurate information, to pass without such a correction as will relieve others from any share of the reproaches which it is the pleasure of a the multitude at this moment to heap upon me and mine.

Referring to the forgiveness which my sense of duty and my feelings impelled me to extend to an erring and repentant wife, you observe, in the course of your temperate and dignified article that, it is said, however that" the last phase of the affair was brought about through the advice of his lawyers?' This is entirely erroneous. I did not exchange a word with one of my counsel upon the subject, nor with any one else. My reconciliation with my wife was my own act, done without consultation with any relative connection, friend or advisers. Whatever blame, if any, belongs to the step, should fall alone upon me. I am prepared to defend what I have done before the only tribunal I recognize as having the slightest claim to jurisdiction over the subject—my own conscience and the bar of Heaven. I am not aware of any statue, or code of morals, which makes it infamous to forgive a women; nor is it unusual to make our domestic life a subject of consultation with friends, no matter how near and dear to us. And I cannot allow even all the world combined to dictate to me the repudiation of my wife, when I think it right to forgive her, and restore her to my confidence and protection.

If I ever failed to comprehend the utterly desolate position of an offending though penitent woman—the hopeless future, with its dark possibilities of danger, to which she is doomed when proscribed as an outcast—I can now see plainly enough, in the almost universal howl of denunciation with which she is follow to my threshold, the misery and perils from which I have rescued the mother of my child.

And although it is very sad for me to incur the blame of friends and the reproaches of many wise and good people, I shall strive to prove to all who may feel any interest in me, that if I am the first man who has ventured to say to the world an erring wife and mother may be forgiven and redeemed, that, in spite of all the obstacles in my path, the good results of the example shall entitle it to the imitation of the generous, and the commendation of the just.

There are many who think that an act of duty, proceeding solely from affections which can only be comprehended in the heart of a husband and a father is to be fatal to my professional, political, and social standing. If this be so, then so be it. Political station, professional success, social recognition, are not the only prizes of ambition; and I have seen enough of the world in which I have moved, and read enough of the lives of others, to teach me that, if one be patient and resolute, it is the man himself who indicates the place he will occupy; and so long as I do nothing worse than to reunite my family under the roof where they may find shelter from contumely and prosecution, I do not fear the noisy but fleeting voices of popular clamor.

The multitude accept their first impressions from a few; but in the end men think for themselves and if I know the human heart—and sometimes I think that in a career of mingled sunshine and storm I have sounded nearly all its depths—then I may reassure those who look with reluctant forebodings upon my future to be of good cheer, for I will not cease to vindicate a just claim to the respect of my fellows, while to those motley groups, here and there, who look upon my misfortunes only as weapons to be employed for my destruction, to those I say, once for all, if a man make a good use of his enemies, they will be as serviceable to him as his friends.

In conclusion, let me ask only one favor of those who, from whatever motive, may deem it necessary or agreeable to comment in public or private upon this sad history; and that is, to aim all their arrows at my breast, and for the sake of my innocent child, to spare her yet youthful mother, while she seeks in sorrow and contrition the mercy and pardon of Him to whom, sooner or later, we must all appeal.

The *Times* thought: "There will be fresh sympathies aroused for the dead man who moulders in his grave unforgiven, while the partner of his guilt smiles her gratitude up into the face of him whose mercy was so tardy while his justice was so swift."[12]

The *Sun*, under the headline "The Sickles Tragi-Comedy," said the "only regret that the public have is, that his vengeance proved so fatal, and that Mr. Key is not alive to witness Mr. Sickles's restoration to sanity."

Chapter Forty-Eight

Excelsior

Mary Chestnut sat with her friends in the gallery of the House of Representatives. "What had that poor man done" she asked, of the gentlemen sitting alone, "as if he had smallpox?"

"He killed Phil Barton Key," someone said.

"No, no," responded another. "That was all right. It was because he condoned his wife's profligacy and took her back."[1]

There were calls and petitions signed to force Sickles to resign from congress. But he had survived the center stage in America's first media circus and was not about to quit simply to gratify some malcontents.[2]

Teresa and Laura stayed in New York while Congress was in session. Sickles rented a small room, had quiet dinners with friends, and avoided the kind of parties he had been famous for hosting the previous session.[3]

Sickles found his voice in the Secession Crisis of 1860. The Republicans, with their refusal to allow the spread of slavery, had won the White House. As expected, a number of southerners were unwilling to accept the result.[4]

Speaking on the House floor, Sickles said, "It will never do, sir, for them to protest against coercion, and, at the same moment seize all the arms and arsenals and forts and navy yards, and ships that may, through our forbearance, fall within their power. This is not peaceful secession. These acts, whosoever or by whomsoever done, are overt acts of war."[5]

Sickles was forceful, "clear" and "logical" in defense of his country, and his words were "attentively listened to by the members and crowded galleries," to "decided effect."[6]

Sickles found himself out of office again a month before shots were fired on Fort Sumter. He recruited three thousand men in a month and was made a Brigadier General. Stationed in Washington, awaiting orders, he heard from Laura: "I hope dear papa that you will write just as often as you can, since we are all so happy when your letters are received. How very fine your soldiers and horses must appear and how glad I should be to see them."

Sickles became close friends with Abraham and Mary Todd Lincoln and was a frequent guest in the White House. He was even invited to participate in Mary's séances in the Red Parlor. Once, he was asked to hide behind a curtain while Nettie Colburn, her spiritualist, was asked to guess his identity: "Crooked Knife," she said. In other words, a "Sickle." There were reports that he may have tried to talk to Key. But he would get no response in this life.

As the war wore on, Sickles was promoted to commander of the Third Corps, one of only seven major generals—and one of only two who did not attend West Point. It was a remarkable rehabilitation for a man who was recently America's most famous murder defendant.

On a rare visit home, General Sickles brought two pressed bouquets, signed by Mary Lincoln to "Miss Laura Sickles."[7]

Teresa may have already been showing signs of consumption, the disease that caused her to waste away, claiming her life at the age of thirty-one.

On the second day of the Battle of Gettysburg, Sickles and his men occupied the low ground to the south. General Meade, his commander, had not seen the land for himself. If the Confederates were allowed to walk into the Wheatfield and Peach Orchard, they could set up artillery and obliterate them all. Sickles sent messengers to Meade, imploring him to come and see the lay for himself, to give them permission to advance to the high ground. At 11 a.m., he went to Meade himself. Meade refused but sent his chief engineer and artillery officer. When he could wait no longer, Sickles moved his men forward. They absorbed the brunt of the attack that day. James Longstreet, leader of the Confederate advance, believed Sickles's move had prevented his victory. As the day neared its end and it looked as though they would successfully absorb the blow, a twelve-pound cannonball came bouncing at Sickles faster than he could avoid it. It exploded and destroyed his right leg. People watching assumed that he had been mortally wounded. Even he thought he was a dead man. His soldiers started to panic, just as victory was in sight, viewing their injured chief. To give them confidence to finish the battle, Sickles, while being carried from the battlefield, lit a cigar and smiled.[8]

Chapter Forty-Nine

The Unwritten Law

—

*"Precedents are almost unanimous in favor of the
assertion that any man has a right to kill the betrayer
of his wife, his sister, or his daughter."*
—St. Louis Globe-Democrat

For a time, the most well-known law in America could not be found in a book.

On the night of the Sickles's trial, a crowd of two thousand revelers had gone to Willard's and asked for remarks from John Graham. He said that they "had shown to the world...that their homes must not be violated." They moved on to the home of Philip Phillips, who told them: "A new era had been initiated in the jurisprudence of the world. An honest, upright and intelligent American jury had established a precedent which all civilized nations would henceforth recognize and be guided by." If a "man violated the sanctity of his neighbor's house he must do so at his peril."[1]

This was not always the case. In 1825, Jereboam Beauchamp killed Solomon Sharp, the attorney general of Kentucky, for seducing his wife before their marriage. Beauchamp was executed seven weeks after being found guilty. It was the kind of homicide that would one day meet with public approval. But not yet.[2]

Eighteen years later, Mahlon Heberton seduced Sarah Mercer, a "beautiful and lovely" though "weak minded" girl, sixteen years of age, leaving her in a house of "doubtful reputation." Her twenty-year-old brother, Singleton, challenged Heberton to a duel. Heberton didn't realize that those were the best odds he was going to get. Instead, he fled Philadelphia under cover of night, driving his carriage onto a ferry to New Jersey. When the boat arrived, Mercer, who had concealed himself aboard, emptied a six-shooter into the carriage, killing Heberton. The Baltimore *Sun* called it a lesson to parents in caring for their daughters, "and what a lesson to the seducer." Mercer was acquitted by reason of insanity after a half-hour of deliberation. "It is remarkable how some people lose all command of their senses, and suddenly recover it again," noted one newspaper. The people of Louisville planned on presenting Mercer with a gold medal. Some proposed a monument to him.[3]

William Myers was married to "one of the loveliest women that ever lived." Three years after Mercer's acquittal, Myers learned of an affair between his wife and lottery salesman D. M. Hoyt. Myers found Hoyt in his basement room of the Exchange Hotel and asked him to sign a pledge to leave the city at once. When Hoyt refused, Myers shot him three times. The *Richmond Whig* wrote: "The injury said to have been inflicted upon Mr. Myers by Mr. Hoyt, in the most delicate relation of life, was of such a character as to justify, in the eyes of all men, the most summary punishment. Truth, surely, as here exemplified, is stranger than fiction." The examining court heard evidence, consisting of proof of the affair, and refused to charge him. "Such a burst of applause took place as we never heard in a court of justice."[4]

Thomas Washington Smith couldn't believe his luck when a beautiful younger woman agreed to be his wife. But she had a secret, the kind it was impossible to keep. Richard Carter, a bank president, was the father. Carter was already married, so Smith was appointed to play the fool. Smith found Carter at the St. Lawrence Hotel in Philadelphia, firing four shots into him. Unlike many defendants acquitted by the Unwritten Law, Smith may actually have been insane. At the end of his trial, he was committed into the care of his sister.[5]

The *New York Herald* said: "Let the race of lotharios beware." It claimed to know of several similar cases where no arrests had even been made. "It may be considered as the *unwritten law* of this country," the paper wrote, "that a man may kill with impunity the seducer of his sister or the paramour of his wife" (italics added). The phrase "Unwritten Law" would not enter common use until the turn of the next century. But its watershed moment was a year away.[6]

Daniel Jarboe and his sister walked down the street on an unpleasant errand. She had fallen for the promises of Rufus Nally and given him what he wanted. Evidence of her deception was more apparent by the day. They found Nally near the Washington Navy Yard, where he worked as a blacksmith. "Do you intend to marry her?" Jarboe asked. Nally refused, "positively and perseveringly." Jarboe shot him, the bullet entering just below his heart. In his final moments, Nally, old enough to trick a woman into bed, wanted nothing more than his mother. He made it to her house with minutes to live. An excited crowd gathered around Jarboe. He told them to be calm and that he was turning himself in.[7]

The trial was heard in Judge Crawford's courtroom. The defense argued that Jarboe was insane and that Nally reached for a weapon, making it a case of self-defense. Prosecutor Barton Key told the jury the "killing was a case not of insanity or self-defense, but an act of revenge. Jarboe's attorneys appealed to jurors with evidence of his sister's seduction. Key, on behalf of the dead man, recited an old Baptist poem:

No longer seek his merits to disclose,
Nor draw his frailties from their dread abode,
There they alike in trembling hope repose,
The bosom of his Father and his God.[8]

Key's efforts to convict Jarboe were "long and protracted." The jury's deliberations were not. They freed Jarboe after fifteen minutes, followed by a "general rejoicing" in the courtroom.

A year later, Daniel Sickles sent Philip Barton Key to his fate. The dam had been building against seducers for years, and now it burst. Sickles forced the conversation into every American living room. What were the consequences of adultery? What were a man's obligations? The Unwritten Law was announced at Washington City Hall and spread throughout the United States.

The temporary insanity defense, popularized in the Sickles trial, became a cornerstone of the Unwritten Law. As with Sickles, the insanity plea opened the door to evidence of an affair. These acquittals were not nineteenth-century juries falling for pseudoscience: it was a belief held with increasing fervency that a man was no criminal who killed the author of his dishonor.[9]

If the victim made any attempt to resist the attack, it would be argued as self-defense. The Sickles lawyers never entirely abandoned this theory, pointing to the Derringer at the scene that did not fit the ball taken out of Key, the fact that Key had reached into his jacket pocket, and that he was known to carry weapons.

In 1867, the New York Constitutional Convention was interrupted by the killing of Harris Hiscock, who had an affair with General George Cole's wife while he was fighting the Civil War. James Brady defended Cole. "All the laws that society can ever make cannot take out of our hearts the instincts that God has put there. Among those instincts we find that of the purpose of preserving the honor and integrity of our family." During his closing, he channeled Cole, saying: "In the blow that I struck and for which I suffer, I strengthened the security of the homes of my fellow citizens as much as I did when I struck against the enemy who would have laid waste our country." It was Brady's last address to a jury.[10]

Cole acknowledged being sane immediately before and after the trigger pull but temporarily insane at the instant of the shooting. The first jury was deadlocked; the second acquitted him. The *New York Times* called it "the most extraordinary verdict ever returned by a jury made up of men supposed to be sane themselves." In the eight years after the Sickles verdict, Cole's defense was able to cite twenty-eight cases of the Unwritten Law. Considering the limited information flow of cases between states, this was a small fraction of the real number and took no account of killers who were never charged.[11]

Daniel McFarland represented the worst of the Unwritten Law. Two years after Cole, he walked into the office of the *New York Tribune* and shot Albert Richardson, an editor. Richardson was set to marry Abby Sage, McFarland's *ex-wife*. Abby and Richardson married on his deathbed, in a wedding performed by Reverend Beecher, with Horace Greeley as a witness. McFarland was a violent drunk who had badly misrepresented his financial situation, an abusive and controlling husband who had made Abby miserable until she divorced him.

Yet McFarland was defended at trial by John Graham, who said this was the third case he'd handled in twelve years where he had "the distinguished honor... of upholding and defending the marriage relation." The brand of the Unwritten Law that excused McFarland's cruel and cowardly act was created by men, for the benefit of men, and one that discounted the agency of women (it was alleged that Richardson had alienated Abby from McFarland). Abby went on to success as an actress, and she once performed at the Lafayette Square

Opera House, which had been built over the Club House and scene of Key's shooting. [Before it was torn down, the Club House served as the home of William Seward, Civil War Secretary of State, and the scene of his attempted assassination.][12]

As with the Mercer trial, the Unwritten Law protected brothers and fathers as well as husbands. William McKaig seduced Myra Black, the sister of his friend since childhood, Harry Crawford Black. McKaig used the secret to keep her as his mistress while he married another. Not only had McKaig refused to marry her, he wouldn't let anyone else do so. He revealed the secret to a man who had proposed to her. Myra became pregnant four years later and told her father. Her father shot McKaig in the arm, but he lived. Enter Harry, brother of Myra, who lived away. Harry Black gunned down McKaig on the main street in front of twenty witnesses. He was acquitted in less than an hour. But state-sanctioned revenge couldn't restore Myra's lost happiness, and she later committed suicide.[13]

The Unwritten Law covered dishonor to sisters and daughters as well as wives. Francis Bartley was killed in his dairy field, quite unexpectedly, by the son of his married lover when he intercepted a love letter. Another Sickles, in Moundsville West Virginia, killed his own nephew when he heard his daughter screaming for help.[14]

Sometimes a legal veneer had to be used, but often the Unwritten Law was invoked directly. Eadweard Muybridge, a protégé of Leland Stanford, traveled a great distance to Calistoga to shoot his wife's lover. "The only thing I am sorry for," he said, "is that he died so quickly." He was mobbed by a supportive crowd at his acquittal.[15]

Some judges would order juries to ignore the Unwritten Law. When George Cline and two accomplices killed the actor "Handsome" Jack Bergin for attempting to rape his wife, the judge instructed the jury "that no evidence could sustain an acquittal." The jurors didn't care. "I have a wife and daughter," one explained. Prosecutors attempted the same thing, such as the one who told a jury: "There is no such defense as the Unwritten Law." The jury disagreed. The American Bar Association held a convention and complained. Nobody cared.[16]

In 1907, an article in the *Virginia Law Register* proposed writing down the Unwritten Law. The Unwritten Law was so strong at this point that "Not one jury in a hundred would fail to acquit" a father who hunted his daughter's seducer for a hundred days. The constant undermining of the jury oath threatened to shake the foundation of the entire system. "Is there any doubt that the common judgement of men fully justifies homicide committed when the provocation is the invasion of martial rights or an attack upon the virtue of the innocent?"

Rather than the continued artifice, would not the interest of justice be better served, it was asked?[17]

Evelyn Nesbit, a gorgeous showgirl, told her husband, Harry Thaw, that she had been drugged and raped by Stanford White. Thaw approached White on the rooftop theater of Madison Square Garden, telling him, "You've ruined my wife." He shot him three times, twice in the face, during the show's finale ("I Could Love a Million Girls"). His first jury hung, and his second found him not guilty by reason of insanity. A twelve-minute silent film, *The Unwritten Law,* was made about the White shooting (it ran into trouble with censors), and the story also became a Broadway play.

The Unwritten Law protected women as well as men. Mary Harris of Chicago defended her own honor against Adoniram Burroughs, who had broken their engagement and encouraged her to join him in a house of ill repute.

Margaret Finn shot her fiancé "on a crowded Los Angeles Street." She was pregnant, and he was leaving her. She claimed not to remember firing the shot but said, "I had placed my honor and my life in his trust and he betrayed that trust" and therefore "deserved death." A judge agreed, dismissing her case without the need for a trial. That same year, Estelle Corwell killed her lover of six years for threatening to expose their relationship. In a trial that featured Wyatt Earp as a defense witness, she was acquitted by reason of insanity.[18]

Clara Falmer, fifteen years old and pregnant, may have seemed the most vulnerable person on earth to the boyfriend who refused to help. He laughed. She shot him dead across the dinner table.[19]

The Law could extend to anyone who aided in the act of dishonor, not necessarily the libertine himself. In 1912, Al Boyce Jr. was shot and killed outside a church in Amarillo. His assailant, John Sneed, was disguised as a bum, "with a heavy growth of beard and wearing overalls." Boyce had made the mistake of seducing Sneed's wife, Lena, and taking her to Canada. Sneed had already killed Boyce's father for helping them escape and was awaiting a retrial after a hung jury. Sneed fired the fatal shot against Boyce as he lay wounded, saying, "I guess you are dead." Sneed would ultimately be acquitted in the cases of father and son.[20]

Ultimately, no place was safe for the libertine. Alfred Hester missed his moment of Unwritten Law glory when Virgil Butt returned fire, killing him in the streets of Portland. But killing the husband only delayed the inevitable. "Butt Convicted of Murder," the headlines said. He was sentenced to death.[21]

Then there are the cases that never made it to trial, like the 1926 Richmond grand jury that refused to indict a railroad flagman who had killed his wife's lover after catching them together in a car. Or the coroner's jury in Kentucky that refused to charge Nancy Murill in 1904 for killing her husband's lover. There's no telling how many were never formally charged or never even arrested, and these stories were much less likely to be covered by the press.

If a killer was arrested and indicted, there were still directed verdicts, where a judge would dismiss the case without sending it to the jury, such as the Georgia judge in 1918 that acquitted J. L. Gibson, who killed his wife's lover after finding their letters.[22]

A defendant who made it all the way to a guilty verdict could expect a comical sentence. One judge, in fining a convicted murderer $5, said: "You are guilty, technically, but I would have done the same thing." When another defendant was fined $500, he was so indignant that he tried to get the verdict overturned, even though a second trial could result in a death sentence.

If a defendant were somehow convicted and given a harsh sentence, there was executive clemency. The Unwritten Law was a manifestation of popular feeling, and elected governors responded with pardons and commutations. Archibald Brown was shot dead in bed with another man's wife. The governor of Kentucky announced that he would pardon the killer if he should he be convicted. Remarkably, the victim was the governor's own son (the grand jury refused to indict). The Unwritten Law was more powerful than a father's love for his son, as well as racial animus in the era of Jim Crow. In 1893, the governor of South Carolina pardoned a black man for the killing of a white man caught having sex with his wife. The Unwritten Law was "as good for the negro as the white man," the governor explained. Speaking of governors, Alabama elected John Anthony Winston, who had been acquitted for a killing under the Unwritten Law years earlier.[23]

A study of a small sample of these cases found that only thirty times out of 201 would a defendant receive a serious punishment. An 85 percent success rate would be astonishing by itself. But that doesn't tell the whole story. The power of the Unwritten Law meant it was asserted even when defendants were lying. It was in these instances, where a jury did not believe the defendant, where the wife or the daughter took the stand to deny the claims of the defense, when the jury would convict. Killers vindicating their family honor, if believed by the jury, were safe.[24]

The Unwritten Law emerged from a society that put a premium on female virtue and entrusted men with the responsibility for its preservation. Thus, men who also killed their wives did so at their peril—like Joseph Steinmetz, who was honeymooning in New York with his wife of sixteen days. After a night of binge drinking, he woke up to find her in bed with a Catholic priest in their hotel. He was convicted of only one count of manslaughter— for his wife.

In 1949, the *Oregonian* wondered whether "a venerable American legal tradition" had been upset by a recent jury. "They failed to acquit Dr. Robert C. Rutledge, Jr., of the murder of Byron C. Hattman, the alleged seducer of his wife. He received a seventy-year sentence. In so doing, they virtually threw out of the window the Unwritten Law." One hundred and five years after the Mercer trial, an unsuccessful Unwritten Law defense in Cedar Rapids, Iowa, made headlines in Portland, Oregon. In fact, the *Oregonian* published a long Sunday feature recapping the history of the Unwritten Law, including the Sickles trial.[25]

The Rutledge case was not the end, as it turned out, but the end was near. Two of the last successful uses were in 1954 and 1958. By coincidence, both killings were committed by dentists.[26]

The beliefs in society that had created and so firmly entrenched and applied the Unwritten Law changed: women were increasingly acknowledged as more than passive participants in sexual affairs. Accordingly, men were seen as something more than villainous corrupters of female virtue. Moreover, expectations regarding female chastity were changing. All of these factored to repeal a law that had never been written.[27]

How many died under the reign of the Unwritten Law? It is impossible to say. The number is in the thousands. No attempt has ever been made to collect every case. Nor could anyone come close. One of the few attempts to study it turned up 201 cases by searching three newspapers for the phrase "Unwritten Law" and the word "trial." But they were simply trying to find enough cases to analyze. The "Unwritten Law" was firmly in place well before it had a consensus term to describe it. Further, that sample is only three newspapers out of many thousands. The vast majority have never been digitized and are not available for searching. Further, not every case would have been covered in the press. Many more would have been reported without explaining the motive or the defense. The true number is and will remain a secret.[28]

★ ★ ★

It was 1893. Champ Clark won his first race to congress and had one more trial before heading to Washington. A St. Louis street car conductor had killed one of his colleagues for seducing his wife. Clark would defend him. "I laid down the proposition flat," he said, "that an American jury would not, and should not, convict under such circumstances." He cited three cases, two of which had been tried in the same courtroom. The third was *United States vs. Daniel Sickles*. The conductor was soon to join the defendants in those cases, freed by the Unwritten Law.

In his freshman class in congress, Clark was surprised to find Daniel Sickles, returned to the House after a thirty-year hiatus. Clark remembered well when his trial was the talk of the nation. He searched for a transcript and found one in the law library of the Supreme Court.

Clark eagerly paged through the dramatic days of the trial. His four-year-old son climbed into his lap and looked over his shoulder. The transcript came complete with the famous drawings from the illustrated newspapers.

"Daddy, who is that man shooting the man lying on the ground?"

"General Sickles." His son often came to the House and knew many of the members.

"The old man who walks on crutches? I'll ask him about it tomorrow."

"No, you must not do that," Clark said. "If you do, he will not give you any more candy."

At his son's request, they traveled to Lafayette Square to see the tree from the picture. They approached the custodian of the park, "who looked old enough to have been in the ark." What tree did Key hide behind when Sickles was shooting him?

The custodian said, "You see that little elm between the two big elms? That little tree is in place of the Key tree. Souvenir hunters cut the bark off the original tree till they killed it."

Clark was as anxious as his little boy "to have General Sickles tell me all about killing Key." He asked questions in private conversations, calculated to lead him to subject of the trial.[29]

Sickles had many stories. He was one of the central figures of the Civil War; an intimate of Abraham and Mary Todd Lincoln; Reconstruction governor of South Carolina, where he fought for black equality in the bosom of Secession; Ulysses S. Grant's ambassador to Spain; an expat in Paris, where he carried on an affair with Isabella II, exiled Queen of Spain; and a frequent visitor to his lost leg at the Army Medical Museum.

But he never spoke about the thing that Clark wanted to know, leaving him to wonder: "Did his memory most frequently dwell on the halcyon days of youth, when he stood on the seashore in New York, watching the stately ships of all nations come and go like great seagulls? Or upon his first successes in New York politics, when he 'ran with the machine?' Or upon the rosy dawn of his congressional career, away back in the 'fifties? Or upon the sudden eclipse of his political sun? Or upon the glorious battle pictures of which he was part? Or upon his brilliant career as a diplomat in foreign lands? Or upon the splendid and peaceful eventide of his turbulent existence? Did he ever think of Philip Barton Key, whom he sent, with his sins fresh upon his head, to the unknown world? I wondered whether, if he could go back to that February morning in 1859, when his pistol shot startled the world, he would do it again. I thought, 'It won't, it can't be long, in the very nature of things, till he must stand, face to face with Key and the lovely woman for whose forbidden love he died, at the judgment bar of God, and his thoughts must be of them sometimes. Does his leonine spirit quail to think of them, or does he justify himself to himself still for that historic killing?' Who knows?"

"He was a fine old man," Clark recalled, "an interesting relic of a day long gone."[30]

Epilogue

Ghosts
of New York

Daniel Sickles had survived them all. He had woken up minus a leg in Washington, with Lincoln by his bedside, and gave him an account of Gettysburg. Sickles had returned to New York on a revenue cutter, traveling the Hudson River to his home on 91st Street. James Brady had made the ride, along with Thomas Meagher, with whom he had served in the war, Emanuel Hart, and Chevalier Wikoff. They made speeches and shared memories. Now that was all he had of them.

Edwin Stanton was appointed attorney general by James Buchanan, giving needed ballast to that administration as it faced the Secession Crisis. But it was as Lincoln's secretary of war that Stanton ensured his name would live forever. He and Brady had died the same year: 1869. Brady had continued as a lawyer in major cases until the last. During the war, he used his rhetorical talents in favor of the Union.

Chevalier Wikoff had no discernible politics and easily made the transition to the first Republican White House. He was arrested for stealing a copy of Lincoln's 1861 state of the Union and selling it to the *Herald*. Sickles served as his attorney.[1]

Reverend Haley served as a cavalry officer in the war and channeled his love for the press into a career, editing the San Jose *Mercury* and starting his own popular paper in Templeton. Haley wrote the definitive account of Johnny Appleseed in an 1871 article for *Harper's*.[2]

Robert Ould became Assistant Secretary of War for the Confederacy, in charge of overseeing exchanges of POWs, and served as the lawyer for Jefferson Davis after Appomattox.[3]

Samuel Butterworth headed west and made a fortune as president of a mining company. He was appointed to the Board of Regents of the University of California, and sponsored resolutions "abolishing all fees and charges" for students and opening them up to women on an equal basis with men. The flowers sent to his well-attended funeral nearly hid the body.[4]

William Stuart/Edmund O'Flaherty, who had chronicled the Sickles trial from DC, found great success in the world of theater back in New York. Among his partners was Edwin Booth, with whom he produced 100 consecutive nights of *Hamlet*. It was said that he could have "written one of the most entertaining volumes of personal reminiscences of 40 years." He and Sickles would sometimes attend theater together in New York. When he died, the *New York Times* called it the "end of a romantic and brilliant career."[5]

There was Teresa, who had died young and left him, and Laura, who had done the same, and Key, who had betrayed him, and who he had brutally killed, and a second family that he had failed and estranged. All were now fading memories.

There were new friends, like Mark Twain, who also tried and failed to get Sickles to discuss the trial. But it was not the same. In his waning days, Sickles was a "prominent figure downtown during the day, hobbling "up the steps of Wall Street offices or down the aisles of the theatre on a pair of crutches." He had entered the world on this island and he would leave it here. In 1819, in the presidency of James Monroe, churches had been the tallest buildings. Now there were sky scrapers, Woodrow Wilson was president, and his city was home to 120,000 souls.[6]

Sickles, his hair and "large moustache" now gray, was a fixture at plays and operas. Gilbert and Sullivan's "Patience" was opening at the Standard Theatre. James Barton Key would play the role of Archibald Grosvenor, a character who was "fatally attractive." Sickles must have thought he had seen a ghost. Key had the same nose, eyes, and mustache of the father who had left him so young, and who existed only in fuzzy memories. Sickles looked down at Key. Key looked up at Sickles.[7]

And the lights went down.

Acknowledgments

M y first thanks are to God, for the opportunity to tell this story and have you read it. "A man can receive nothing unless it has been given him from heaven." (John 3:27, NAS)

Writing my first acknowledgments in five years, it occurs to me I have more people to thank than ever. Most notably my brilliant and beautiful wife Hannah, to whom this book is dedicated. With her came a wonderful new family: parents Tom and Cindy Lawther, brother Cole (Backstreet forever), sisters Samantha Jasinski, Maddie Kirelawich, and Alex Finley, their husbands Jim, Billy, and Phil, our nieces, Jessica and Kate, and nephews, Willie and Colin.

Then there's the amazing family I had before, and am pleased to report, still have: my sainted mother Anna DeRose, who raised us on her own and is now enjoying retirement, and sister Catherine DeRose, the smart one.

Kimberly Beare, Amy Kalman, Mikel Steinfeld, and Maria Strohbehn read this first and their feedback made it a better book. Your reward will be reviewing bad first drafts going forward.

Steven Drexler, handwriting expert, teamed up with me to help identify the mysterious R. P. G., the Iago of our story who probably got away with it.

When asked to visit a nineteenth century murder scene, Abby Livingston didn't ask too many questions. Everyone needs a friend like Abby.

For all the researchers, curators, and librarians who gave me assistance, particularly Dan Boudreau at the American Antiquarian Society and Dale Stinchcomb in the Harvard Theatre Collection.

For the team at Regnery: Stephen Thompson, superlative editor, gentleman, and scholar; Anne Mulrooney, for the incredibly smooth and professional final edits process; Nicole Yeatman, Tim Meads, and Jennifer Duplessie, publicity and marketing ninjas—if you're reading this, it's probably because of something they did; or maybe because of Josh Taggert's beautiful cover art; but certainly because of publisher Alex Novak's enthusiasm for this story.

For Adam Chromy, advocate and friend, who wears every hat of a literary agent with aplomb, and makes you feel like you're his only client.

Abraham Lincoln was right when he said, "The better part of one's life consists of their friendships." The better part of mine has included: Jon Anderson, Alex and Allie Benezra, Elliot Berke, Clint and Shawnna Bolick, Mark and Wendy Briggs, Bill and Debbie Cheatham, Chuck Coolidge, Josh Daniels, Nolan Davis, Dominic Draye, Jeremy and Robyn Duda, Rob Ellman, Ashley and Connie Fickel, Tom Forese, Tom and Ana Galvin, Ruben Gallego, Justin Herman, James Hohmann, Eric Johnson, Ken and Randy Kendrick, Adam and Orit Kwasman, Heather Lauer, Whitney Lawrence, Dylan Leffler, Heather Macre, Simer and Vicki Mayo, Danny and Bonnie Mazza, Adele and Fran Ponce, Tysen and Kellee Schlink, James Slattery, Evelyn Slomka, Jay Swart and Carol Perry, Don Tapia, Trey and

Elise Terry, Jim and Kitty Waring, Katie Whalen, Justin Wilmeth, Megan Wojtulewicz, and Jess Yescalis. For David and Caroline Van Slyke and everyone in small group, for my friends in the Abraham Lincoln Association and at President Lincoln's Cottage, for our friends in the British American Project, for all my former law students, and for the Blue Comet, Arizona's premiere bar trivia team.

And for you, the reader. You have made possible this extraordinary chapter in my life.

Notes

OVERTURE

1. Playbill for *"Sickles: or, the Washington Tragedy."* TCS 66 (403), Houghton Library, Harvard University.
2. *Evening Star*, May 28, 1859.
3. *Boston Journal*, April 14, 1859.
4. *Appleton's Annual Cyclopaedia and Register of Important Events*, v. 42, 450.
5. *The Era* (London), May 29, 1859.

CHAPTER 1

1. Thomas Keneally, *American Scoundrel* (New York: Random House, 2002), 27.
2. *Globe*, February 24, 1859, 1324.
3. Benjamin Perley Poore, *Reminiscences of 60 Years in the National Metropolis* (Philadelphia: Hubbard, 1885), 2:25.
4. *New York Times*, March 15, 1859; Press January 19, 1859.
5. *New York Times*, February 28, 1859.
6. W. A. Swanberg, *Sickles the Incredible* (New York: Scribner's, 1956), 6; *Tribune* February 26, 1859; *Cincinnati Commercial Tribune* February 28, 1859; *Plain Dealer*, March 5, 1859.

7. *New York Times* obituary 1884; *Press* January 19, 1859; John Forney, *Anecdotes of Public Men* (New York: Harper Brothers, 1873) 1:368; Crain, Caleb. "The Courtship of Henry Wikoff; or, a Spinster's Apprehensions." *American Literary History*. Vol. 18, No. 4 (Winter, 2006), 659-694.
8. *Trial Day*, 14.
9. Virginia Clay-Copton, *A Belle of the Fifties* (New York: Double Day, 1905), 73, 86.
10. Clay-Copton, 97–98; *Press* January 24.
11. *Trial Day*, 7; Tribune, March 2, 1859.
12. Unknown author. "The Dobbs Family in America" (London: John Maxwell, 1865).
13. Poore, 2:26; *New York Times*, February 28, 1859.
14. *Leslie's*, March 26, 1859; Poore 2:26; *New York Times* February 28, 1859; *Harper's* March 12, 1859.
15. *Trial*, Days 7 and 8.
16. *Harper's*, March 12, 1859.
17. *Trial Day*, 9; Star April 11, 1859.

CHAPTER 2

1. *Harper's*, April 9, 1859.
2. *Harper's*, April 9, 1859 (This was the first attempt to tell Sickles's life story, and many of the earliest details of his life are attributable to this article. It has served as the foundation of every subsequent biography); Brown, William [Editor] "History of Warren County." (1963); "Printer's Devil," Historically Speaking blog, obtained online: https://idiomation.wordpress.com/2011/08/10/printers-devil/.
3. *Harper's*, April 9, 1859.
4. GWD Daniels to Sickles, NYHS, 1853.
5. *Harper's*, April 9, 1859.
6. *Harper's*, April 9, 1859.
7. Hathi Trust catalog obtained online: https://catalog.hathitrust.org/Record/000529340.
8. Keneally, 4.
9. Classic FM; Renee Montagne, "The Librettist of Venice," https://www.classicfm.com/composers/mozart/guides/da-ponte-facts-gallery/venice; *Harper's*, April 9, 1859.

10. Edgcumb Pinchon, *Dan Sickles: Hero of Gettysburg and "Yankee King of Spain"* (New York: Doubleday, 1945), 12-13.
11. Later known as New York University.
12. *Harper's*, April 9, 1859.
13. *Commercial Advertiser,* February 3, 1840; *New York American,* January 31, 1840.
14. Keneally, 10.
15. *Harper's*, April 9, 1859.
16. *Harper's*, April 9, 1859; Golway.
17. *New York Evening Post (Post)*, May 14, 1844; *Sober Second Thought, June 8,* 1844.
18. Anonymous. *The Life and Death of Fanny White: Being a Complete and Interesting History of the Career of That Notorious Lady* (New York: 1860), obtainable online: https://iiif.lib.harvard.edu/manifests/view/drs:2968201$1i.
19. *Harper's*, April 9, 1859.
20. Keneally, 26.
21. Anonymous, *The Life and Death of Fanny White*.
22. Sickles to J.H. Herbach, January 28, 1859, Library of Congress.

CHAPTER 3
1. *The Ladies' and Gentlemen's Etiquette*, excerpted at susannaives.com; *London Daily News*, March 31, 1854.
2. Keneally, 18–19.
3. *American*, September 26, 1832; Pinchon 12; Keneally, 4.
4. *New York Times,* March 15, 1859; Keneally, 21.

CHAPTER 4
1. Keneally, 26; *Reflector*, January 14, 1853.
2. Forney, John Wiley. *Anecdotes of Public Men* 1:317-319 (New York: Harper and Brothers, 1873).
3. Chris DeRose, *The Presidents' War* (New York: Lyons Press, 2014), 57.
4. Buchanan, *The Collected Works* (Indianapolis: Liberty Fund), 9:31.
5. *Daily Union*, July 31, 1853; *Inquirer*, August 1, 1853.
6. Keneally, 33.

7. *Manchester Courier and Lancashire General Advertiser*, March 9, 1853.
8. Teresa to Sickles, August 1853, New York Public Library.
9. Buchanan to Harriet Lane, September 30, 1853, found in *Works*, 9:61-2.
10. *London Times*, April 1, 1859; *Boston Journal*, March 2; *London Daily News*, April 18, 1854; *London Morning Advertiser*, April 20, 1854.
11. *Morning Chronicle*, February 13, 1854.
12. Pinchom, 849-900.
13. *Morning Post* (London), August 31, 1854.
14. *Albany Journal*, January 11, 1856 and February 1, 1856; *Tribune*, February 9, 1856; February 16, 1856.
15. *Leslie's Illustrated*, May 3, 1856.

CHAPTER 5

1. *Alexandria Gazette*, May 21, 1856.
2. McKinsey, Folger. *History of Frederick County, Maryland*. 306-307; Leepson, Marc. *What So Proudly We Hailed: Francis Scott Key, A Life* (New York: St. Martin's Press, 2014), 193; Ferris, Marc. *Star-Spangled Banner: The Unlikely Story of America's National Anthem*. (Baltimore: Johns Hopkins, 2014); *Daily Journal* (Wilmington), June 4, 1856; Leepson, Marc. *What So Proudly We Hailed: Francis Scott Key, A Life* (New York: St. Martin's Press, 2014), 193; Dubovoy 459.
3. *Alexandria Gazette*, April 9, 1844; Sina Dubovoy, *The Lost World of Francis Scott Key* (Bloomington, IN: WestBow, 2014).
4. *Saturday Visitor*, April 12, 1845 (the number of children given is usually four; but Ellen was reported as having been buried with one of her children. Therefore, the Keys must have had five).
5. *Sun*, March 3, 1846; *Alexandria Gazette*, January 29, 1846.
6. *Alexandria Gazette*, March 4, 1844; *Daily Union*, June 20, 1845 and February 3, 1847
7. Stanley C. Harrold, *The Pearl Affair: The Washington Riot of 1848*. Records of the Columbia Historical Society. Washington D.C., Vol. 50, (1980), pp. 140-160.
8. Daniel Drayton, *Personal Memoir of Daniel Drayton* (Boston: Osgood, 1875), 33-34.
9. Drayton, 64.

10. Drayton, 45-46.
11. Drayton, 65-68.
12. *National Intelligencer*, July 17, 1849; *Globe*, March 27, 1843.
13. *Evening Journal*, September 7, 1853.
14. *Intelligencer*, March 22, 1855; *Baltimore Sun*, March 22, 1855.

CHAPTER 6

1. *Leslie's*, July 19, 1856.
2. *Herald*, May 25, 1856, May 26, 1856, and June 6, 1856; *Daily Union*, June 20, 1845; *Richmond Whig*, June 13, 1856.
3. Ghosts of DC, http://ghostsofdc.org/2012/09/20/philemon-herbert/; Erin McHugh, *Political Suicide: Missteps, Peccadilloes, Bad Calls, Backroom Hijinx, Sordid Pasts, Rotten Breaks, and Just Plain Dumb Mistakes in the Annals of American Politics* (New York: Pegasus, 2016).
4. *Washington Reporter*, March 23, 1859.
5. *Tribune*, July 14, 1856.
6. *Albany Evening Journal*, October 10, 1856 and October 12, 1856; *Herald*, July 19, 1856; *Schenectady Reflector*, April 1; *Tribune*, November 4, 1856.
7. *New York Times*, November 5, 1856.
8. United States senators were chosen by state legislators until the adoption of the Seventeenth Amendment in 1913.
9. *Schenectady Reflector*, February 6, 1857; Swanberg 1-2.
10. Swanberg, 1-2.
11. Poore, 2:26.
12. *Boston Evening Transcript*, March 9, 1857; Swanberg 21.
13. Swanberg, 6.
14. *Herald*, June 6, 1870; World, June 6, 1870; *Intelligencer*, June 1, 1849; *Manufacturers' and Farmers' Journal*, February 7, 1853; *Daily Pennsylvanian*, March 19, 1853.
15. Swanberg, 7.
16. *Trial Day*, 7.

CHAPTER 7

1. Lonnie Hovey, *Lafayette Square* (Washington, D.C.: Arcadia, 2014), 9; *Albany Evening Journal*, February 28, 1859.

2. *Munsey's Magazine*, v. 20; Hovey, 42. Most biographies of Sickles
    refer to this home as Stockton House. They are one in the same;
    Busey, 212; *Metropolitan*, February 10, 1820 and May 9, 1820;
    Washington Gazette, November 1 and December 11, 1820.

CHAPTER 8

1. *Globe*, February 26, 1859.
2. Crouthamel, James, and Jackson, Andrew. "James Gordon Bennett,
    the New York Herald, and the Development of Sensationalism." *New
    York History*, Vol. 54, No. 3 (July 1973), pp. 294-316; *Albany
    Journal*, April 12, 1859.
3. John David Lawson, *American State Trials* (St. Louis: F. H. Thomas,
    1914), 636.
4. *Trial Day*, 15; *Star*, February 26, 1859.
5. *Globe*, March 28, 1859.
6. *Trial Day*, 14.

CHAPTER 9

1. Poore 2:26; Richard Henry Dana, *To Cuba and Back: A Vacation
    Voyage* (Boston: Osgood, 1875).
2. *Boston Herald*, December 18, 1857.
3. *Boston Evening Transcript*, February 6, 1858; *Tribune*, February 6,
    1858; *The States*, February 6, 1858; *Herald*, February 7, 1858; Clark,
    41.
4. Clay-Copton, 114; Champ Clark, *My Quarter Century of American
    Politics* (New York: Harper Brothers, 1920), 41.
5. *Star*, March 1, 1859.

CHAPTER 10

1. *Trial*, April 12, 1859.
2. *Trial Day*, 8.

CHAPTER 11

1. Clay-Copton, 86.
2. Clay-Copton, 134.
3. Clay-Copton, 128.
4. *Trial Day*, 15.

5. Henry Watterson, *Marse Henry* (New York: Doran, 1914), 63.
6. *Herald*, May 15, 1858.
7. *New York Times*, November 20, 1858.

CHAPTER 12

1. *American Traveler*, March 12, 1859; *Historic Washington Homes*, 255.
2. *Leslie's*, 3/12; *Public Ledger* (Philadelphia), September 8, 1843; *Daily Evening Transcript* (Boston), September 9, 1843.
3. *Alexandra Gazette*, April 21, 1859; *Sacramento Daily Union*, June 12, 1865; *Daily True Delta*, November 17, 1864.
4. John Charles Fremont, *Memoirs of My Life* (Chicago: Belford, 1887), 27.
5. *Lloyd's Weekly Newspaper*, April 24, 1859; *Plain Dealer*, March 3, 1859; *Diary of Laura Crawford Jones*; *New York Times*, April 21, 1859; *Boston Journal*, March 2, 1859.
6. Lawrence, 679.
7. *Tribune*, March 3, 1859; *Louisville Daily Courier*, March 4, 1859.
8. *Trial day*, 13; *Tribune*, March 3, 1859.

CHAPTER 13

1. *Leslie's*, March 12, 1859.
2. *Press*, April 14, 1859.
3. Lawson, 623.

CHAPTER 14

1. Elizabeth Lomax, *Leaves from an Old Washington Diary* (New York: Lyons Press, 2014), 57.
2. *Trial Day*, 10; Milles, Quincy T. "Cutting Along the Color Line." 22.
3. Poor, 2:26.
4. *National Intelligencer*, February 28, 1859; *New York Herald*, February 28, 1859.
5. The actions of Sickles, Wooldridge, and Butterworth on February 27 are drawn from statements published by the latter two in the *New York Times* and elsewhere on March 2. Butterworth was the closest eyewitness to the shooting and saw the all of it, and his account is

primarily relied upon for its exact details. It is supplemented by eyewitness testimony from Day 4 of the trial.

6. Clay-Copton, 97.
7. Newsome, A. R. "Letters of Lawrence O'Bryan Branch 1856-1860." *North Carolina Historical Review* 10:1 (January 1933) pp.44-79. Branch to his wife, February 27, 1859.
8. *Trial*, 21; *Time*, February 28, 1859.
9. Statement of Robert Walker; *Trial Day*, 15.
10. *Boston Evening Transcript*, April 13, 1859.
11. *States*, February 28, 1859.
12. *Trial*, day sixteen.
13. *Daily Tribune*, March 2, 1859.
14. New York *Times*, February 28, 1859; *Boston Traveler*, March 1, 1859.
15. *Washington Union*, March 1, 1859.
16. *Harper's* April 12 1859.
17. Hives, 2.
18. Tim Krepp, *Capitol Hill Haunts* (Washington, D.C.: The History Press, 2012).
19. Joseph T. Kelly, *Memories of a Lifetime in Washington* (Records of the D.C. Historical Society) 134-5; Green, Constance McLaughlin. 217.
20. *Daily Tribune*, March 1, 1859; *Trial Day*, 11.
21. New York *Times*, March 2 and March 4, 1859; *Boston Evening Transcript*, March 1, 1859; *Commercial Advertiser*, March 1; *Commercial Advertiser*, March 2, 1859; *Herald*, March 1, 1859.
22. March 15, 1859.

CHAPTER 15

1. Richard Kielbowicz, *Technology and* Culture, Vol. 28, No. 1 (Jan., 1987), pp. 26-41. *News Gathering by Mail in the Age of the Telegraph*, 29.
2. Richard Kielbowicz, *Technology and* Culture, Vol. 28, No. 1 (Jan., 1987), pp. 26-41. *News Gathering by Mail in the Age of the Telegraph*, 29, 37; Standage 45-46.
3. Standage, 45-46.
4. Standage, 148.
5. *States*, March 2, 1859.

6. *New York Times*, March 5, 1859.
7. *New York Times*, January 15, 1859; *New York Times*, January 25, 1859.
8. *New York Times*, March 1, 1859.
9. *Cincinnati Commercial Tribune*, March 14, 1859.
10. *Star*, March 1.
11. *Daily Standard*; *Commercial Tribune*; *Louisville Daily Courier*, all of February 28, 1859.
12. *Leslie's*, March 12, 1859; *Sun*, March 4, 1859; *Herald*, March 28, 1859.
13. *Boston Journal*, February 28, 1859.
14. *Herald*, February 27, 1859; *Cincinnati Commercial Tribune*, March 1, 1859.
15. Diary of Laura Crawford Jones.
16. The British English world "gaol" means the same as the American English word "jail."
17. *San Francisco Bulletin*, July 18, 1857; *Evening Mail* (London), August 18, 1854; *Atlas* (London), November 11, 1854.

CHAPTER 16

1. *Harper's*, March 14, 1859.
2. *Daily Union*, March 1, 1859; *Evening Post*, March 1, 1859.
3. *Boston Evening Transcript*, March 1, 1859.
4. *Daily Tribune*, March 1, 1859.
5. *American Traveler*, March 1, 1859.

CHAPTER 17

1. William Marvel, *Lincoln's Autocrat* (Chapel Hill: North Carolina Press, 2015), pp. 6-7, 8, 30, 37, 43-44, 55, 102; *Daily Union*, January 4, 1859.
2. *Press*, April 6, 1859; Sun, April 16, 1853; *Journal of the Executive Proceedings of the Senate of the United States*, 10:155; *Tribune*, December 14, 1882.
3. *American State Trials*, 12:499.
4. *Reflector*, March 4, 1859; *New York Times*, March 2, 1859; *Evening Journal*, February 28, 1859.

CHAPTER 18

1. *Tribune*, March 2, 1859.
2. *Tribune*, March 5, 1859.
3. *Leslie's*, March 12, 1859.
4. *Tribune*, March 3, 1859; *Leslie's*, March 12, 1859; *Commercial Advertiser*, March 2, 1859.
5. *Pennsylvanian*, March 4, 1859; *Pittsfield Sun*, March 17, 1859.
6. *Evening Post*, March 2, 1859.
7. *New York Times*, March 12 and March 4, 1859.
8. *Tribune*, March 2, 1859.
9. *Waltham Sentinel*, March 11, 1859.

CHAPTER 19

1. Reprinted in the *Star*, March 10, 1859.
2. *Star*, March 2, 1859.
3. Reprinted in the *Star*, March 8, 1859.
4. *Baltimore Sun* editorial reprinted in the *Union Democrat* (Manchester, NH), April 5, 1859.

CHAPTER 20

1. *Boston Journal*, March 2, 1859; March 15, 1859.
2. *Herald*, March 26, 1859; *Schenectady Reflector*, March 4, 1859; *Pennsylvanian*, March 2, 1859.
3. Reprinted in the *Star*, March 8, 1859.
4. *New York Times*, April 14, 1859, quoting the *Times* of London.
5. *The Letters of Jesse Benton Freemont*, 213.
6. *Herald*, March 17, 1859.
7. *New York Times*, March 15, 1859.

CHAPTER 21

1. *Tribune*, March 2, 1859.
2. *Times*, March 7, 1859.
3. *Tribune*, March 2, 1859; Diary of Laura Crawford Jones, Library of Congress.
4. *States*, March 6, 1859.
5. *Washington Reporter* (Washington, PA), April 13, 1859.

CHAPTER 22

1. Leslie's, March 19, 1859.
2. *The Tribune.*
3. National Anti-Slavery Standard, March 12, 1859.
4. States, March 7, 1859; "Lafayette Square." Records of the Columbia Historical Society.

CHAPTER 23

1. *Star,* 1859.
2. *Inquirer,* March 14, 1859.
3. *New York Times,* March 15, 1859.
4. *Albany Journal,* March 8, 1859.
5. *Harper's,* March 19; *New York Times,* March 15, 1859.
6. *Boston Traveler,* March 14, 1859.
7. *New York Times,* March 15, 1859.
8. *Tribune,* March 2, 1859.
9. *New York Times,* March 15, 1859.
10. The encounter with Laura in his cell is described in *Harper's,* March 19, 1859.
11. *Harper's,* March 19, 1859; *Herald,* March 10, 1859.
12. *New York Times,* March 3, March 6, and March 11, 1859; *Times Picayune,* April 15, 1859.

CHAPTER 24

1. *Leslie's,* March 19, 1859; *Harper's,* March 19, 1859.
2. *Tribune,* March 2, 1859; *Lesile's,* March 12, 1859.
3. *Daily Pennsylvanian,* March 7, 1859.
4. *Congregationalist,* April 15, 1859.

CHAPTER 25

1. *Evening Post,* March 24, 1859; *Manufacturers' and Farmers' Journal,* June 13, 1859.
2. *Centinel of Freedom,* March 8, 1859.
3. *Manufacturers' and Farmers' Journal,* March 24, 1859.
4. *Lowell Citizen and News,* March 16, 1859.
5. *Star,* May 10, 1859.
6. *Pennsylvanian,* March 4, 1859.

7. *Lowell Daily Citizen,* April 6, 1859.
8. *Weekly Miners' Journal,* (Pottsville PA).

CHAPTER 26
1. Bonn's *Handbook of Washington,* 74.
2. *Evening Post,* March 16, 1859; *Star,* March 14, 1859.
3. *Leslie's,* March 26, 1859.
4. Poore 2:27; *New York Times,* April 9, 1859.; The *Sun,* November 20, 1857; *Washington Union,* November 25, ; The *States,* June 28, 1858.
5. *New York Times,* March 15, 1859; *Evening Post,* March 16, 1859; *Albany Journal,* March 15, 1859.
6. *New York Times,* March 16, 1859.
7. *New York Times,* March 17, 1859.
8. *Star,* March 18, 1859; *Albany Journal,* March 18, 1859.
9. *Evening Post,* March 5, 1859.
10. *New York Times,* March 23, 1859.
11. *New York Times,* March 23, 1859.
12. *States,* March 24, 1859.
13. Harvey Crew, *Centennial History of DC* (Dayton: Crew, 1892), 735.
14. Lawrence Gobright, *Recollection of Men and Things at Washington, During a Third of a Century* (Philadelphia: Claxton: 1859), 192.
15. *New York Times,* March 25, 1859; *Star,* March 25, 1859.
16. *Morning Post* (London), April 12, 1859.
17. *American Traveler,* March 12, 1859.

CHAPTER 27
1. *Evening Post,* March 26, 1859; *Harper's,* April 9, 1859.
2. *States,* March 26, 1859; March 18, 1859; *Leslie's,* March 19, 1859.
3. Diary of Laura Crawford Jones
4. *Louisville Daily Courier,* April 4, 1859.
5. *Boston Courier,* May 12, 1859.
6. *Evening Post,* April 9, 1859, reprinted from the *London Examiner.*
7. *Traveler,* April 15, 1859.
8. *New York Observer,* April 16, 1836; David Anthony, The Helen Jewett Panic, American Literature, vol. 69, no. 3 (September 1997), pp. 487-514.
9. *Massachusetts Spy,* April 6, 1859.

10. *Providence Evening Press*, April 5, 1859; *Boston Journal*, April 11, 1859.

CHAPTER 28

1. *States*, April 6, 1859; *New York Times*, March 15, 1859.
2. *New York Times*, April 7, 1859; *Press*, April 8, 1859; *Trial Day*, 4
3. *Herald*, April 4, 1859.
4. Swanberg, 69.

CHAPTER 29

1. *Union*, April 5, 1859; *Manufacturers' and Farmers' Journal* (Providence), April 4, 1859; *Albany Evening Journal*, April 4, 1859; *New York Times*, April 7, 1859.
2. *Press*, April 6, 1859.
3. *Evening Journal*, April 4, 1859; *Sun*, April 6, 1859.
4. *Sun*, April 6, 1859; *New York Times*, April 7, 1859; *Press*, April 8, 1859; *Intelligencer*, April 5, 1859; *Intelligencer*, April 5, 1859; *Intelligencer*, April 5, 1859; *Intelligencer*, April 5, 1859; *New York Times*, April 8, 1859.
5. *Daily Union*, October 2, 1859.
6. *Post*, April 6, 1859.
7. *Herald*, April 4, 1859; *Daily Union*, April 5, 1859.
8. *New York Times*, April 5, 1859; *Union*, April 5, 1859; *New York Times*, April 6, 1859; *Press*, April 6, 1859; *States*, April 5, 1859.
9. *States*, April 4, 1859.
10. Lawson, 497; *New York Times*, April 7, 1859; Poore, 2:26.
11. *Press*, April 6, 1859.
12. *New York Times*, April 5, 1859.
13. *New York Times*, April 5, 1859.
14. *New York Times*, April 5, 1859.
15. *Daily Union*, April 5, 1859; *Intelligencer*, April 5, 1859.
16. *New York Times*, April 6, 1859.
17. Transcript, March 26; *New York Times*, April 6, 1859; *Post*, April 7, 1859.
18. See, e.g., *New York Times*, April 5, 1859.
19. Joseph T. Kelly, *Memories of a Lifetime in Washington*, 134-35.
20. *States*, April 5, 1859; *Inquirer*, April 6, 1859.

21. *New York Times*, April 6, 1859.
22. *Evening Journal*, April 6, 1859; Union, April 6, 1859.
23. *London Daily News*, April 20, 1859.
24. *New York Times*, April 7, 1859.
25. *New York Times*, April 7, 1859.
26. *Cincinnati Commercial Tribune*, April 11,1859.
27. *New York Times*, April 7, 1859.
28. *Star*, April 7, 1859. This was sharply at odds with what the *New York Times* reported. The *Star* attributes this to the prosecution digging into the reasons behind a juror's expression of bias, without similar follow-up from the defense; *New York Times*, April 7, 1859.
29. *New York Times*, April 7, 1859.
30. *Herald,* April 8, 1859.
31. *Herald,* April 11, 1859.

CHAPTER 30

1. *States*, April 8, 1859; *New York Times*, April 7, 1859; *New York Times*, March 15, 1859; *Inquirer*, April 9, 1859.
2. *Post*, April 7, 1859.
3. *Post*, April 7, 1859.
4. *New York Times*, April 8, 1859.
5. The transcript of the trial of Daniel Sickles (*Trial*) was prepared by Fleix Gregory De Fontaine and published by R. M. De Witt (New York: 1859). Unless otherwise specified, descriptions of events during the trial can be found in this transcript; *New York Times*, April 8, 1859.
6. *New York Times*, March 15, 1859; *Press*, April 8, 1859; *New York Times*, April 6, 1859.
7. *Tribune*, April 9, 1859.
8. *Salem Register*, April 21, 1859.

CHAPTER 31

1. *Columbian Register* (New Haven), April 23, 1859.
2. *Boston Evening Transcript*, April 11, 1859.
3. *Star*, April 8, 1859.
4. *New York Times*, April 9, 1859.

CHAPTER 32

1. *Herald*, December 25, 1844; *National Police Gazette*, March 3, 1849.
2. *Sun*, March 13, 1849.
3. *Albany Law Journal*, v. 49, p. 260; *New York Sunday Times*, reprinted in *The Musical World*, 29:58.
4. *New York Evangelist*, November 14, 1850.
5. *Coos Republican* (Lancaster, NH), December 1, 1857; *Irish American Weekly* (New York), November 20, 1858; *Weekly Herald*, December 26, 1857; *American State Trials*, 12:498.
6. *Boston Journal*, April 9, 1859.
7. *Tribune*, April 12, 1859; Sun April 11, 1859.
8. *Boston Journal*, April 23, 1859.
9. *Plain Dealer*, April 13, 1859.

CHAPTER 33

1. Paul Barron Watson, *Marcus Aurelius Antonious* (Los Angeles: Hard Press, 2012), 76–78.
2. LaRue Munson, "Insanity as a Defence in Criminal Cases," *American Law Register*, v. 25, no. 8, 449–55; Roberty Aitken and Marilyn Aitken, "The M'Naughten Case: The Queen was Not Amused," *Litigation*, v. 36, number 4, Requirements, Relations, Representations (Summer 2010), pp. 53-56; Richard Moran, "The Founding for the Insanity Defense: The Cases of James Hadfield and Daniel M'Naughtan," *Annals of the American Academy of Political and Social Science*, v. 477, the Insanity Defense (Jan. 1985), 31–42.

CHAPTER 34

1. *Daily Confederation*, 1859.
2. *Philadelphia Inquirer*, 1859.
3. *Post*, 1859.
4. *Cleveland Plain Dealer*, February 7, 1859; *Evening Star*, January 19, 1859.
5. *Evening Star*, February 9, 1859.
6. *Trial*, 39.
7. *Trial*, 39.
8. *Atlas and Daily Bee*, April 5, 1859.

CHAPTER 35

1. *Albany Journal*, April 11, 1859.
2. *Albany Journal*, April 13, 1859.
3. Paul Wylie, *The Irish General; The Greatest Brigade* (Oklahoma City: University of Oklahoma Press, 2011); Thomas Craughwell, *The Greatest Brigade* (Beverly, MA: Fair Winds, 2011).
4. *New York Times*, April 15, 1859.
5. *Spy*, April 13, 1859.
6. *States*, March 26, 1859; *Tribune*, April 13, 1859.
7. *Alexandria Gazette*, April 13, 1859.
8. *Alexandria Gazette*, April 13, 1859.

CHAPTER 36

1. *New York Times*, April 14, 1859.
2. *New York Times*, April 15, 1859.
3. *New York Times*, April 18, 1859.
4. *Star*, April 19, 1859; *New York Times*, April 18, 1859.
5. *Boston Journal*, 1859.
6. *New York Times*, 1859.
7. Diary of Laura Crawford Jones (Library of Congress, Washington, D.C.).
8. *Papers of Jefferson Davis*, 244.
9. *Press*, April 14, 1859; *Star*, April 13, 1859.
10. *Press*, April 14, 1859.

CHAPTER 37

1. *New York Times*, April 13, 1859.
2. *Trial*, 48, 51.
3. Horatio King, "My Recollections of War Times," *Blue and Gray: The Patriotic American Magazine*, vol. 2, p. 290.
4. *Trial*, 51.
5. *Cincinnati Daily Commercial*, March 1, 1859.

CHAPTER 38.

1. *Trial*, 58.

CHAPTER 39

1. *Independent Democrat,* Concord (NH), April 17, 1859.
2. *New York Times,* April 18, 1859.
3. *New York Times,* April 19, 1859.
4. *Trial,* 70.
5. Henry Clay Whitney, *Life on the Circuit with Lincoln* (Boston: Estes and Lauriat, 1892), 183.
6. www.thelincolnlog.org, April, 1859; lawpracticcofabrahamlincoln. org, *Champagne County v. West Urbana, Illinois*; *People v. Patterson.* Travis Lewin and Tyler Hite, "Lincoln's Second to Last Murder Case: *People v. Patterson,*" American Bar Association, www.americanbar.org.

CHAPTER 40

1. *Worcester Palladium* (Mass.), April 20, 1859.
2. *Trial,* 70
3. "Center Market's Chaotic Exuberance," http://www. streetsofwashington.com/2010/05/center-markets-chaotic-exuberance.html.

CHAPTER 41

1. *Boston Recorder,* 1859.
2. Correspondence of Benjamin Perley Poore to the Boston Journal, reprinted in the *Maine Rural,* May 7, 1859.
3. *Evening Press,* Providence (Rhode Island), April 20, 1859.

CHAPTER 42

1. *Star,* April 22, 1859.
2. *Vermont Chronicle,* 1859.
3. *Herald,* April 22, 1859.
4. *Times,* April 14, 1859.
5. *Albany Journal,* March 8, 1859.
6. *Sun,* April 22, 1859.

CHAPTER 43

1. *Frederick Douglas's Paper* (NY), April 22, 1859.

2. Reprinted in *Milwaukee Daily Sentinel*, April 22, 1859.
3. *Herald*, April 23, 1859.
4. *Herald*, April 23, 1859.

CHAPTER 44

1. *Milwaukee Sentinel*, April 22, 1859.
2. *Marvel*, 108.
3. *Herald*, April 24, 1859.

CHAPTER 46

1. *Morning Advertiser*, May 10, 1859.
2. *Herald*, April 27, 1859.
3. *Morning Advertiser*, May 10, 1859.
4. *Morning Advertiser*, May 10, 1859.
5. *Herald*, April 27, 1859.
6. *New York Times*, April 27, 1859.
7. *Morning Advertiser*, May 10, 1859.
8. *New York Times*, April 27, 1859.
9. Edwards Clarke, "James T. Brady," *The Galaxy*, May 1, 1869: 716–29.

CHAPTER 47

1. *Herald*, April 28, 1859.
2. Crawford to Ellis Lewis, April 28, 1859. Crawford papers, Yale.
3. *Herald*, May 7, 1859; *Boston Journal*, April 28, 1859; *Star*, April 30, 1859; *Star*, May 16, 1859.
4. *Herald*, May 27, 1859.
5. *Dollar Weekly Mirror*, June 18, 1859.
6. *Alexandria Gazette*, May 7, 1859.
7. *Boston Post*, May 2, 1861.
8. *Herald*, July 19, 1859.
9. *Daily Confederation*, August 14, 1859.
10. *Herald*, July 12, 1859.
11. *Daily Confederation*, August 14, 1859.
12. *New York Times*, July 21, 1859.

CHAPTER 48

1. Mary Chestnut, *Mary Chestnut's Civil War* (New Haven: Yale University Press, 1981), 379.
2. *London Daily News*, August 22, 1859.
3. Keneally, 204-05.
4. *New York Times*, January 8, 1861.
5. Keneally, 211.
6. *New York Times*, December 14, 1859.
7. Keneally, 219.
8. Keneally, 284.

CHAPTER 49

1. *Star*, April 27, 1859.
2. Ireland, 130.
3. *Sun*, February 13, 1859; April 8, 1843; *Maine Cultivator and Hallowell Gazette*, July 1, 1843; *Daily Atlas*, May 8, 1843.
4. *American and Commercial Advertiser*, September 29, 1859; *Spirit of Jefferson*, October 23, 1846 and October 30, 1846.
5. *Intelligencer*, January 2, 1858; *Herald*, January 21, 1858 and January 22, 1858; *Sacramento Daily Union*, December 19, 1857.
6. *Herald*, January 22, 1858.
7. *Sacramento Daily Union*, June 20, 1856; *National Intelligencer*, July 29, 1856.
8. George Alfred Townsend, *Washington Outside and Inside*, 309.
9. Robert Ireland, "Insanity and the Unwritten Law," *The American Journal of Legal History*, vol. 32, no. 2 (April 1988), pp. 157-172.
10. *Remarkable Trials of All Countries*, 345.
11. Lawrence M. Friedman and William E. Havemann, "The Rise and Fall of the Unwritten Law: Sex, Patriarchy, and Vigilante Justice in the American Courts," 61 Buffalo Law Review 997 (2013); *Daily Argus*, April 24, 1868; Ireland, 31.
12. "Murder by Gaslight," http://www.murderbygaslight.com/2010/07/richardson-mcfarland-tragedy.html; records of the Library of Congress.
13. "The Black-McKaig Homicide," http://www.murderbygaslight.com/2013/03/the-black-mckaig-hommicide.html.
14. Robert Ireland, "The Libertine Must Die: Sexual Dishonor and The Unwritten Law in the Nineteenth Century United States," *Journal of*

Social History, v. 23, no. 1 (Autumn 1989), pp. 27-44, 27 (Ireland 1); Friedman 1017, 1018; *Kansas City Times*, October 29, 1909.

15. Friedman, 1010-11.
16. Friedman, 1032, 1036, 1044.
17. *Virginia Law Register*, June 1907, 107.
18. Friedman, 998, 1024.
19. Friedman, 1021-22.
20. Friedman, 999.
21. *Richmond Times Dispatch*, October 1, 1916.
22. Friedman, 1030.
23. Friedman, 1018-20, 1025, 1036, 1040.
24. Friedman, 1026.
25. *Oregonian*, October 16, 1949.
26. Friedman, 1047.
27. Friedman, 1045-46.
28. Friedman, 1003.
29. Clark, 38-39.
30. Clark, 50-51.

EPILOGUE

1. *New York Times*, February 15, 1862.
2. Thomas Kirwan, *History of the Seventeenth Regiment, Massachusetts Volunteers*; William Kerrigan, *Johnny Appleseed and the American: A Cultural History*, 169; *Cincinnati Daily Gazette*, October 17, 1871.
3. *Charleston Mercury*, April 5, 1862; *Daily Naitonal Republican*, August 11, 1862.
4. *Los Angeles Herald*, September 5, 1875, reprinting from *S. F. Bulleton* of 6th inst; *Daily Post* (San Francisco), May 7, 1875.
5. *New York Times*, December 29, 1886.
6. Stephen Fiske, "Offhand Portraits of Famous New Yorkers,", 284.
7. Fiske, 287; *Tribune*, January 6, 1882.

Index